APARTHEID MEDIA

Disinformation and Dissent in South Africa

APARTHEID MEDIA

Disinformation and Dissent in South Africa

John M. Phelan

Lawrence Hill & Company
WESTPORT, CONNECTICUT

Library of Congress Cataloging-in-Publication Data

Phelan, John M.
Apartheid media.

Includes index.
1. Government and the press—South Africa. 2. Freedom
of the press—South Africa. 3. Apartheid—South Africa.
4. Anti-apartheid movements. 5. South Africa—Politics
and government—1978–   . I. Title.
PN4748.S58P4 1987   323.44'5   87-11831
ISBN 0-88208-244-4
ISBN 0-88208-245-0 (pbk.)

Published in the United States of America
by Lawrence Hill & Company, Publishers, Inc.
520 Riverside Avenue, Westport, Connecticut 06880

1   2   3   4   5   6   7   8   9   10

Printed in the United States of America

Contents

ACKNOWLEDGEMENTS

This type of book requires many different kinds of help from a variety of institutions and people. I have been fortunate in finding extraordinary generosity, and not a little courage, in almost every quarter my quest took me.

For financial assistance I am indebted to my own university, Fordham; to its McGannon Center for Communication Research; to the Westinghouse Education Fund; to the World Association of Christian Communicators. For research assistance I am indebted to Yale University, Columbia University, New York University, the American Civil Liberties Union Communications Media Committee, and the Committee to Protect Journalists, all located in the United States of America, and to Witwatersrand University, the University of Cape Town, Rhodes University, the South African Institute of Race Relations, the Centre for Applied Legal Studies and the Interchurch Media Programme, all located in the Republic of South Africa.

Prof. Roland Stanbridge of Stockholm's Journalisthögskolan I and Rhodes Scholar Shaun Johnson generously gave me the use of much of their unpublished research.

I am particularly grateful to Ramsay Milne, Cheetah Haysom, Charles Barry, and their families, for starting me off with excellent contacts for this project. Rene DeVilliers was of very special help in the Cape area and Professor Mavis Taylor and her family were imaginatively hospitable and generous with care and concern. Father Basil van Rensberg was unstinting in sharing both acute observations and good cheer.

Moore Crossey, Africana Curator of the Sterling Memorial Library, and Leonard Thompson, Charles J. Stillé Professor of History Emeritus and director of the Southern African Research Program, both at Yale University, were accessible, stimulating, and spectacularly informative. Professor William Foltz, director of the Center for International and Area Studies at Yale, graciously extended my research affiliation for an additional year.

Michael Traber, editor of *Media Development,* was the catalyst and conscience of this entire project, although I do believe certain of the views and observations offered in this book cannot meet with his agreement. As he knows, I am grateful for his friendship and frank criticisms.

Richard Huett's professional and personal guidance was cool and warm in the right places. He is a treasured friend and resource.

I try not to let on too much, but I am appreciative of my wife's patience and sympathy and of the affectionately irascible technical aid perpetually available from Mary Jo, my daughter.

All of these good and worthy people are of course off the hook of responsibility for any errors, omissions, oversights, etc., in and of this book.

Many others have helped, and I trust they will forgive me for not including them in the above very short list.

PREFACE

SINCE 1948 South Africa has become more and more of a police state for everyone as it has become more and more steeped in a disastrous commitment to apartheid. Desmond Tutu has said that the whites will not be free until all the blacks are free. Some people may take this in some sort of Augustinian spiritual sense: the whites will not be morally free of the burden of guilt until the blacks are free of the shackles of apartheid. True as this may or may not be, Tutu's statement is also true in the more literal sense of parallel liberties. The political liberty of every white is hostage to the political liberty of every black. For in order to maintain the manifestly unjust system of racial preference and racial prejudice, the National Party regime of South Africa has had to stifle more and more forms of legitimate democratic dissent, no matter what the color of its provenance.

Tutu's remark is true in a more discomfiting sense as well. No one rules except by opinion. Therefore, so long as the effective political majority of any country countenances the subjugation of any portion of the populace, no momentarily favored individual or group is safe from the talons of Draco. One thinks of all those palace coups and vengeful bloodbaths from Nero to Pol Pot. More generally, then, so long as some of us are slaves, all of us are slaves.

For Americans and the British, South Africa's spiral down into chaotic despotism is more than just another episode of a failed dream in a new world. It is a cautionary tale, for their nation is very like our own, with the same heritage of freedom, a very similar code of laws, the same moral principles of protection for the individual, and parallel judicial limitations on state absolutism. South Africa's laws spring from the same source as our own; they share the same light.

And they have a darkness very much like ours, from the slavery of the last century to the economic racialism of today. South Africa's apartheid system, bolstered and maintained by a shadow government of military and security forces, directed by unaccountable executives and secret committees, is a response to a political-economic situation not very unlike our own.

Many South Africans are afflicted with a hysterical paranoia which blames their indigenous violence and unrest principally on "outside agitators." Sound familiar? The ruling elites of Afrikaner civil servants and government officials and, for the most part, English-speaking businessmen have a long-standing fear of being overrun by an alien mass of "Bantu"—native Africans—which has led the country into both apartheid and a host of other compromises with their heritage of freedom for all. Anyone familiar with America's treatment of native Americans—"Indians"—in the last century and of immigrant Hispanics in recent decades knows that we not only have a similar situation but have devised similar solutions. The obvious parallels between the plight of American blacks and South African blacks may have blinded us to more sweeping and more threatening linkages. With its unresolved conflicting provisions, the U.S. Immigration Reform and Control Act of 1986 seems an imitation of the typically schizoid measures of the South African Parliament. A member of the American House of Representatives, disgusted with the compromises but trapped by the perceived expediency of final passage for the bill, said, "I am going to hold my nose and I am going to vote for this conference report."

Most major decisions in South Africa are made by its State Security Council, supported by a network of local security committees. In that country, one may have to hold one's nose, but is more and more relieved of the onus of voting (and if you are black, you have never had the problem in the first place.)

Our own executive branch has a National Security Council, and it appears to have been quietly quite busy without bothering to inform the people or its representatives of its actions, plans, or purposes. In fact, former National Security Adviser John Poindexter believed he had a patriotic duty to "disinform" the American press and people in the national interest.

Thus there are in South Africa as in the United States two contending forces: on the one hand, a marred heritage of universal freedom and an early commitment to open government in the public interest with strict limits on state power; on the other hand, a nationalistic security psychosis coupled with a fear and hatred of the "foreigner"—even though he or she may be a fellow citizen. The conflict comes to a boil in our first freedom, the freedom of the press. Just so in South Africa, where the antiapartheid struggle, in its earlier cold stages and now in its increasingly hot phase, is a media war between dissent and repression, propaganda and truth, state control and individual free expression, secrecy and openness.

There is a still broader meaning to Tutu's statement about whites not being free until blacks are free. In their starkly differing ways, the nuclear threat and satellite communications are forcing us to be one world, with common concerns and a common fate. In a nation, it has always been true that if all are not free then none are free. Now it is becoming true of the globe. Human rights violations in China or Chile are threats to all of us. This awareness sparked the sanctions and disinvestment drive of the international community against the National Party regime in South Africa. The form and force of that drive, as that of Amnesty International's more general permanent campaign for human rights, could only be conceived in the living context of the startlingly new global media environment.

Although we may not yet have a free flow of information, or a new world communication order, we do have global media warfare, with nation-states contending not merely for territory and capital, but for a favorable press and upscale world audience ratings as well. Despite the oft-noted ominous side to this, I see it as a development full of hope. The apartheid media wars are being fought on the global as well as the domestic scale, and it gives greater hope to dissenters. So, too, of other domestic struggles between freedom and repression, as I hope to finally demonstrate.

Throughout the world, the media are avaricious for scandal in high places—thank God—and love to cover dramatic protests—thank the Lord again. There may well be a meretricious motivation in all this, but the end result is to inform the discriminating and concerned public. Many journalists have a sense of vocation in keeping the mighty honest and holding the feet of public officials to the fire of public scrutiny. In America, we may find this at times tinged with an air of self-righteousness and pharisaical smugness. South Africa's embattled press and very brave journalists may give us an insight into the true moral grit required to carry out the ideals of a free and responsible press in a country that began much as ours.

South Africa, particularly in the way its government reacts to critical press coverage, shows us a direction in which we are already heading but may still turn away from.

If we are very, very vigilant.

APARTHEID MEDIA

Disinformation and Dissent in South Africa

ONE

The Devised Divisions of South Africa

Foreign Yet Familiar

There is no calculus for injustice, no measure for atrocity. In the Gulag Archipelago starving prisoners have been known to cut off pieces of their own flesh simply to taste a bit of red meat. Idi Amin required some of the condemned of Uganda to perform sexual acts of his own devising before they were pounded to death by cheerfully wielded sledgehammers. In Uruguay there are professional torture centers, not unlike clinics in appearance and administration, to which prisoners of conscience are taken on a bureaucratically constant schedule to have their neurological systems meticulously ravaged. The list can go on and on, with greater or lesser vividness, until long after our sensibilities are numbed.

Most acts of savagery, like the structure of the atom or the size of the universe, surpass our imaginative grasp. The worst victims shrivel our capacity for sympathy, since they have lost the last shred of dignity necessary to evoke the remnant of hope for realistic remedy.

It is for this reason that we Americans, with our history of slavery and racism, so readily recognize and facilely revile the apartheid system of the Republic of South Africa. It presents a familiar scale of misery and a nostalgic form of injustice. True, black men have been beaten to death slowly or killed instantly for no offense beyond their color. But most of us have no realistic comprehension of what it must be like to be beaten to death or even to observe such a process.

Social discrimination and economic exploitation we know.

The Law

You are at a posh bar in Johannesburg, "Jo'burg," the largest city in South Africa and the one to which the largest black city in Africa, Soweto, is subserviently appended. It is the commercial center of the country, spiked with high-rise hotels and office buildings, wrapped round with expressways, and plagued by downtown parking problems. You are alone, attended by a white bartender in crisp red and gold. Behind you at a cocktail table are four young businessmen, slightly tipsy, bantering boyishly in Afrikaans. Two tables away a solitary black man, tweed jacket and trim beard, nurses a tall beer, with a paperback book open before him. Casually, one of the mustachioed businessmen tosses a peanut on the black's table; it bounces insolently to the side of the hand holding the paperback, black wrist in white cuff. There is no reaction. The whites' loud talk is abruptly hushed, punctuated by muffled snorts of derision. Soon, another peanut hits the table, another hits the book, a fourth plops menacingly on the padded shoulder of the tweed jacket. The barman studiously polishes glasses. You are transfixed, uncertainly alarmed, angry, a bit anxious. After three or four eternal minutes, the white men return to their conversation, and the black man perdures in his impassive posture.

What has happened is against the law.

If you had insisted on complaining and the white men had persisted in their little prank, the police might well have arrived, embarrassed at your presence, avuncularly annoyed with the young men, scrupulously correct with the black man, probably a visitor but possible a native South African businessman himself (South Africa does have the largest black middle class in Africa). Boys will be boys. Best ignore the whole thing. The black man may have some trouble later; be disinvited for his own good from this bar. You suddenly find your voice and make some overly loud banal remark to the barman, who agrees with hysterical bonhomie. Law and order have been restored.

The Law. The law is the key to our perpetually selective outrage at South African apartheid. White South Africans, even during the recent years of increasing township violence and repressive emergency measures, present themselves to the world as the embattled custodians of civil order in a continent notorious for whimsical massacres. As this is written, far more Africans have died of starvation in Chad and Ethiopia, because of deliberate government policies, than have died in all the impoverished South African homelands put together. Yet racism is enshrined in the South African legal system, however many decent people try to circumvent it, just as racism is against U.S. law, however many Americans practice it.

The Law. South Africa is a police state and was so long before recent states of emergency were declared: a Poland with palm trees. You are lucky if the police formally arrest you, for then you must be charged. In that case, you can get a lawyer and perhaps be released on bail pending trail. But any policeman of senior rank (in the state of emergency, any policeman or soldier) may "detain" you—throw you in jail for ninety days without charges, then renew the detention for another ninety days, then for another. Why have they come for you? You may never know. Perhaps you are suspected of being a terrorist, which is so broadly defined in the Terrorism Act that anyone who "embarrasses" the government can be legally considered a terrorist. Perhaps you are just a suspicious character, or a valuable witness to something you know nothing about. Your white skin is no protection here. Although all the laws are differentially enforced, the security laws do not observe apartheid.

Knowing this, you are amazed at the rarity of uniformed policemen. Johannesburg is a cosmopolitan center, yet one can arrive at Jan Smuts Airport, take a cab the many miles through the suburbs to the business center, and the only uniforms observed will have been on customs officials, bus drivers, doormen, and bellboys. Curiously, this visible absence creates the apprehension that there are even more policemen, in mufti, than the government could possibly muster. Doubt about real identities is a national state of mind.

You are digging into scrambled eggs and bacon at high noon on a well-windowed connecting structure between two bustling department stores in the main shopping center of downtown Jo'burg, not far from the railroad station. It is thronged with blacks, a few white faces in the milling crowds. Your white companion points to a traffic light just below. A few weeks ago, you are informed, he was robbed at the height of the rush hour right there, a knife to his white throat from behind, while another black robber went through his pockets deftly. Eight stitches took care of the farewell slash across the chest. Passersby minded their own business. Police? None were about in uniform, as usual, and undercover men on more important security detail would not reveal themselves for such a trivial cause. They might have come forward if the white man had been foolish enough to pursue his attackers into the railway station, packed with bustling blacks hurrying to get home before the witching hour when special passes would be required for staying in the white center of Jo'burg. The white man might be stopped from running into a black area, for his own good. It might be against the law.

You are standing on a hill overlooking a Scarsdalish inner suburb of Jo'burg. Your companion this time is a white executive, known as a liberal who pays blacks and whites alike for equal work. He is a patriot, too, proud of his country's material accomplishments, pleased with the recent relaxations of petty apartheid, the Jim Crow segregating of public facilities. Making a broad proprietal gesture over the scene of tree-shaded lanes and discreet estate fences, bourgeois comfort wrested from the unforgiving red earth of Africa, he smiles confidently. You mention freedom. (At that time and place, no state of emergency had been declared.)

"Ah, yes," he admits, "the two of us could be standing here on this balmy winter day and a car could pull up and we could be hustled off, perhaps never to be heard of again. But it would be most unlikely. The police are not mad dogs; they would need a pretty convincing argument to detain us."

"Or," you suggest, "a plausible anonymous accusation."

He makes a gesture of exasperation at this naive visitor.

"Yes, yes, but, well, we are under siege from all over the world. The entire continent has vowed to bring us down. The Soviets consider us the key to the entire southern tier. And what about your CIA and FBI? Don't you think they keep tabs on subversives? In any event, the detention laws are perfectly legal—and necessary."

You recall that the South African Broadcasting Corporation, the SABC, the state monopoly for radio and television, had the night before run an American Defense Department film version of their latest report on "Soviet Military Power," with Secretary Caspar W. Weinberger issuing dire warnings as animated hammer-and-sickle emblems marched menacingly down the coast of Africa. There was little possibility, within this closed system, for the South African executive to see a broadcast rebuttal to this particular view of the world.

It is a pity, for this man is decent and honest; he is remarkably candid in his willingness to discuss the existence of the Security Police and the awesome extent of their powers. South Africa is a vast land, bigger than France and Germany combined. It has three mountain ranges of great beauty, an endless seacoast that joins two oceans, red deserts and white deserts, deep forests and high savannahs, Irish-green vineyards and Utah-bleak scrub country. It has one of the largest seaports in the world at Durban on the Indian Ocean and one of the most dramatic scenic harbors of the planet at Cape Town on the South Atlantic. Johannesburg itself is an African Denver, six thousand feet above the sea on the high veldt, straddling the Reef or Rand, a deep rock backbone veined with gold. No matter where you go, the topic of the Security Police is met with the same fearful freeze that the topic of cancer evokes elsewhere.[1] Horrible thing. Dreadful. Could get any one of us at any time. But it is in rather bad taste, depressing and neurotically morose, to go on about it. Chances are you will be passed by—unless you are foolish enough to take unnecessary risks.

The avoidance of politically heated topics is mightily encouraged by the law itself. Just as South Africa is a police state without too many police in evidence (and, as a matter of fact, with fewer police per capita than New York City), so, too, many of its political prisoners are not in jail. Rather, they are *banned,* a form of punishment unique to South Africa. Banning admits of different degrees, but it is fundamentally a form of house arrest and a stripping of political rights. In some cases the banned person may not be with more than two people at once. It is a crime for anyone to quote him or her, even from the unbanned past. The banned are nonpersons.

Although banning is more humane than solitary confinement in a sternly administered prison, it has a more chilling effect on civil liberties in general because, as it were, it makes of the entire country a prison. The invisibility of the police makes you think they are everywhere. The invisibility of the banned makes you think that any odd passerby may be one of the damned—a prisoner in mufti.

The emergency decrees and the detention of more than 30,000 people, as of the end of 1986, only underscore the obsession of the authorities with legal forms for their own essentially lawless behavior. What the various fine details of the decrees and regulations do is to put a theoretical boundary around the areas of draconian repression. But there remains yet another device for legal illegality, and that is the virtually duplicate shadow government that operates beyond the knowledge of the legislature or court system. It is the intricate system of security management so characteristic of totalitarian states. China had its Red Guards who stood watch over every function to guarantee political orthodoxy; Nazi Germany had the ever-present party loyalists in all levels of the government, education, and the military sworn to the leader; Stalin had his political commissars who told generals what to do. A secret real government makes a mockery of the facade of legality of the surface government. And of course, mutatis mutandis, there is the same alarming propensity in the American leadership, from Nixon's "Plumbers" to Reagan's National Security Council.

In South Africa, the agency of fear is the State Security Council. Chaired by State President P. W. Botha, the SSC expands and contracts at the whim of the leadership from a central core of the ministers of defense, foreign affairs, police, and justice and their lieutenants. This central organ reaches out to the smallest village through a tight network of a central Working Committee, an operations Secretariat, a dozen regional Joint Management Centers, three score subregional JMCs, and 448 local JMCs, each of which has an intelligence committee, a political-social-economic committee, and a communications committee. These local intelligence committees are the nerve centers of control through domestic spying and the use of informers: all the information is funneled to the National Interpretation Branch in the SCC Secretariat in Pretoria.

It is ironic that this shadow government, with the Orwellian title of the National Security Management System, is practiced by Botha's Nationalists in a sort of mirror image of the black African National Congress and other antiapartheid groups, who are delegitimizing the official local black town councils and setting up what the government selectively brands "kangaroo courts." The Nationalists have a kangaroo kingdom of their own devising, while the "real" government of elected representatives is a sort of elaborate charade without power or punch. This emasculation of duly elected officials (if only by whites) reached near completion in the new emergency regulations of December 11, 1986, which abolished one of the most sacred aspects of the quasi-Westminster system that the Nationalists used to boast of: freedom of debate and speech in the legislature. This abolition was accomplished in a typically "legal" way: Legislative speech is still privileged, but only in the actual chamber; if reported elsewhere, it may be judged "subversive," and is thus punishable. Open court proceedings, the sole surviving arena for uncensored reporting, may no longer be reported, if detainees are involved, until after a verdict is reached.

Clockwork Censors

You have just finished a succulent broiled fish fillet washed down with a delicate Cape version of Macon Village at the Civil Service Club in Cape Town. Your table is on a glassed-in veranda overlooking the Botanical Gardens, beyond which are the dignified whitewashed silhouettes of the Parliament buildings. Towering over the entire scene is Table Mountain, for the moment trailing a plume of silken vapor. Cape Town, physically, is a place of enchantment. It combines the best features of Bermuda, San Francisco, and Vancouver: salt sea air, red flowers, royal palms and tall pines, misty parks, booming surf, crowded and hunched mountains shoving their shoulders into the city. At times, silver curtains of sun showers sweep down one street, leaving its neighbor bone-dry.

You have been lunching with Tony Heard, the editor of the *Cape Times,* one of the principal English-speaking opposition papers, which has more than once been punished by the government for its lack of cooperation. Heard himself has been detained and arrested for violating press laws. Gerald Shaw, the distinguished assistant editor, is also present. As with so many South Africans, they are gracious hosts as well as witty and earnest conversationalists. After lunch you stroll the few blocks to the editorial offices. Once there, Heard makes an ambiguous gesture toward a word-processing station, which Shaw activates; the printer rasps into life and spews page after page of dense text, which mounts steadily in the tray. When it finishes, Heard hands you the packet. It is an updated version, fresh this day, of the various regulations that control the press and the latest list of the banned, the unquotables.

"High tech," he says, with resigned irony.

The Law. You recall being in the offices of John Dugard, the celebrated civil rights advocate and human rights activist, professor of law at Witwatersrand University in Johannesburg, whose Centre for Applied Legal Studies has been the principal instrument for appealing censorship decisions. It had come as a surprise that his highly critical, yet massive scholarly work, *Human Rights and the South African Legal Order,* had not been banned. Wryly, he had mentioned that the book had probably passed muster because of its scholarly technical nature. But the dust jacket of the book was not so fortunate. It quoted the endorsement of a scholar who had subsequently been banned. So all the dust jackets had to be stripped from the book, an expensive and time-consuming process. Thus the great utility of the up-to-the-minute list provided for Tony Heard, who could hardly afford to dump entire editions of the *Cape Times.* Gulliver in Laputa could not have run across anything more meticulously absurd.

Of course, the need to avoid quoting nonpersons is but a minor itch amid a raging eczema of regulations. Laws unrelated to communications have censoring codicils. Acts primarily concerned with the police or prisons, as we shall see, forbid the reporting of "false" information concerning them. No information about nuclear energy can be reported at all. The Internal Security Act bristles with direct hostility toward even the most gentlemanly versions of press inquiry. Tertius Myburgh, editor of the Johannesburg-based but nationally circulated *Sunday Times,* told me, with baffling good humor, that he was given a suspended three-month sentence for merely printing the facts of a case that was known the world over: the aborted coup of the Seychelles and the subsequent amnesty granted the failed mercenaries, some of whom were South African intelligence agents. Publishing the names of intelligence agents is illegal.

It is the Publications Act, however, which embodies most of the regulations that affect freedom of expression in South Africa. Like any act of Parliament, it is crammed with details, exemptions, exceptions to exemptions, procedural rules, and conditions for the suspension of procedural rules; nevertheless, the sweep and scope of the repression is breathtaking. It embraces all media and even includes "objects" which may be seen as expressive of an idea or political position. The grounds for banning any form of expression are extremely broad and vague. Anything that might cause "ill-feeling" among the different races is reason for finding an utterance or object "undesirable." T-shirt slogans, key-ring emblems, films, audiotapes, videotapes, song lyrics, plays, cabaret skits, even government broadcast material, are all subject to banning just as much as the obviously threatening political speeches, books, socially critical novels, and works of scholarship. There are stretches of blank pages in locally published encyclopedias.

Paradoxically, however, it is in keeping with South Africa's curious mixture of Draco and due process that abundant criticism of the government flourishes, as do scathing condemnations of the central policy of apartheid. There is a handful of small opposition parties and a coalition of the disaffected, called the United Democratic Front, in this overwhelmingly one-party country. National Party members and government officials are quick to point out that this toleration of vigorous criticism is unusual for Africa. Although the picture is complex and the freedom is both subtly and crudely curtailed, they are sadly correct in the context of sub-Saharan Africa. Without one-tenth of the regulations or one-hundredth of the bureaucracy to enforce it, the rest of Africa has a much less free press, because the media that manage to exist there are either state owned and operated or bribed into compliance. Worse, many African media are bullied into submission by totally unpredictable extrajudicial state terrorism.[2]

The cultural shape that freedom of expression assumes in the legal climate of South Africa is therefore of unique interest. Some countries have unabashed state censorship. Some countries have a bought-and-paid-for press, whatever the official policies. Still others have a sacred tradition of freedom of expression in religion, morals, and political affairs that may or may not foster an encouraging milieu for countercultural modes of expression. Astonishingly, South Africa shares in all these characteristics, sometimes tilting toward freedom, sometimes toward repression. It has a legal culture cognate to our own yet in some ways alien to it. The differences are for the most part technical, stemming from the former Westminster system and the Dutch-Roman elements in the area of common law.

Imagine, if you will, a United States Department of Public Media, which would operate all the radio and television stations in the country and make all the programming decisions. All broadcasters, from television anchorpersons to station janitors, would be federal employees, like park rangers or Pentagon public relations colonels. Now imagine, beyond and above this legion for communication control, a United States Department of Public Expression which could act on its own or respond to anonymous complaints about any book, magazine, newspaper, statue, painting, poster, videotape, song lyric—in short, about any "object" which might "express" anything. The department would then be free to ban the sale, distribution, even the possession, of any "object" because it was "un-American" or "anti-Christian" or "undemocratic" or "depraved" or "communistic." Further imagine a Federal Media Appeal Board, which would review the censorship decisions of the government, now gently chiding the department as too narrow-minded, now castigating excessive leniency. Finally, picture these agencies of repression presiding over a plethora of varied media that in no way resemble the great gray yea-saying of totalitarian states, but rather remind one of our own vulgar and sassy, bright and brave, deep and honest confusion of voices. In some ways the media spectrum of South Africa is broader than our own, because the churches and universities there are in the mainstream of political debate and their spheres of influence are less narrowly construed than our own.

In this hysterically anticommunist country, with state-run higher education, there are scores of Marxist professors, some of the vulgar variety. A city block distant from "Wits"—Witwatersrand University—there is a bookstore that specializes in Marxist literature and revolutionary tracts. On the other side of the railroad tracks, quite literally, is Khotso House, the headquarters of the South African Council of Churches (SACC), which provided Desmond Tutu with the strong and secure antiapartheid platform that led to the Nobel Prize and his elevation to the Anglican primacy of South Africa. Until it was banned during the most recent state of emergency, SACC published *Ecunews,* filled with thoughtful yet uncompromising denunciations of many government actions and policies, particularly the forced removals of blacks from newly declared white areas.

There is a large number of civil rights lawyers who donate their services or work for much lower fees than other work would garner in order to obtain due process for the detained and arrested, particularly among the poor blacks. During the mass detentions of the summer of 1986, platoons of such lawyers brought countless court actions. The South African Institute of Race Relations, a rough counterpart of the American Civil Liberties Union, issues a broad program of scholarly books and statistical surveys that are implicit condemnations of state-sponsored racism. Its massive annual survey of issues, topics, and events, crammed with careful documentation, is the standard reference work for recent history. Ironically, the institute published a study of censorship in 1983 that itself would have to undergo the censorship process from the Directorate of Publications.

Perhaps because of the climate of censorship, theater is more politically conscious in South Africa than in the United States, reminding one more of Czechoslovakia. *Woza Albert,* written and presented by two spectacularly energetic young black Africans, is a dazzling set of skits and mime that works off the single premise of Christ staging the Second Coming in South Africa; it is comic apocalyptic that sizzles with satire. Produced at the Market Theatre in Jo'burg, which features protest plays as well as Neil Simon-type imports, *Woza* (rise up) *Albert* (Albert Lutuli, a revered Christian Zulu chief, African National Congress president, and Nobel laureate) has toured, uncensored, South Africa and the world. *Country Lovers* and *City Lovers,* two of six short films adapted from Nadine Gordimer short stories and locally produced, are well-wrought cries of controlled outrage against sexual apartheid. Despite an on-again-off-again censorship status, these films have been screened all over the world. Finally, there is the globally noted irony of exhibiting the imported superhit *Gandhi* before segregated audiences.

The letter of the censorship laws, like the letter of the security laws, is meticulously detailed, yet the spirit of their application seems capricious. Dissident South Africans develop a sense of what is currently getting by, and the brave push against this moving edge until they meet rock.

Cultivated Babel

You are walking down a "street" in Crossroads, the disputed no-man's-land some miles from Cape Town, teeming with black squatters in cardboard or plywood hovels stapled over with plastic garment bags. There is not a blade of grass in the compacted dust. There are no sewers. Amazingly, there is a heroic form of cleanliness here, and no foul odors flavor the sere air.

Crossroads has a dogged civic pride born of its very insufficiency. The government has been bulldozing the hovels and trucking people further out from the city, claiming, among other things, that no sanitary facilities are present or providable. The "approved" more distant locations impose a crippling commute. Khayalitsha, the latest, has neat rows of cinder-block and corrugated tin shacks, with plumbing. It is built on sand, surrounded by high barbed wire, the stark grounds spiked with immensely tall lighting poles that cast an alien sodium vapor glare at midnight: a Stanley Kubrick set for a futuristic nightmare.

You have also driven through Langa, built closer to town, but meant only for men, not families. The men are stored, not housed, in concrete bunkers, like sides of beef. They are often drunk, always angry. Here you did receive some taunts, some menacing gestures, on a late smoky Sunday afternoon. Unlike these pitilessly planned places, Crossroads is a home, however squalid.

You enter a large cinder-block building, once owned by the international self-awareness movement, Transcendental Meditation, now used as a community center. You have come to see live protest theater. The blacks, advised by two white women students from Cape Town University, are to put on a play in their own tribal language; its general drift, if not clear from the action, will be explained by locals at your side. No set, few props, a bare wall. The story is about a family going to jail for living in a white area, about unrequited love, about sickness, about revenge and rage. To get the girl who rejects him, the protagonist must present to his medicine man the testicles of a white man; these he duly obtains from the policeman who has been hounding his family. *Exeunt omnes* to that plaintive African chant that has a hint of the Gregorian. After the performance, the shy young actors gather around you, thinking you might be an agent from the big time.

You stroll over the dirt floor, chatting in English with the gently mannered and friendly black actors, heading for the door. Outside, the young white woman adviser is angry. She had asked them to present a more authentic play, one about displaced native life. This was patched-up Americanized theater of rage, staged to meet your assumed American liberal expectations.

Your black African guide for the day, a social worker, pulls up in a battered Volkswagen and lurches you toward Nyanga, another black area, but legal, with semipermanent buildings, even some struggling gardens despite the drought.

The guide is a handsome, compact man from a different township, Guguletu, established and settled; he was born there thirty-two years ago. At the time, it was thought to be on the list of areas to be declared off-limits for blacks, who would be subject to "relocation"—forced removal.

"We will have to fight. We just won't go."

He says this matter-of-factly as you begin walking through a scrubby field to an old white farmhouse, ramshackled and sagging, in need of paint, but generously proportioned and graced with a wraparound veranda. There must be fifteen or so men lounging about, smoking with the air of drained combatants between battles. Inside, in what must have been the front parlor, a grizzled thin black man is playing a battered but tuned upright piano. You are led into a further room, quite large, dusty, filled with clay figures. This is the Nyanga Community Art Center. The next room, not quite so large, is filled with paintings and sketches. There is no attempt to sell or promote anything. Modestly, but knowingly, the works are discussed, the voices soft and serious. The eyes of the speakers are intense, as are the rapid hand movements, commanding you to carry away a message: These people are not beasts of burden. They have sensitivities, dreams for their children, social aspirations, even bourgeois pretensions.

The next day you are back in Cape Town, in the shadow of Table Mountain, driving through a bright neighborhood of middle-class homes, with front yards, plantings, dogs, people chatting on front steps. It would remind you of a Creole area in New Orleans except for the vigor of the salt air. The district is designated for "coloured" people, as those of mixed white and black ancestry are classified under apartheid. Awaited in one of the homes, you are met with casual and natural hospitality. Soon you are sipping a beer, your back against the refrigerator door, as the women bustle and the children shriek around you, getting ready for dinner. Pat, the father of the family, is expertly filleting a fish he caught that morning. Over his shoulder, he talks to you about his great love, the Afrikaans language: its earthy flavor, sexual frankness, its connections with manor life and with an earlier, seemingly happier, time for his people.

Pat is a high school teacher who refuses any longer to teach Afrikaans, the language of the oppressor. This is a sad thing, since until recently Afrikaans was the first language of the "coloured," many of whose ancestors were the slaves of servants of Boers-Afrikaners, or, of course, Afrikaners themselves. Disowning the language is painful, but beyond that, the "coloured" are beginning to dissociate themselves from their very name. If they cannot be white, they might as well be black, true brothers to the oppressed underside of apartheid. The category is of course hardly scientific, bundling a loose mixture of black, white, imported Malay, Indian, and East Asian. Historically, however, it is quite real.

The Afrikaners have always had a special affection for this group, roughly comparable to the "decent white" regard for the blacks in the older American South. One of the major precipitators of the current political crisis was the passing of the new constitution, which gave the Indians and the "coloured" each a Parliament of their own (about which Thomas More's comment on the Parliament under the Tudors is most apt: like the male teat, decorative but useless). The regime still hopes to use the "non-white/nonblack" groups as buffers between themselves and the angry Africans. In time, they promise the "coloured" full political rights, something they had over fifty years ago, when at least the men had a real vote.

At dinner, switching over to the superb Cape wine, you are bathed in a happy family babble of teasing, dispute, conversation, Pat's strong teacher-voice cutting through to you, still talking about the beauty of Afrikaans, which is a language concocted from Dutch, German, and French, with a certain Flemish fullness to it. As with Norwegian, Afrikaans literature is inaccessible to the world because so few read it.

A local priest drops in, obviously very close to the family. (Pat is the church organist.) He has come to take you back to your hotel, but first he sits down to share dessert, charm the children, tease the ladies, and argue with Pat about his abilities as a fisherman. Later, out on the street, slightly muzzy from the wine and beer, you get in the priest's car and are driven off serenely, as he waves back to dozens of families that know and apparently love him. As you leave the area for the open road, roaring along with the rest of the traffic, the priest turns to you seriously and begins to talk about his country.

The "coloured" number a bit over two-and-a-half million, mostly clustered around the Cape. This is almost exactly equal to the number of Afrikaners spread around the country. Although they predominate among Cape whites, Afrikaners are nevertheless concentrated in the Orange Free State and the Transvaal, the high veldt of the northeast, the center for mining, finance, and government administration.

The English-speaking whites (he goes on) are spread all over the country, but they predominate in Natal, the province containing Durban, the major commercial port. As in India, English is the unifying medium. All ethnic groups can deal with it, at least as a second language, although it may be utterly foreign in some isolated rural areas. Generally, the English are in commerce and the professions; the Afrikaners are farmers or in government service. Although more Afrikaners are getting into business, they among the whites would have the most to lose if the African majority ruled, for they would lose their government jobs. Productive whites may be welcome to stay in a new black order, but it is doubtful they would man the bureaucracy.

The Afrikaners are a tight-knit white tribe, descendants of Dutch, German, and French Huguenot settlers, as well as some blacks, no doubt. The English are in fact predominantly British, but the term is used to embrace all whites who are not Afrikaners. The Catholic priest telling you about all this is himself something of an anomaly since he is an Afrikaner, virtually all of whom are members of the Dutch Reformed Church, "the National Party at prayer."

He looks levelly at you for a moment, his eyes off the road. Overseas, you are told, the impression one might have is of an overwhelmingly black country dominated by a few clever and cruel whites. Not quite so simple, although it is essentially correct in the moral sense. Nonblacks, to put it that way, number about eight million. The 26 million or so blacks (the census is not terribly accurate about them, just as the United States census is not very accurate about its Hispanic population) are tribally fragmented over a vast, mostly desert landscape. Many of the few (about ten million) who are close to the major cities or in so-called white rural areas have been forcibly relocated to the homelands, often remote, allegedly ancestral, tribal reservations like the Transkei, Bophuthatswana, or Venda. These territories are being converted into separate countries, although the international community looks upon these artificial fiefdoms as internal colonies. The regime had high hopes for this plan until, under foreign pressure, it suspended, at least momentarily, the policy of denying blacks citizenship in their own country.

Whatever the cosmetic packaging of the policy, to the regime it certainly was and may still remain a plausible foundation for maintaining white supremacy. Should it succeed, the role of the "coloured" would be pivotal, giving the urban whites a strong local plurality vis-à-vis the urban blacks. If the "coloured" decide they are black, as it appears they are doing, thanks to both the United Democratic Front and the sledgehammer politics of the Nationalists, then the game is clearly up.

Petty apartheid, the Jim Crow practices in public facilities that are truly being phased out in the larger cities (where they matter), are trivial and largely irrelevant to the grander strategies of both apartheid and liberation, a point sometimes lost on American liberals who remember the U.S. civil rights activism of the sixties. The priest suddenly pulls over to the side of the road. "You've got to see something."

You drive back a bit, still in the central area of Cape Town, only about a half-hour's brisk stroll from your hotel. You have entered a sea of rubble, level and combed, the size of Harvard Yard, its emptiness emphasized by three widely separated standing buildings: the priest's own Catholic church at one end, a mosque to the east, and an abandoned Episcopal church, now used as a community art center, further to the south. This is what is left of the notorious District 6, a "coloured" area once densely packed with a bustling community. It was declared too close to the center of things, too poor, too unsanitary, a hotbed of crime. The people were moved out to more planned, more controlled, more remote places. And then the bulldozers came in and leveled everything. To the north, where the rubble rears up toward Table Mountain, a new row of luxurious townhouses, reserved for whites, had just been erected.

It is this kind of action that makes "coloured" solidarity with the blacks rather than with the whites more likely. Pat's family, in this scheme, is between a rock and a hard place, deprived of their language and left only with another white one, English; deprived of their local habitation and name.

The priest has a professionally cheerful manner as he ticks off these observations, but his eyes are sad, flickering over smashed walls that you suppose might have housed memories of parish life, good and bad. Now there is a void. He drives you back to your hotel in five minutes.

White on White

The Mount Nelson Hotel in Cape Town is a rambling Bermudan pink structure, approached up a long drive guarded by soaring royal palms and surrounded by its own garden, which is alive with songbirds even in winter. Inside, past a very efficient porter who disarmingly resembles Monty Python's John Cleese, there are cozy, hearth-dominated tea lounges, walls and drapes in flowery pastels. It is veddy, veddy British, and the black and Indian staff serve with the style of the Savoy.

You are reminded that the British ruled South Africa for centuries under a variety of political arrangements and at the cost of some bloody battles. The last battle was against the Boers, the Afrikaner settlers, whom the British defeated and kept down for generations with their inimitable class system. Only a few years ago, to speak Afrikaans in these rooms or in a posh shop was an admission of hairy-backed country-bumpkinism. Afrikaners do not forget this, especially since they turned the political tables on the English in the 1948 elections, when the National Party began its first uninterrupted climb to consolidated power. Among many other more obvious things, apartheid is an attempt to restore the legal and social bondage of the darker-skinned that had been self-righteously diminished by the long arm of Victorian conscience, which was eager to "improve" natives.

Pieter Dirk Uys, a cabaret satirist who often does his stand-up routines in drag, plays an upper-class English matron who between bonbons confesses her enormous hatred of apartheid—and of blacks, too, of course. Dirk Uys, an Afrikaner, does an Afrikaner matron as well as a merciless rendition of every verbal and facial tic of the state president, whom he can uncannily resemble. As in Moscow or New York, the great causes have left in their wake small hates and parlor grudges that the Directorate of Publications is just as happy to have lanced in public.

So the apartheid is not just a question of black or white. It is the codified summit of a complex ziggurat of caste and culture, language and bloody history. It is an ingenious exploitation of African tribalism, that most intense form of the universal human need for in-group–out-group dichotomies which animates petty practices and energizes grand ideologies. Prison life, for instance, is rife with conflicts between rival gangs, and the warders encourage it. They, in turn, are part of a civil service caste system that recalls Evelyn Waugh's satiric view of the British army.

Apartheid is defined by its inventors as separate development and defended as a protection for disparate cultures. This formulation, if applied on a global scale, is alarmingly parallel to the language of apartheid's archenemies, Third World members of UNESCO and the United Nations, who have been demanding a "New World Communication Order" that will honor local cultures and oust the "information imperialism" of that great vulgar leveler, Western mass culture, with its mouthwash, blue jeans, and James Bond movies.

Unhappily for ideologues on both sides of the argument, tribalism is not a total principle of social organization in the modern world, however fervently some form of tribalism, in Africa or Lebanon or Ireland or Iran or Israel, is invoked. People cannot help belonging to a variety of cultures and groups in different degrees at the same time. A Frenchman may eat an American hamburger, see a British movie, revere a German philosopher, enjoy Spanish music, use Japanese technology. Look at any nation, even a Denmark, which banks on cultural homogeneity, and ethnic diversity appears. On a grander scale, India, China, Malaysia, and Polynesia have all mixed and mingled cults and customs over the centuries. The high-tech communication distribution systems developed by the West and Japan may pour images of Madison Avenue all over the globe, but those very images are ladled from a huge melting pot of the creative and kitschy by hordes of ethnically diverse contributors.

The South African media system is part of this diversity and part of this unity, but it exists within a symbolic apartheid system of its own.

Media World

At one end of the media spectrum is the South African Broadcasting Corporation, SABC, the state monopoly for all television and almost all radio; it serves as an arm of the state, much more so than French television does and only slightly less so, if these things can be measured, than Soviet broadcasting. At the other end are the print organs of the black labor unions and black communities, which focus on specific grievances that stem from daily coping with life under apartheid. In the middle are the establishment presses: First come the fiercely loyalist Afrikaans press, which has a mildly dissenting wing on the right, growing less mild each day of township unrest. Next come the English newspapers and magazines, which range from apolitical sex-and-soccer tabloids to brave antiapartheid journals, mostly from the left. Student and church publications are politically aware, usually from a sharply left or right viewpoint, and have a much greater influence than do similar organs in America. Finally, there are the nonbroadcast audiovisual media, from rock and reggae records to videotapes, live theater, and funeral orations. Although these formats favor either apolitical entertainment or moral uplift, they nonetheless offer instances of both the most extreme state propaganda and the most radical rejections of the establishment, especially through the unique form of black protest theater.

In surveying the media world of South Africa, one must bear in mind that most South Africans cannot or do not choose to read.

In a country with an educated white population of over four million, with a middle-class mixed race group of about two million, a significant number of Asians and the largest black middle class in Africa (admittedly a small part of the total black populace), the largest single print run is under half a million, for the weekly *Sunday Times*. The largest daily, *The Star*, runs well under a quarter million. None of the Afrikaans dailies exceeds ninety thousand. The solitary newsmagazine, *The Financial Mail*, modeled on Great Britain's *Economist*, reaches thirty thousand. *Frontline*, an English liberal feature magazine similar in style to Clay Felker's original *New York Magazine*, has a readership of ten thousand.

Books are very expensive in South Africa, partially due to the censorship laws (a banned person's books are all retroactively contraband), which have made remaindering impossible, and partially due to the high cost of importing books. Outside of schools and churches, there are few bookstores in the country, although, as in the United States, drugstores and newstands have paperback racks.

Once the literacy factor is accounted for, however, one must not underestimate the indirect, and for that reason perhaps more powerful, influence of the press. American broadcast news would have to invent *The New York Times*, and even the *New England Journal of Medicine*, if they did not already exist. So, too, South African audiovisual media depend on print for their ideas and most of their facts.

The most important influence of the mass media system, however, is its intrinsic marketing mentality, beyond and behind any fundamental moral conflict about apartheid. It forms the assumed unquestioned background to everyday life, dominating the public images and inner fantasies of black and white, of South and North Africans, of American, French, and Japanese. In this context, Tom Selleck and Frank Sinatra, Pele and Jimmy Connors, Donna Sommers and Ralph Lauren are more important than Archbishop Desmond Tutu or State President P. W. Botha. Despite the increased global coverage during the state of emergency and the heightened curiosity provoked by tighter press controls, most people outside of South Africa have not paid much heed to either of them, but probably are aware of Sun City, the African Las Vegas in Bophuthatswana. Here whites and blacks dance and drink together and watch Vegas acts like those of magician Doug Henning or, until the boycott of the mid-eighties, Sammy Davis, Jr. As we shall see, the commercial transformation of publics into markets makes T-shirt slogans and rock lyrics, which fall under the all-seeing eye of the Directorate of Publications, far more influential than Professor Dugard's scholarly skewering of the legal system.

Although losing ground to the secularizing influence of the media, the churches still provide the single major forum for the apartheid struggle, which at a time of increasing violence still remains more a matter of words and symbols than of guns or fists. Although the Cape Parliament formally disestablished the Anglican Church in 1875, both it and the Dutch Reformed Church have a history of ecclesiastical leadership in civil affairs. With the ascendancy of the Afrikaners and the National Party, it became the increasingly reluctant task of the Dutch Reformed Church of South Africa to demonstrate that the status quo was the will of God. Virtually all the other ethnic groups, black and white, have their own churches, from Catholic to Congregationalist. Most of these are politically united under the banner of the South African Council of Churches (SACC), which, as noted, has gone far beyond declaring apartheid a heresy as an idea and fundamentally anti-Christian as a policy (which it has repeatedly done in a variety of forums). SACC supports a string of media beyond its own churchly publications. It gave an initial grant to *Frontline;* it produces videotape documentaries and editorials decrying substandard conditions for the black population; it regularly sends abroad exposés of government repression. In effect, SACC serves as an antiestablishment church.

The government has struck back with the Eloff Commission. South African commissions are similar to American congressional investigating committees in powers and purpose, but they are totally creatures of the executive arm, and their members are not necessarily elected officials. As in a previous investigation of a dissident church group (Beyers Naude's Christian Institute), this commission zeroed in on the finances of SACC and found irregularities. It also accused the body of actively supporting terrorism. It did fall short of urging the government to declare SACC an "affected organization." This is a legalism which would forbid SACC to accept foreign money. Since SACC is greatly dependent on funds from the World Council of Churches and other outside sources, such a ruling would have been crippling.

Both sides share the conviction of American clergy and politicians that the mass media are their most effective instruments of control, for "winning hearts and minds." Interestingly, as the churches at home and abroad condemn apartheid with rising intensity, the South African Broadcasting Corporation has turned more and more of its religious programming within. Christianity is projected as a private inner choice with no social consequences. The programmers may have gotten their cue from the corporately run American media, who find it convenient to present morality as private, something that should not be socially or politically "imposed" on others. Churches are for charity, not justice.

United Stands

Under South African law, powerful political parties opposed to the nationalist regime, by definition, may not exist. To the right, the Conservative Party is gaining strength. But its quarrel with Pretoria is hardly about the premises of apartheid, but about the tactics of accommodation to growing black power. At the other end of the political spectrum, the Progressive Federal Party has long waged an honorable campaign against state-sponsored racism. Nevertheless, it has done so within the parameters of the existing order. Radical opposition that calls for immediate, universal suffrage in a unitary state is the province of outlawed and exiled parties like the African National Congress and the South African Communist Party.

If a fundamental principle of organization informs the strategy of apartheid, it is that *groups* have separate turfs, each with their own distinctive rights and rules. Hence, many "enlightened" whites are in favor of some sort of federalism, which would cede territories to different groups—whites, Zulus, Indians, "coloured," and so forth—within which universal suffrage would be granted. Then each group would have some sort of weighted representation in a national body, perhaps like the U.S. Senate, where each state, despite significant differences in size, population, and economic stature, has an equal voice.

Because apartheid is based on the primacy of groups, mainstream opposition is ideologically committed to the notion of equal rights for each individual, regardless of color or race. It is on this account that the ANC and others reject the term "coloured" and prefer to call all nonwhites black, as both a sign of solidarity and, paradoxically, of each individual's separate legal and moral existence apart from group identification. This focus on the individual (quite apart from certain tendencies toward strong-arm fascist tactics) has made Chief Gatsha Buthelezi's Zulu political party, Inkatha, unpopular with the mainstream opposition, even though it is opposed to white supremacy and constitutes the largest single political party in South Africa. Inkatha seeks group rights and group turf. As a powerful group with an existing territory (KwaZulu) and government, any future movement away from apartheid would place the Zulus in a much more favorable position than other blacks.

Because no political party can be formed legally in order to oppose apartheid, creating alliances of established groups such as unions and churches is the necessary tactical choice of the mainstream opposition. It is thus an irony that the opponents of apartheid have emphasized *group* membership in their fight for individual rights.

The current cycle of violence and repression was set off in 1983 by the campaign against the government's proposal for a new constitution, which in the end was adopted (blacks had no vote in this, or any other, referendum). The campaign was spearheaded by the United Democratic Front (UDF), a coalition of churches, student organizations, labor and trade unions, comprised of over six hundred *groups* with a cumulative membership of about two and a half million. Dr. Allan Boesak, the head of the "coloured" division of the Dutch Reformed Church, the *Sendingkerk,* Fr. Smangalisu Mkatchwa, the executive secretary of the Catholic Bishops, Cyril Ramaphosa, the head of the National Union of Mineworkers, and others, became leaders of the UDF, because they were already leaders of legal constitutuencies. Thus the opposition to the separate group politics of apartheid ironically depends upon the power of groups, of interlocking coalitions.

As with the churches, the labor unions had become platforms for the struggle against apartheid by default, once trade unions became legal for blacks on the recommendation of the 1979 Wiehahn Commission and were the only alternative to black political parties, which had been harassed and legislated out of existence. Since 1979 the number of black unionists had burgeoned from fifty thousand to almost one million, and strike man-days (blacks only) had jumped from twenty thousand to well over a million by 1986.

The government acquiesced to the Commission in its own self-interest, of course, seeing the creation of black trade unions as a chance to incorporate black labor demands into the system of controls the state has at its disposal. Originally, the unions by law were to exclude migrants, be of one race membership, be subject to state registration and financial regulations, and refrain from all party political activity. In fact, the unions organized both migrants and other races and mounted prominent political platforms. This created and still creates some internal disagreement between the populist and "workerist" elements in the union, since the latter

The Devised Divisions of South Africa

feel that the antiapartheid struggle detracts and distracts from the primary union goal of better wages, benefits, and working conditions for its members. Because eight hundred miners were killed in 1986 in accidents such as "rockbursts" and gas emissions, these needs are not trivial. Nonetheless, the election of 1987 and the preceding repression have fueled the populist cause further.[3]

As with the South African Council of Churches and the United Democratic Front, several unions since 1985 have formed a coalition of their own called the Congress of South African Trade Unions (COSATU).

COSATU replaced another coalition of unions, the once powerful Trade Union Council of South Africa, whose more exclusively "workerist" emphasis was seen as increasingly irrelevant during the states of emergency. Earlier still, a politicized union coalition, the South African Congress of Trade Unions, openly allied with the ANC, had been driven into exile. COSATU has successfully blended both "workerist" and populist aims.

On the economic side, COSATU aims to unify disparate small unions, form unions among the unorganized, and to establish a national minimum wage. On the political side, it aims to fight homeland policy, influx control, and pass laws while continuing to seek Pretoria's recognition of the ANC as the bargaining agent for the nonwhite population in the process of power sharing. Ironically, unions pose a threat to blacks in the homelands in the economic sense, even as they are allies for their political liberation, due to the fact they will exclude the unemployed from a chance to enter the labor market, just as they will exclude more immigrant workers in the frontline states, a conflict Pretoria hopes will grow.[4]

With a half million members and a campaign to organize industrywide single unions, COSATU is easily the most powerful element within UDF and a force that the government must reckon with. Before the 1987 election, Cyril Ramaphosa, whose National Union of Mineworkers is the largest union in COSATU, told Alan Cowell of *The New York Times* that the burgeoning numbers and community support of the black unions, a well as the symbiotic relationship they had with their employers (whose own associations, such as the Urban Foundation, Federated Chamber of Industries, and the Association of Chambers of Commerce, were pressuring Pretoria to ease up on labor for the sake of good business) would make it very unwise for the government to increase repressive measures.[5]

Pretoria still has some very strong cards to play. Despite the strength of COSATU's numbers, in its strongest area, the mines, only half of the 600,000 workers are unionized, and there are 400,000 on the waiting list for employment in the mines. In January 1986, 20,000 workers who went on strike in a platinum mine in the homeland of Bophuthatswana were summarily dismissed. For its plan to succeed, COSATU must organize a labor force of six million, 80 percent of which is non-unionized. There are no strike funds to speak of.[6]

The depressing and unforeseen swing to the right in the elections of 1987 has dimmed opposition prospects further.

Prague Spring Revisited

By the end of 1986, most of South Africa was in a declared state of emergency, and the press had been completely smothered by December 11 under layer upon layer of bureaucratic blankets. It was believed that most of the townships, the black urban ghettos near major white cities, were ungovernable, with black collaborationists—policemen, town councilmen, and others—abandoning ship in fear of their lives. The U.S. Congress had voted for sanctions, and more and more American companies were pulling out of South Africa. In what was seen as a defiant gesture of desperation, President Botha called for elections on May 6, 1987.

The period of the campaign was perceived from abroad as a period of further decay of National Party power, with furious defections to the extreme right at the mere suggestion of accommodation to black demands and some spectacular defections to the left. The Nationalist regime's ambassador to Great Britain, Denis Worrall, resigned his post in order to run against Botha's party for a White Assembly seat.

Most spectacular of all, Willem de Klerk, editor of *Rapport*, a widely read Afrikaans weekly supportive of the regime for years, and brother of F. W. de Klerk, National Party leader, also resigned his position in protest against the slowness of the party to accommodate the demands of the moderate left within the establishment, such as the abolition of pass laws. David de Villiers, a distinguished Afrikaner journalist and a former managing director of Nasionale Pers, the more powerful of two Afrikaner press chains loyal to the National Party, also resigned his position to serve as campaign adviser to Ester Lategan, yet another defector. To add to the sense of disintegration of support for Botha's policy of *Romanita* (agree and delay), over thirty academics at Stellenbosch University, the Afrikaner Harvard, signed a reform manifesto calling for the granting of full political rights to blacks through peaceful negotiation.

While Botha was losing on the political front, his policies were also being thwarted by the courts.

On March 10, 1987, police entered the offices of Johannesburg's leading daily, *The Star,* in an attempt to seize all editions carrying an advertisement urging public support of those detained under the emergency powers. But the paper, under editor Harvey Tyson, refused to permit the confiscation, citing lawyers' opinions that offending phrases (calling for release of the prisoners) had been deleted from the ad and that the call for release had been placed in a front-page editorial in the same editions. While the presses were rolling and police were standing by in the pressroom, Tyson and the paper's lawyers went to the Supreme Court to get a restraining order. They got it and the paper went to press.

But it was in April, just two weeks before the election, that the most stunning blow to Nationalist policies of censorship and stifling of dissent was dealt. On April 24, 1987, the Supreme Court of Natal at Pietermaritzburg declared the press restrictions of June 12, 1986, and December 11, 1986, to exceed the powers of the President. Also set aside were the rules against advertisements promoting banned organizations. The regulations of December 11 were found by the court to be particularly vague in defining what were "subversive statements," "security action," "unrest." The judgments were the results of actions brought against the government by the United Democratic Front and the Release Nelson Mandela Campaign.

Law Professor John Dugard, a constant critic of the judiciary (his magisterial *Human Rights and the South African Legal Order* and many other public statements and scholarly articles have sought to debunk what he believes to be the "myth" of the South African judiciary's independence) has noted that the Natal decision, and others like it, show a new character forming among some judges. Dugard believes that this development resulted from the pressure of the civil rights lawyers, the loss of black confidence in the courts, and the criticism of the International Commission of Jurists that the South African courts have been legitimizing apartheid.

It looked like a Prague spring was at hand. But it was not to be. On May 6, 1987, whites chose Botha again, and any electoral defections of note were to the right. Although P. W. Botha's party garnered only 52.28 percent of the popular vote, it gained seven seats to form a majority of 123, a total of 101 seats more than that of the new opposition, the Conservative Party.

As for the court ruling against censorship, it may have been a Pyrrhic victory: Acting on legal advice, ABC, CBS, Visnews, Independent Television News, Reuters, the Associated Press, *Time* and *Newsweek* covered a peaceful demonstration at the University of Cape Town that was violently dispersed by the police. Claiming that the regulations were still in force pending appeal, police arrested at least thirteen journalists at the scene. Many believe new rules, technically within the guidelines of the Natal ruling, will soon replace the overruled regulations.

The white elections of May 6, 1987, showed the still forceful appeal of the *laager* [the ring of covered wagons under "native" attack] mentality. Michael Buerk, the BBC-TV correspondent whose vivid pictures of protests and police retaliations led to his being deported by Pretoria (as was his Independent Television News counterpart), told Robert MacNeil on the May 25th *Mac-Neil-Lehrer News Hour* that this "spectral shift to the right" was a manifestation of "fatalistic defiance" of world condemnation on the part of the Afrikaners (and many other whites as well).

The emergency regulations had kept the whites "more ignorant than ever" of what was going on in their own country. Buerk noted that the "tolerance on the margins of apartheid" would be eroded further as a result of the election and that the cyclical violence that has characterized South Africa for the last hundred years would speed up drastically, with shorter and shorter lapses into periods of quiet desperation.

Dr. Allan Boesak of the United Democratic Front felt that the blacks would be more irreversibly alienated by the regime—not even comforted by the sporadic court rulings that had forced government repressions to stagger in legalistic spurts: "For every ruling in our favor, the South African government has a new law. . . . It is something happening in a remote courtroom out of the reach of the people.[7]

The Congress of South African Trade Unions (COSATU) had its headquarters in Johannesburg ripped to shreds the morning after the election by two powerful explosions. The previous week, COSATU offices throughout the country were raided by police. During the election period, COSATU meetings and rallies had been banned. A month before the election, six railroad strikers were shot by police.[8]

The struggle continues.

In what follows, I will try to show part of what counts for so much in this and other struggles for freedom around the world: the power of speech and press, both high-tech and humble, to force respect for freedom on those who would crush it.

NOTES

1. The writer has visited all the major cities and many of the towns and villages in every province of the Republic, as well as the "homelands" of Ciskei and Transkei. Interviews, shared meals and quarters, journeys, brief and lengthy encounters, were experienced with scores of South Africans. Rev. Bernard Spong of the Interchurch Media Programme, who shares my professional interests, was particularly informative and gave me entry to all the relevant and generous people at Khotso House, including, of course, the heroically accessible executive secretary, Bishop Desmond Tutu. Official South Africa was, I should add, both correct and cordial. My impressions and recollections are of course my own. I wish to emphasize that no one to whom I spoke ever favored any violent overthrow of duly constituted authority, although many were deeply opposed to apartheid on moral and humanitarian grounds and were well known to the authorities for this reason.

2. Since this point is often made as a justifying boast by the Nationalist regime, it is often either ignored or denied by opponents of apartheid, especially if they are white and safe. Black African journalists and authors outside South Africa are not helped by this selective and ultimately self-undermining tolerance.

Nigeria, the most populous black African country, has had a particularly sad history of press repression, particularly under the former military junta headed by Major General Muhammadu Buhari, whose infamous Decree Number 4 against criticism of the government was the pretext for a number of detentions of journalists, some of whom died under mysterious circumstances. When President Ibrahim Babangida took over the government in August 1985, he immediately repealed this decree. This was taken as a signal by my former student and friend, Dele Giwa, who had suffered for his journalistic courage and integrity, to try yet again with a new weekly newsmagazine, *Newswatch,* with the help of fellow journalists Ray Ekpu, Yakubu Mohammed, and Dan Agbese. The magazine was a sensation, which made us very proud of Dele, who was editor-in-chief. The new government was not very happy with this exercise in press freedom and made threatening noises. That did not daunt *Newswatch.* On October 19, 1986, Dele Giwa was blown apart by a letter bomb. There is a widespread belief, and fear, that the bomb originated with the Nigerian security police. It was a message for other critical journalists, but we hope that Dele Giwa, who wore his bravery lightly, who was warmly affectionate as well as coldly analytical, stands for a more enduring message to journalists and dissenters everywhere.

The March–April, 1987, issue of *Africa Report,* which was devoted to the question of press freedom in Africa, made for depressing reading. In our context the following items from this issue are of interest.

Nigeria has had a consistent history of press repression under a succession of otherwise diverse governments. Nigeria's Minister of Information and Culture, Prince Tony Momoh, has declared that "President Ibrahim Babangida's administration has consistently regarded the press as a true partner in progress." Less diplomatically, Nathan Shamuyarira, Minister of Information, Posts and Telecommunications for Zimbabwe, has routinely given notice to all foreign correspondents in his country that they will be deported for writing "negative" reports.

Robert Mugabe, highly regarded for many of his leadership qualities, has nonetheless (through the Mass Media Trust) effectively nationalized all but one of Zimbabwe's newspapers. Despite his early promises of press freedom, he has also introduced emergency powers that control what reporters can write and where they can go, detained reporters for long periods without charges, expelled a number of journalists, and refused entry visas to others. Kadoma, a suburb of Harare, Zimbabwe's capital, was the site of an agreement on treatment of the press by the frontline states (black-ruled African countries bordering South Africa). The terms of the Kadoma Declaration banned foreign journalists based in South Africa from all the signatory states, and assured admission to all states for any journalists admitted to one. Although even South African-based correspondents have been welcome in Zambia and Zimbabwe for ANC press conferences, at times of domestic troubles they are unwelcome and even banned. Many authorized in Zimbabwe are still waiting for permission to enter half of the frontline states which keep them at bay.

Jeune Afrique, a Paris-based magazine that allegedly covers and is distributed throughout francophone Africa, is heavily tied to the governments it must report on. Many of the magazine staffers are also, either directly or indirectly through public relations agencies, employed as "flacks" by the African governments. The company that owns *Jeune Afrique* also runs its own agency, DIFCOM, which does the same work, often with the same people. This is evident in the appearance of the copy, loaded with "advertorials" and so labeled. The newshole itself is a long glowing testimony to the "Sage of Africa," Ivory Coast President Houphouët-Boigny, Senegal's Abdou Diouf, Congo's Denis Sassou-Nguesso, and others, among whose entourages the reporters often travel. It is noteworthy that few of the reporters are black.

Oliver Chimenya, a black journalist under both Smith and Mugabe, has said that all African leaders, black and white, "have fallen victim to controlling their own press."

For broader overviews of the African press and media, I refer the reader to:

Frank Barton, *The Press of Africa: Persecution and Perseverance* (London: Macmillan), 1979.
David Lamb, "Some of the News That is Fit to Print," *The Africans* (New York: Random House, 1982), pp. 245–257.
W. Steif and T. Mechling, "A Precarious Freedom," *Commonweal,* 112:429–31, Aug. 9, 1985.
W. Steif, "Stop the Press," *The Progressive,* 48:32–4, December, 1984.
Sanford J. Ungar, *Africa: The People and Politics of an Emerging Continent* (New York: Simon and Shuster, 1985), esp. pp. 115, 263.
Dennis L. Wilcox, "Black African States," *Press Control Around the World,* edited by Jane Leftwich Curry and Joan R. Dassin (New York: Praeger Special Studies, 1982), pp. 209–32.
———. *Mass Media in Black Africa: Philosophy and Control* (New York: Praeger, 1975).

3. "COSATU Marks First Anniversary," *Africa News Special Report,* December 8, 1986, pp. 6ff.

4. *Art. cit.,* p. 21.

5. Alan Cowell, "The Struggle: Power and Politics in South Africa's Black Trade Unions," *The New York Times Magazine,* June 15, 1986, pp. 14ff, p. 18.

6. *Art. cit.,* p. 22.

7. John D. Battersby, "Botha Landslide Worries Foes," *The New York Times,* May 10, 1987, p. 2.

8. *Ibid.*

CHAPTER TWO

Uncovering Apartheid

War Is Peace

Ted Koppel has had conversational gridlock with the apartheid regime.

He has had trouble with both of the Bothas, P. W., the former prime minister, now state president, and R. F., "Pik," the foreign minister.

Early in 1985, the headmasterly interlocutor expressed indignation to P. W. Botha that black people were not allowed to travel freely throughout the land. More recently, during the state of emergency, he expressed bewilderment that he and his colleagues were denied access to places where the news of protest and conflict was to be had.

Each of the Afrikaner officials smiled indulgently and answered Koppel with tired courtesy: Of course, blacks were free to travel anywhere in the country. The minister assumed one would understand this was so if they had the money (which would also be true of the United States) and the proper documentation (which may also soon become true in America in response to the presence of illegal aliens). More significantly, he left unsaid that the blacks could not reside anywhere outside areas specifically designated for their race (nor could the whites, few of whom, however, were clamoring for admission to townships or homelands).

Pik Botha was not so lucky when he extended an avuncular invitation to Koppel to "come and see for yourself." Koppel instantly shot back that he had just been denied a visa. Without missing a beat, Pik went on to outline the menace of communist subversion.

Each encounter is instructive of apartheid doublethink. As we shall see, each also presents a plausible model for what some fear may become the shape and state of American government-press relations.

It would be dangerously simplistic to dismiss these politicians as barefaced liars. What characterizes and creates their behavior (and that of not a few of our own politicians and officials) is a very special mentality which makes what they say literally true but hardly the truth. It is physically possible and legally conceivable for some blacks to travel all over South Africa. But it is not bloody likely for the vast majority.

As for the other Botha, he was absolutely right: Editorials lambaste the government day after day in very forceful terms. Like William J. Casey when he was running the CIA, Botha restricts his notion of the freedom of the press to opinion. Access to information and the public conduct of public government are quite different matters. The government is the only judge of what types of information are not going to damage the "security" of the nation. In 1986 journalistic big guns Seymour M. Hersh, who exposed the My Lai incident in Vietnam, and Bob Woodward, who gained fame during the Watergate scandal, both received personal calls from then CIA director Casey, warning them of possible criminal prosecutions if they published classified material on intelligence matters. At the time, both men were working on books in this area. One wonders how less prestigiously placed researchers and writers would react to such calls, especially in the light of the two-year sentence contemporaneously meted out to Samuel L. Morison, of Navy intelligence, for providing American satellite pictures of a Soviet aircraft carrier to the definitive *Jane's Defense Weekly*. Benjamin Bradlee, the *Washington Post* editor who managed the Watergate coverage, voluntarily suppressed much background on another recent espionage case, that of Ronald W. Pelton of the National Security Agency, as a result of direct persuasion from the administration. Such informal pressure and voluntary compliance are a part of a long tradition, from advance notice of D-Day during the Second World War to suppression of preparations for the Bay of Pigs disaster. But as Daniel Schorr has pointed out, the Reagan administration wants to change this voluntary self-censorship to a legal obligation with criminal sanctions.[1] For this purpose, William Casey sought to apply to the press the severe penalties of the Cold War Communications Intelligence Statute of 1950, which was designed to protect codes relating to intelligence communications. At the same time, Senator Ted Stevens (Republican, Alaska) proposed a bill that would allow the government to confiscate all property used in the publishing of such information, which could include CBS or *The New York Times*. Casey told the *Washington Monthly* that the government needed to have "greater control" over all publications.[2] The South African apartheid regime is following exactly the same line in principle.

In this regard, the South Africans, though far more restrictive in actual practice, are more refreshingly candid in the formulation of their laws, one of which can rule treasonous (that's right, treasonous) the publication of information that may be embarrassing to the government.

After the brutal killing of Black Consciousness Movement leader Steve Biko in 1977, while under the custody of South African prison officials, the government passed a law making it illegal to reveal the findings of an inquest, because that was the way the facts of his death had emerged. It was already illegal to publish, without permission of the officials involved, anything pertaining to the conditions of prisons or the status of prisoners. Closing an embarrassing window after some revealed disgrace has long been a mark of the regime's ad hoc concept of press laws.

In 1950, two years after the Nationalists came to power, the police fired on a demonstration of the African National Congress at a May Day parade. *The Guardian* reported the next day that "they [the police] slaughtered the people like cattle, stabbing them from behind and shooting them in their backs as they ran." The Suppression of Communism Act, passed shortly thereafter, gave the government the power, and the excuse, to close down *The Guardian* and other leftist papers, such as *Advance, New Age, Spark,* and *Fighting Talk.* The Defiance [of apartheid regulations] Campaign of 1952, which created a lot of publicity, brought about the Criminal Law Amendment and Public Safety Acts, which punished both defiance and the reporting of defiance of apartheid.

In 1965 *The Rand Daily Mail* published three articles exposing the torture and maltreatment of political prisoners. Empowered by the newly amended Prisons Act, the police raided the editorial offices, removing sworn affidavits, tape recordings, and photographs. The source of the stories was banned, the editor and reporter were fined, and the paper had to pay £116,000 in legal costs. In 1973, journalist Roland Stanbridge received information from an unimpeachable source that a law lecturer arrested for distributing ANC literature was being tortured under interrogation with genital shock treatment and severe rubber truncheon beatings. This information was imparted in the presence of a police warden, who did nothing to silence it—and with good reason. When Stanbridge went to his editor, he was told to forget the story because of the Prisons Act.

In 1976, the Soweto school boycotts and unrest were most vividly reported by the black *World,* which was closed in 1977 under the newly amended Internal Security Act.

These central historical events set the template for the present cycle of press repression.

The story of South Africa's systematic repression of free expression through the very instruments that saw it come to fragile

Uncovering Apartheid

birth in the eighteenth century—the rule of law—can serve as a cautionary tale for Americans, who share a similar colonial history and legal heritage. The tale also gives tangible dimension to the black liberation struggle, one more instance of the injunction that none of us is free until all of us are free.

Although the historical and geopolitical conditions are dramatically diverse, the operative principle behind the barring of the press from Soweto and Grenada is the same. Stay out! We cannot guarantee your safety, and you can endanger other lives: we are at war!

The intense crisis in government-media relations of the summer of 1986 was the product of both long-term forces and short-term events. In the latter perspective, the current cycle began in the fall of 1984 with black deaths and clashes with police in the Eastern Cape area. This led to the declaration of a series of states of emergency, applied selectively to different sectors of the country. By July 21, 1985, when a broader state of emergency was declared, irritation with the press, particularly foreign broadcasters, was beginning to boil. In September Ray Wilkenson of *Newsweek* was exiled for "telling half-truths." On September 10, *The Star,* the largest circulation daily in the country and one of the principal, if not the bravest, oponents of the regime, printed an article by David Braun which presented the government's point of view and hinted that soon steps might be taken, including the ousting of foreign correspondents who "frequently [transgress] basic principles and ethics of journalism." The article was followed in October by one more strong speech by President Botha about the flagrant animosity and unfairness of reportage in and of South Africa; Botha particularly singled out television as an inciter of violence. The following week *South African Digest,* a government handout issuing from Botha's office, reprinted the Braun piece prominently under its "Viewpoint" heading.

On November 2, the government declared sweeping press restrictions. Television, radio, and photojournalists were banned from entering the thirty-eight districts under emergency law. All other reporters had to obtain permission from the police to enter the areas with or without police escort. Satellite transmission of material without its being cleared was forbidden. Topics, as well as locations, might be declared off limits on an ad hoc basis. The penalty for violating these and other regulations was a possible jail term of ten years and a fine of R10,000. It was also clear that the 170 accredited foreign journalists would be reduced in number through one means or another.

The violence did not abate after these measures. The hotpoints on the calendar of grievances, from anniversaries of individual deaths to commemorations of national disgraces like the 1960 Sharpeville massacre or the 1976 Soweto uprising, coupled with increasing labor unrest and a rising tide of international calls for economic sanctions, produced the June 12, 1986, crackdown in which over a thousand people were detained and which extended the state of emergency to the whole country. Journalists were singled out second only to antiapartheid activists or "terrorists." From now on, all journalists, print as well as broadcast, were to be excluded from areas of unrest, which could be so designated by the police at their discretion. Furthermore, the new order prohibited the "announcement, dissemination, distribution, taking or sending within or from the Republic [of] any comment" that reflected poorly on any government official or member of the police or armed forces or that might incite anyone to take part in any unlawful strike, boycott, form of unlawful protest, civil disobedience or statement that might engender feelings of hostility or weaken confidence in the government! There is more, but one gets the idea. Lest there be any doubt, David Steward, the steely, urbane chief spokesman for government press relations, told his audience in Room 159 in Pretoria, the amphitheater where the opposing estates meet: "We're not kidding!" A former diplomat who had spent many years in New York City, Steward's voice had an uncanny American twang to it on this occasion. Two weeks later, Steward's boss, Louis Nel, announced that the government was prepared to close down permanently any local medium and to expel any foreign medium that violated the new regulations. Since the government had impounded the entire runs of *The Weekly Mail* and *The Sowetan* the day after Steward's remark, nobody thought Nel was kidding.

Like so many of the repressive Nationalist moves, this further clampdown on the press, part of a new state of emergency declaration, was prompted by additional pressure from outside. This time it was the Commonwealth Mission, known as the Eminent Persons Group, which was visiting the country at the time. It called upon Pretoria to release Nelson Mandela, the imprisoned leader of the banned African National Congress, and to open negotiations with the ANC, or else face the probability of economic sanctions by British Commonwealth nations, some of them South Africa's largest and most important trading partners. News of the new martial law was handed as a bulletin to the two cochairmen of the mission, Prime Minister Malcolm Fraser of Australia and former Nigerian head of state Gen. Olusegun Obasanjo, even as they were announcing the failure of their initiative to move Pretoria.

By December 11, 1986, further and even stricter press regulations were put into effect. Now reporters who happened to be on the scene when violence or any other "subversive activities" broke out would be obliged to run away "out of sight."! Heretofore privileged statements made in the legislature would only be privileged within the actual chamber. Open court hearings on detentions could not be reported until after a verdict had been reached. Any meeting could be declared "restricted," and thus any announcement beforehand or report afterward could become automatically "subversive." Already forbidden to go into "affected areas," reporters were now barred from reporting on the "aftermath" of violence. Journalists were finally subject to grave penalties if they spied on "armaments" or security "appliances."

The proximate justification for the tightening of an existing noose was provided by the newly established Bureau of Information's report that content analysis of South African papers for November 1986 showed a pronounced tilt toward revolutionary forces and a bias against government. David Steward compared this type of reporting to the alleged antiadministration coverage of the Vietnam war. He stated that, then as now, revolutionaries seek to mobilize the masses through the media to prevent the restoration of law and order.[3]

American correspondent John Madison, in a cleared satellite transmission for National Public Radio's *Morning Edition* of December 23, 1986, pointed out that the real reason for the stricter regulations—which as usual were selectively applied, *The Sowetan, City Press,* and *Weekly Mail* being hardest hit—was to prevent coverage of the growing number of alternate community structures set up by blacks to bypass black township councils and other surrogate setups serving Pretoria. The United Democratic Front's initiative to get blacks to turn off their lights and boycott stores in a "Christmas Against the Emergency Campaign" was seen as particularly pernicious by the government, which wished to squelch any coverage of it. Madison noted that this year the UDF explicitly condemned past excesses of the "comrades," the violently militant young blacks, who "enforced" what was meant to be a voluntary exercise.

Each new turn of the screw follows the same Laputan logic of National Party censorship. New forms of protest dictate specific new laws to squelch them. For example, on January 8, 1987, the seventy-fifth anniversary of the African National Congress, many newspapers ran full-page ads urging the government to remove the banning of this organization, the chief militant foe of the regime. The next day the government enacted a law making it "subversive" to publish reports or run advertisements that might "improve the image" or "defend the policies" of any banned organization.[4]

The laws themselves are in turn enforced in a variety of ways, from the draconian to the whimsical. In the township violence, journalists often just happen to be in the way of police who may be firing buckshot or rubber bullets at crowds. Foreign reporters are not exempt: Mike Hornsby of the (London) *Times* was lacerated with buckshot. Then police will simply pick up ("detain"—no charge is required) reporters for a short time to keep them from a story, as they did Alan Cowell of *The New York Times*. If they are black, like Theophilus Mashiani, a television soundman for Worldwide Television News, they may be held in custody for weeks; if they are black editors or newsmen for black local media, like the eminent Zwelakhe Sisulu (son of Walter Sisulu, who has been in prison with Nelson Mandela since 1964, and for the same reasons), they may be held indefinitely. TV crews have been pushed up against walls by the police and told to shove their (expletive deleted) press credentials.

Percy Qoboza, former editor of the banned *World* and now editor of the beleaguered *City News,* has had his phone cut off in the middle of calls to newsmen in New York. All of Soweto was cut off during periods of the state of emergency, because of "technical difficulties" according to the Bureau of Information.

Sometime in the spring of 1986 the South African Security Police began driving BMWs in the townships. In a land of sledgehammer law enforcement, this had an almost admirable elegance about it. The elegance came not from the manufacturers of the car, but from their habitual users: foreign television crews who were covering stories. To the "children," the increasingly militant teenage blacks who hurled rocks at cars and burned to death suspected collaborators, white men driving into black areas in plainclothes were either police or journalists. If they drove BMWs, they were journalists, friends to be helped; if they drove other models, they were the dreaded and hated Security Police. By switching cars, the police managed both to confuse the blacks and to get them to do their job of harassing the press as a bonus. A further result was that rental car companies no longer were willing to issue to TV crews insurance against smashed windows and pocked bodywork. Having rocks thrown at you "gets your attention," as Simon Stanford of NBC-TV News put it during a cau-

Uncovering Apartheid

tious drive through Soweto in August 1986. Stanford, a soundman, and Tony Wasserman, the cameraman, stopped by a peaceful field to shoot a horse-drawn wagon cutting across the dusty road. "Wallpaper" is what they call it: stock background footage for possible later use.[5] Under the regulations then in force, even if they could avoid rocks, they could not avoid arrest if they filmed or taped areas where there was trouble, or any area within a bit over a mile of a "strategic point." Since every post office, police station, firehouse, city administrative office, and many other types of buildings are "strategic," nothing but "wallpaper" is safe.

These regulations, aimed at the more vulnerable electronic media, with their dependence on visible hardware, were buttressed by the regulations imposed on June 12, 1986, which made it illegal to publish any "subversive" statement. Just what a "subversive" statement was would have to be determined by lawyers, according to David Steward, who ran school for the press every day in a manner reminiscent of the "Five O'Clock Follies" run by the U.S. Army for the press in Vietnam. "Minority White Regime" was one example he offered, since there were nonwhite cabinet ministers (without portfolio) under the new constitution. Some few days later, *The Sowetan* was advised that the blank white spaces it was running to indicate unprintable stories were themselves subversive. When Bishop Desmond Tutu urged that America disinvest in South Africa, that, too, was subversive. He said just that over ABC-TV and was asked if the interview violated the new regulations. "Yes," Tutu replied with weary defiance. For the moment, he was allowed to get away with it. ABC, according to Roone Arledge, head of the News Division at network headquarters in New York, was prepared to lose its Johannesburg bureau as the penalty. The government did ask for the names and addresses of the journalists associated with the broadcast, but proceeded no further.[6]

CBS, which had spent $100 in legal fees in 1984 for its part now had legal firms on retainer in each of the three major South African cities. The television people have tried to fly over interdicted areas, only to be turned back by police. They have tried telephoto lenses, in fruitless defiance of the law, which explicitly forbids their use as well.

These restrictions and harassments have had their effect. When the emergency began in 1985, the American networks ran sixty stories in August on the morning and evening news. By November, when more severe restrictions were imposed directly on the press, the spots went down to twenty. Soon after the restrictions, thirteen blacks died in Mamelodi during a protest; fourteen were shot dead in Queenstown, presumably by police gunfire. These and so many other incidents received no television coverage, and under the later very stringent rules, no news coverage at all. For the great world outside of South Africa, as well as for the domestic television audience, they might as well not have happened.[7]

Freedom is Slavery

Critics of the sensationalism of television have a test case on their hands in South Africa. Some even credit an American, John Hutchinson, professor of international relations at UCLA, who was hired as a consultant to the regime, with "getting these sjamboks [police whips and canes] off the screen." On the one hand, television coverage is regarded as mindless: peace talks in the Middle East are reduced to the opening and closing of limousine doors; the Geneva summit is shrunk to a contrasting style show. John Corry, a television critic for *The New York Times,* noted that the restrictions might help television by leading to more thoughtful coverage and lessening unexplained and perspectiveless scenes of charging police, burning tires, and rock-hurling youths. Mike Boettcherr of the NBC-TV bureau in Johannesburg admits as much: "We may have less stellar pictures, but I think this makes us do better stories."[8]

On the other hand, Allister Sparks, the former editor of *The Rand Daily Mail* and current correspondent for the *Washington Post,* noted that the lack of television coverage has moved South Africa off the screens and thus off the front pages of the world (as of December 1985) and only exacerbated the general decline, in his eyes, of the print press, which sins by omission—despite the courageous efforts of a few papers like *The Cape Times* and *The Weekly Mail,* a low-circulation shoestring paper that popped up to "replace" the deceased *RDM.* Sparks pointed to the articles published by *The Star,* an Argus publication that is considered part of the English opposition press, which gave currency to the canard that television reporters actually paid blacks and others to protest in dramatic ways for good footage. When the government was challenged to produce one proven instance of this alleged practice, it provided none.[9] Many whites, according to NBC and other television journalists, furiously protest that the television people are stirring up violence.

Shortly after the first imposition of media restrictions, on November 2, 1985, which were aimed mostly at television, Louis Nel, then deputy minister of information, opined that the restrictions had "not undermined democracy." He assigned them a causal role in reducing the number of "serious incidents of unrest (by government count)" from 2,790 in October to 1,435 in November. The independent and respected South African Institute of Race Relations (SAIRR), however, had counted November 1985 as the second most lethal month in fifteen months of sustained unrest: 99 blacks and people of mixed race killed, as opposed to 85 in October. More generally, the SAIRR noted that the unrest kill rate had more than doubled after the July 21 declaration of a state of emergency, from 1.67 per day to 3.44 per day.[10]

When I lunched with the brave and distinguished editor of *The Cape Times,* Tony Heard, in the Civil Service Club of Cape Town in 1983, he made a strong point of the paper's need to make money and of his excellent record in this regard. It gave him the authority, he said, to stand up to the pressures placed on the board of directors by the government to restrain the *Times's* coverage of events embarrassing to the National Party government.

At that time *The Rand Daily Mail,* internationally recognized as one of the best South African newspapers and one of the top twenty papers in the world, had not yet been closed down because of financial troubles—very real troubles, but not trouble brought about solely because of economic causes. *The Mail* had been the principal exposer of "Muldergate," the government's secret use of taxpayers' money to buy favorable coverage, largely the brainchild of former Minister of Information Cornelius "Connie" Mulder. In the manner of the *Washington Post's* relentless coverage of Watergate, but under significantly greater duress and danger, *The Mail* had revealed the millions of rand poured into *The Citizen,* an English-language paper supportive of the National Party but otherwise having no economic reason to exist. This was the centerpiece of a host of other shady public relations schemes, including the attempted purchase, through an American agent, of *The Washington Star.*

A foreseeable result of these revelations, according to the legal pattern of South Africa, was the establishment of an advocate general to investigate government corruption who had virtually absolute power to gag any reportage of the cases he was investigating.

In the result, Mulder's career, which had been targeted securely on the prime ministership, was ruined, but *The Rand Daily Mail* is closed, whereas *The Citizen* is still being published.

The immediate aftermath of *The Mail's* closing was a microcosm of the general trend in the South African mainstream English press. The owning chain, SAAN (South African Associated Newspapers), replaced it with a bland new paper, *Business Day,* which Raymond Louw, the last editor of *The Mail,* considers "right wing and insensitive."[11] Reaching only a sixth of *The Mail*'s final circulation, *Business Day* is being kept on the stands despite the existence of the same "economic" reasons that justified closing its predecessor. Many former *RDM* journalists prefer the streets to a job on the new paper. Some have pushed out on their own, however, marking the second trend of the South African press, a move to smaller as better, with less to lose and more chances to innovate.

The Weekly Mail averaged 12,000 circulation in its first year, but went up to about 15,000 in 1986, with an occasional peak of almost 20,000. It is put together by a dozen young turks, most of them white, who also own it. So far, they have been toughing out the stiff emergency rules. After an entire issue had been impounded by the police for the first time, the paper made its spirit and astonishing good humor remarkably evident in its returning banner headline:

OUR LAWYERS TELL US WE CAN SAY ALMOST NOTHING CRITICAL ABOUT THE EMERGENCY, **BUT WE'LL TRY:** Pik Botha told US television audiences this week that the South African press remained free [in the Koppel interview already alluded to]. We hope blank blank blank blank blank was listening. They considered our publication subversive. If it is subversive to speak out against blank, we plead guilty. If it is subversive to believe there are better routes to peace than the blank, we plead guilty.

Glenn Frankel of the *Washington Post* visited the offices of *The Weekly Mail* in June, right after the big crackdown on the media, and reported that the paper is put out by the staff, their lawyers, and the Security Police. Rather than have themselves second-guessing the complex and deliberately vague censorship regulations, the editors, Anton Harbor, twenty-seven, and Irwin Manoim, thirty-one, have the lawyers go over the copy, which takes them about five hours. (One more reason for having a weekly schedule.) On a given day before the paper goes to press, two security men arrive and ask to see a copy of the paper, which they insist on paying for. Sometimes they say things look all right; sometimes they just leave. Sometimes the paper gets printed with unforeseen deletions demanded, sometimes it is not allowed to be distributed.[12]

The constant presence of lawyers and his own irresistible and baffling optimism have made Manoim a bit of a legal bloodhound:

Uncovering Apartheid

he reviewed the practical bible for South African journalists, *Kelsey Stuart's The Newspaperman's Guide to the Law,* in its latest updated version (constant updating was necessary during Stuart's life, and now, after his death, is essential in the legal wonderland of Nationalist legislation) and the thrust of his review was that efforts have long been too timid in accepting the widest interpretation of the laws. Manoim cites the example of how few mainstream editors would ever dream that Nelson Mandela can be quoted, so they never do so. Bizarrely, under the law according to Stuart, he can be quoted, so long as the quote does not forward the cause of his banned organization, the ANC. Since Mandela is in prison, he himself cannot be banned—and thus he can be quoted.[13] Joseph Heller, meet Franz Kafka.

Heard recently talked about his own mature anxieties in covering the riots and demonstrations ripping through the Cape during emergency regulations, even before the first stage of special restrictions imposed on November 2, 1985. It was still October when *Cape Times* reporter Peter Dennehy was dispached to cover a banned (under the state of emergency and hence illegal) meeting. He was detained by the police for not leaving the area when instructed to do so. Heard was called by the police, who told him that Dennehy would be locked up incommunicado for fourteen days. This intimidating information was actually a relative courtesy when one recalls that most detainees simply disappear, with their relatives and employers left guessing about their fate. In the event, Dennehy was released at the end of the day, but the point had been made.

Foreign correspondents, having the protection of their international organizations and the possible notice of the world, are treated with more care. But the New York-based Committee to Protect Journalists has documented dozens of cases of assault, detention, breakage of equipment, and general harassment of reporters in the early months of 1987 alone.

Heard also pointed out some of the Kafkaesque aspects of state intimidation of the press. Suppose, he says, a doctor complains to your newspaper that one of his patients has been severely beaten by the police. You must "clear" this with the police themselves or get their side of the story. The police will routinely deny the story and then go after the doctor for subversive rumormongering, one of the many categories of offense under the Internal Securities Act, as amended. Even a less abrasively critical paper, like *The Star,* has faced intimidation on this score. *Star* reporter JoAnne Richards was served a subpoena requiring her to reveal the names of the doctors whom she had used as sources for her story that many of the detainees had been beaten and carried the evidence on their bodies. This action was taken despite the fact that the original report had been submitted to the police before publication and the paper had obligingly printed police comment that such allegations were not credible. Had the reporter failed to comply with the subpoena, she could have been jailed for up to five years. The law was not put to the test in this instance only because the medical people voluntarily came forward. Of course, South African journalists do not have the protection of so-called shield laws in refusing to identify their sources. This exposure has a powerful, chilling effect on investigative reporting, and, if truth be told, even on routine reporting.

In this atmosphere, it is all the more admirable to see the coverage that Heard's paper and others have given to the anti-apartheid struggle. Gerald Shaw, assistant editor under Heard, visited the United States in the fall of 1985 with a thick folio of exemplary newspaper pages from *The Cape Times,* with dramatic photographs and vivid on-the-spot stories of police, army, and mob violence, created under fire and published with great courage. Two years prior to that, when I visited black editor Joe Latagkomo of *The Sowetan* (produced by blacks for blacks, but owned by Argus, the large white media conglomerate), he shoved a copy of that day's edition across his desk toward me and asked me if I saw any evidence of censorship. I said that I did not. With courteous but fatigued patience, this brave tired man pointed out a headline, "Girl Sjamboked by Strange Men." Only the police sjambok people (that is, beat them with whips), but since the police would deny it and the girl might be intimidated into changing her story, "Strange Men" are accused. The black readers knew exactly who was to blame. But, of course, no names and certainly no indictments were to follow.

This was thus at once an example of the failure and the triumph of South African newspaper censorship.

We will see in another chapter the staggeringly oppressive and bizarre methods and effects of censorship on all of the other media and possible vehicles of communication (from audiotapes to T-shirts). Newspapers, our current concern, are singled out for a special type of control.

Self-Discipline

"Newspapers" are defined in South Africa as periodicals that appear more frequently than once every five weeks. As such, they must be registered, and that requires the posting of a bond of

R40,000 that may be confiscated if the organ violates any one of a number of complex rules or is simply judged, by often anonymous watchdogs, "subversive" or "provocative" or "embarrassing." Automatically, many periodicals, which do not have the wealth or the will to push against that repressive edge, dare not publish more frequently than once every five weeks.

After negotiations with the government in 1983, a Media Council was created to give some semblance of "self-regulation" to the control of newspapers. More than one hundred vaguely worded laws affecting the press already carried harsh penalties, which could be imposed with very meager procedural or judicial restraint. Control would now be further enhanced with the powers of the council, which could impose a penalty of R10,000, a crippling amount for the smaller papers most likely to be critical of the government.

Unlike the previous voluntary Press Council, the Media Council has half of its members chosen from the public, and proceedings can be initiated upon any complaint from any person; also unlike its predecessor, the Media Council does not have legal counsel available to those accused of improper behavior. In the past twenty years, these "self-regulating" bodies, from Press Council to Press Board to Media Council, have been exploited at an increasing rate.

In the first ten months of its operation, the council was handed 89 complaints; of these, 23 were resolved between the parties through mediation and two were upheld, 17 were rejected, and 21 were adjudicated by the body; the remainder lapsed or were withdrawn.

What sort of case was adjudicated?

The police complained to the council that the *Pretoria News* ridiculed them by heading an editorial about their Namibian counterinsurgency team, KOEVOET, "Mad Dogs?" Wilf Nussey, the editor, when hauled before the board, indicated that he was only questioning the abuse of power, not the existence of the unit, and that the alleged abuses were based on a number of separate allegations. "When there is such a weight of accusation and allegation, the existence of the allegation itself is a fact which deserves comment." The council found the editorial based on facts that "may or may not be true," and thus that it had violated clause three of the code of conduct, which requires comment to be based on "truly stated facts."[14]

If we look upon the emergency decree restrictions on the media as an acute form of repression of freedom of speech, and if we see the major laws curbing access to information as a permanent tactic to maintain this repression, then the Media Council is a strategy for implementing, without the minimal safeguards imposed by adversarial legal proceedings, an integrated political philosophy that assigns a particular role to news media (the strategic manipulation of other media is handled by another instrument, the Publications Act and its agency, the Directorate of Publications).

Like so many other notions exploited by the apartheid regime, such as anticommunism, the idea of a media council (also called press council or news council) is borrowed, in this case from Western Europe, and then given that weird Orwellian twist. We in the United States tried something like it in the seventies called the National News Council, but it failed to gain sufficient support from the media. Ironically, in its origins the news council is a libertarian idea. The power of the press to damage reputations and cause considerable suffering to innocent bystanders can only be restrained, in free societies, by the libel laws, which are not easily accessible to the unsophisticated or the unmoneyed. A press council is the institutionalization of an ombudsman who is to protect the public from the mistakes or the malice of the press. The council is not a court of law and cannot impose legal penalties and will not deal with a case that is before any court. All that happens if a complaint is found to be accurate is an apologetic retraction published with the same degree of prominence as the original mistaken report. The American version could not get even that much cooperation from our at times arrogant media and merely sought to get its findings published in some prominent paper of record, like *The New York Times*. This lack of acceptance, coupled with an increasing flooding of their docket by organized one-issue lobbies and radical political groups on the right and left, sank a noble effort, which had been launched by the impeccably liberal Twentieth Century Fund. In South Africa, the Media Council, the latest version of a self-regulating body, came about through the recommendations of the Steyn Commission of Inquiry into the Mass Media, appointed by P. W. Botha.

Like congressional investigating committees in the United States, South African commissions of inquiry have broad subpoena powers and are backed by the full power of the state. And as in the United States, depending on the political climate, they can be McCarthyite instruments of intimidation; the Steyn Commission was in this mold.

Steyn Strategy

The Steyn Commission was started less than a year after P. W. Botha became prime minister (having been minister of defense).

In August 1979, shortly after assuming office, Botha told the nation that since there was a "Marxist drive which aims at controlling the subcontinent," he needed the assistance of the private sector to fully support the government in establishing national security.[15] The press was crucial to this program. Accordingly, on December 5, Botha appointed a six-man commission to inquire into newspaper reporting of defense matters, a mandate that was widened into a general inquiry into all the news media. This commission was headed by Justice M. T. Steyn, a senior member of the Afrikaner Broederbond, the secret ultranationalist brotherhood to which so many top political leaders belong (including every prime minister, for instance). Steyn had previously served as administrator general of Namibia, and all the other members of the commission were military men. In announcing the commission, Botha said: "South Africa is entering a new phase of the total onslaught of its survival, which is being waged on the military, political and psychological fronts. . . . [The communications media play] an extremely important role in building up or breaking down the nation's morale." In the same statement Botha more than hinted at how he thought the media were doing so far: "[There is] a gradual and systematic denigration of the South African Defense Force [which] has become a priority objective of our enemies and their agents."[16]

"Total onslaught" became a catchphrase for the regime's mentality as well as their own strategy—the ironic suggestion being that it was not clear "who was slaughting on whom." One half of the ponderous report of the commission was dedicated to the theology of the total onslaught, reminiscent of some of the more extreme tracts of Cold War America.

Botha had not been secretive about his plans. In a White Paper written under his aegis at the Defence Ministry in 1975, he had pointed out the vital role of the media in militant enemy ideologies. In 1977, in another White Paper, he assigned a crucial role to the media in securing the active cooperation of the populace.[17] General Magnus Malan, then head of the Defence Force (and now defense minister), was singing the same song. Shortly before Steyn was established, he often referred to "the battle for the soul of the people" in the context of media and total onslaught. Only six months after the Steyn Commission was given its original broad mandate, it was renewed and expanded further to determine whether "the mass media meet the needs and interests of the South African community and the demands of the times and, if not, how they can be improved."

The final report on this later mandate, called Steyn II, elicited howls of protest from all members of the press when it was presented in early February 1982, since it called for a register of journalists as well as a much more powerful General Council to replace the Press Council then in effect. It was one of the few occasions when the generally supportive Afrikaner press protested loud and long against an administration initiative. The government backed off, just a bit, and the present Media Council was born. The register of journalists, the sort of licensing system dear to the hearts of the Soviet bloc (another irony) and many Third World countries (a different sort of irony), was dropped. The banning order system, of course, used so brutally on both journalists and sources, but particularly on black journalists, as we shall see, makes the register superfluous anyway, although it may have reduced the paper work on John Vorster Square (police headquarters).

Granted that the "total-onslaught" view rings a dreadfully familiar American bell, its particular view of the press has that special Afrikaner spin. McCarthy and company wanted to weed out the un-American journalists because they attacked the status quo. Botha and company certainly want to stamp out criticism, but that is not enough. They want cheerful collaboration in selling the administration line to the population, a view ironically characteristic not only of rightist dictatorships but of many socialist states as well, where journalists are state employees, park rangers with pencils. This totalitarian view, however, can be astonishingly expressed in a context of "free press" rhetoric only in South Africa, a bizarre circumstance that becomes somewhat comprehensible in the light of the development of the press in South Africa and its unusual version of bilingualism.

Since the disturbances of the middle eighties, Americans now know that the South African whites are split between English speakers and Afrikaners. For the Afrikaners, their language is something very special. They have erected the only monument to a language (their own) in the world. For the entire history of the country the Afrikaner-Boers were either a poor minority or a self-exiled struggling band of pioneers. After the Boer War, their status as vanquished peasants was emphasized. The growing cities and their modernization were making English speakers rich (on very cheap black labor). The Boers were either farmers, very few of them prosperous, or civil servants, humbly secure. Their language was a comical kitchen Dutch to the effortlessly superior English, the world-class masters of the snub. Their newspapers, not unlike the Hispanic press of the United States, were instruments of identity, solidarity, and community.

The anti-British-Empire aspect of this identity came to prominence during the European world wars, when the country, under British influence and power, sided against Germany, where the sympathies of the Afrikaners often lay. There was an open rebellion against the government on the part of the more militant. When one of the more aggressive rebels, who had fired on a government installation, was executed (singing a hymn, quite bravely), Afrikaner resentment was at fever pitch and expressed itself in the formation of a Dutch paper, *De Burger,* in 1915, which carried so much Afrikaans copy that its name was soon Afrikaanized to *Die Burger.*[18] D. F. Malan, a minister of the Dutch Reformed Church, the elected editor, was simultaneously chosen to head the National Party in the Cape. That position led to the national cabinet and the premiership (under a previous form of government).

As a commercial enterprise, the Afrikaner paper was no match for the established English papers, which had a circulation five or more times greater and what now would be called an upscale readership appealing to advertisers. But the Afrikaners were not in journalism for the money; the newspaper was an organ of the National Party.

The same pattern held true in the other center of growing population, Johannesburg, in the Transvaal, but in a more extreme form. *Die Transvaler* was first edited by H. F. Verwoerd, later prime minister and principal founder of the concept and program of apartheid, and at the time of his editorship the head of the Transvaal wing of the National Party. The pattern remains true today: A. P. Treurnicht, head of the conservative offshoot of the Nationalist Party, once a cabinet minister and member of Parliament, was, before that, editor of *Hoofstad* in Pretoria and, earlier, of *Die Kerkbode,* the journal of the Dutch Reformed Church.

Even the financial side remains the same, mutatis mutandis. Nasionale Pers and Perskor, its now much weakened rival Afrikaans publishing empire, do not make much money, and even lose money on the majority of their papers. Their profits come from government contracts to print telephone directories, glossy Bureau of Information booklets, and, since 1983 for Nasionale Pers, ownership of black papers in English.

The English publishing companies, South African Association of Newspapers (SAAN) and Argus and some few independents, outpublish all Afrikaans newspapers fifteen to six. Durban, the third largest city, Kimberly, the diamond capital, Pietermaritzburg, and East London, a traditional center of opposition, have no Afrikaans papers at all. Even in areas that are heavily

Afrikaner, like the Orange Free State, no city is without an English paper. This has grown more painful to the Afrikaner leadership because 90 percent of Afrikaners now live in cities, where they are exposed to the "bad influence" of the English press. The English speakers, outnumbered among whites six to four, dominate the newspaper field commandingly. Worse yet, in the regime's worried reckoning, 99 percent of blacks, 95 percent of Indians, and 75 percent of so-called coloured who read newspapers read them in English.

With this background and this predicament, it is clear why the Afrikaner elite and other supporters of apartheid can see newspaper criticism and even lack of wholehearted support as bordering on the treasonous. And they have long memories which make them see the English as hypocritical in their espousing of independent, objective journalism.

Prior to the outbreak of the Second World War the editor of the *Cape Argus* criticized Neville Chamberlain's policy of appeasement. The owners fired him for doing so, on the unhidden grounds that the English papers had always to back the British government since the Afrikaner papers were so anti-British.[19] After the war broke out, *Die Burger* and *Die Transvaler* both chastised Nationalists who showed Nazi sympathies, but some editorials in the *Transvaler* followed the same line that Nazi shortwave propaganda was urging on South Africa. *The Star* accused it of "speaking up for Hitler," and Verwoerd sued for libel in the British-influenced court system. He lost, and the court declared: "He did support Nazi propaganda, he did make his paper a tool of the Nazis in South Africa, and he knew it."[20]

The regime either ignores or punishes impoverished organs like the United Democratic Front's newsletter, which has screaming banner headlines like "Stop Killing Us!" or "End Apartheid Now!" It is hugely frustrated by *The Star* heading a story, "Disobey Unjust Laws—Tutu." For the regime, the non-Afrikaans-speaking whites are committing suicide, which will incidentally be the genocide of the Afrikaner. As Piet Cillie told me (and doubtless many others before and since) in his office at the Journalism School of Stellenbosch University: "The British seek to use the black man to break the back of the Afrikaner!" This came out during a long, amiable discussion about journalism education, and it came out with volcanic force.

Shutting down *The Star,* though conceivable under the state of emergency, would signify the beginning of the end of any possibility of cooperation from the indispensable English media. The numbers (in this case average sales per issue from the Audit

Bureau of Circulation for the first six months of 1984) tell just how indispensable:

The Argus	106,476		Beeld	96,656
The Cape Times	72,096		Die Burger	79,383
Daily Dispatch	35,032		Die Transvaler	21,094
The Daily News	91,841		Die Vaderland	47,063
Eastern Province	Herald		Die Volkblad	27,969
	31,050			
Evening Post	24,573			
The Natal Witness	24,829			
The Natal Mercury	65,299			
Pretoria News	27,186			
Rand Daily Mail	118,381			
Sowetan	102,416			
The Star	180,895			

Among the weeklies, *Rapport,* published jointly by Nasionale Pers and Perskor, has an impressive 413,793, but is still beaten by *The Sunday Times* (481,131) alone and is overwhelmed by the other seven major weeklies, all of which are in English or Zulu. (I have omitted the many papers, most of them published in English or in one of the black languages, having a readership of less than 10,000.)

These comparative circulation figures, however, should not fuel the illusion that oppositionist papers are economically clobbering the Afrikaner press. SAAN, weakened by the closing of *The Rand Daily Mail,* has been further debilitated by its circulation battles with the Argus Publishing Company. Argus itself was forced to close *The Sowetan Sunday Mirror* due to pressure from the rival *City Press,* a newly resurrected paper intended for blacks now bizarrely owned by the Afrikaner chain, Nasionale Pers. Thus the loss of *The Rand Daily Mail* readership, which may have powered *The Star*'s leap to a circulation exceeding 200,000 was a Pyrrhic victory for Argus, which in turn lost to the Afrikaner owners of the "black" *City Press* and the "white" *Citizen,* papers that are "English" only in language. The Afrikaner chains, which profit from lucrative government printing contracts, thus were the ultimate beneficiaries of the politically forced closing of *The Rand Daily Mail,* since what Argus picked up with one paper it lost to them through its own closings. With the latest emergency press restrictions of 1986, which as of this writing seem destined to get worse, oppositionist newspaper publishing is becoming almost impossible as an ecomically viable enterprise. Even well before the more restrictive rules, Raymond Louw called 1985 the "Year of the Chop" for South African journalism, not merely because the paper he edited *(RDM)* was closed, but because, altogether, 200 out of 1,800 journalists in the country were fired.

And, of course, whatever the economic picture, it was never mere money that made the Nationalists prize the Afrikaner press. It was always its solidarity with the party. Given the changes of the times, how does the government now see this prized quality and how does it try to sell it to the other media?

Contrived Consensus

In the latest political newspeak, Pretoria's blueprint for journalism is something called *consensus politics,* which is opposed to the perceived characteristic of the English press, *confrontational politics.*

Consensus politics has gained official currency since the installation of the new constitution, which was adopted in a 1983 plebiscite that of course included only whites. The new constitution, touted by the Nationalists as a step toward a fuller franchise, abolished the old Parliament, which was composed exclusively of whites elected by whites. The new legislature is tricameral. The old Parliament is now the new White Assembly, with two other separate (and not equal) bodies representing the Indians and the "coloured." Since these latter bodies can only advise the government, the real legislative power remains with the White Assembly. Largely due to the outrageous provision that the blacks have no chamber even in this charade, the campaigns for and against the new constitution had a great deal to do with heightening the tensions to the fever pitch they subsequently reached. A further ominous change, perhaps unnoticed in the racial main theme, was the vastly increased power given to the executive, which is transformed from a Westminster model of ministerial government to a Gaullist-style state presidency.

It was in this context of centralizing power plays that the government used the terms *consensus* and *confrontational,* announcing that the press would henceforth be excluded from meetings of standing parliamentary committees. The ruling, it was announced, would aid consensus politics by avoiding the danger of confrontational politics. Shortly afterward, Chris Heunis, minister for constitutional development and a member of Botha's inner circle, urged the media to seek political consensus.[21]

It is interesting that as some blacks have gained a tenuous

control of some township affairs, they have formed a not unsimilar view of the press.

Michael Massing, a contributing editor of the *Columbia Journalism Review,* who was closely watching South African press affairs in late 1986 from both the editorial desks of the mainstream press and the townships, reports the feeling among white and black journalists that press freedom might not show any signs of improvement for a long time, no matter who is running the country. He cites the example of a reporter who reported that a black boycott, according to one leader, had outlived its usefulness. He soon found himself before "several hundred angry people" at a local "people's committee" he was persuaded to attend. The reporter, considering himself lucky to have escaped unharmed and alive, hid out until things cooled down. Massing further feels that Robert Mugabe's example of curbing the Zimbabwe press will be followed by whatever black group gains control of Pretoria by, for instance, nationalizing the Argus newspaper chain. An Indian reporter told Massing that then one could look forward to "dreary accounts about agriculture."[22]

The current masters of the media version of the political consensus concept are best represented by Riaan Eksteen, director-general of the SABC, the state monopoly in television and quasi monopoly in radio. His news division is refreshingly forthright about its being strictly a mouthpiece for the government, à la TASS. He told the Press Club of Cape Town that SABC policy was consensus politics and a conscious avoidance of confrontational politics. With this model even the Afrikaans press would have to shape up (Eksteen is, of course, one of the most senior of the Broederbond.)

The Afrikaans press is not monolithic, and the extreme right wing pulls no punches in damning even the appearance of conciliatory moves by the Botha regime, but by and large its variety is invisible to the outside observer. The colorful Piet Cillie, in his years as editor of *Die Burger,* often opposed Prime Minister Verwoerd, who of course replied in *Die Transvaler.* Cillie is famous for his remark that he (meaning the Afrikaans press in general) was married to the National Party in the sense that neither party would think of divorce but might often think of murder. At the end of the day, however, the Nationalists could hardly find a more loyal son (to mix the metaphor) than Cillie. Willem de Klerk, who edits the popular *Rapport* and who is credited with loosening and enlivening the *verkrampte* (that is, ultra-conservative) *Transvaler* under his *verligte* (that is, somewhat liberal) editorship, is often held up as a relatively free-thinking Afrikaner journalist, who will hardly bow to the National Party. Relatively speaking, this is true. But here is an example of his viewpoint in 1982, from *Rapport* (February 7): "The onslaught requires us to pass harsh security legislation and stronger press discipline in the interest of community discipline." And in 1978 his weekend column qutoed in *The Rand Daily Mail,* June 20: "If blacks continue to spit at the ground when whites present proposal after proposal, if blacks meet every political advance with protests and more demands, if terror increases . . . and black leaders amuse themselves about our fear and tell us the day of reckoning is at hand, then the cord will snap."

Consensus politics may be best seen by taking a look at the way Afrikaans papers treat a government proposal and contrasting it with the way an English paper reacts to the same proposal; then by comparing their way of commenting on an incident of violence with that of a black paper.

The government proposal was made in May 1986 and was relevant to dissatisfaction with the absence of blacks in the new constitutional legislative arrangement. The unrest was an example of black-on-black violence in the so-called squatter camp of Crossroads on the Cape.

Die Burger:

The National Council Bill, which is published today for general information and comment, is a particularly important reform initiative, which can decisively lead South Africa out of the present situation of unrest to a more peaceful future in which the country's full potential can be realised.

From the start is can therefore be a powerful instrument to ensure the equal inclusion of Black South Africans in a new constitutional dispensation.

May 23, 1986

The same proposal viewed by the moderate English *Sunday Tribune:*

. . . If he is sincere about the council, he will realize it is not up to him to select leaders, but up to the Blacks themselves.

If the council is to have any chance of success, the key lies in the credibility of the Black membership. If the Blacks demand Nelson Mandela, then for the sake of the country, the President should release Mandela to take his place on the council.

. . . By doing so he would start along the road towards the trust he so desperately needs if he is to go down in history as the man who saved his country from certain destruction.

May 25, 1986

Uncovering Apartheid

Die Volksblad:
Built on the belief that an Almighty God decides the fate and future of this country—not on the sand of hatred, discrimination, and unfairness—the National Council can become a monument for peaceful coexistence.

May 23, 1986

And now the Afrikaner view of the Crossroads violence:

Beeld:
. . . The police's present role in Crossroads is to keep the quarrellers apart, but it should also be a lesson for people who maintain that peace and order will return automatically to the Black residential areas as soon as the police and army withdraw.

May 23, 1986

Die Volksblad:
Radicals, mostly youths, have through terrorism, intimidation, necklace murders and firearms, established a culture of violence. They dictate boycotts, stay-away actions and keep the area in turmoil.

May 22, 1986

A black paper, *Evening Post:*

Security Forces already have virtually unfettered powers of arrest and detention, yet the Government finds it expedient to add yet another repressive measure to the statute book. . . . innocent people could be locked up for three months before reasons for their detention have to be given to a review board.
This Bill is unnecessary and should be scrapped.

May 23, 1986

The National Council Bill question serves as a litmus test for editorial policies. The Afrikaans papers hail the move as a way of getting the blacks (who will be appointed to it) into government, without the messy business of the black vote coming up. The English opposition takes the measure as an opportunity to bash Botha for his lack of trust but does not for a minute reject this latest fine-tuning of the apartheid apparatus as objectionable in principle. The occupation of the Crossroads squatter camp by police is a chance for *Beeld* to pronounce on a human error in the terms of antiseptic sociology—something the National Government has grown adept at ("deurbanization," "influx control, "own affairs"). The black papers simply reject the entire *status quo* as the frame for the *status questionis*.

(For fuller quotations on these issues, see Appendix I.)

Another style of reluctant accommodation to the "concensus" politics pressure of government is found outside the newspaper format. The magazine *Frontline,* to my mind, represents the American style of accommodation to pressure, within the obviously draconian press regulations of South Africa. First of all, *Frontline* has the glossy look of the innumerable city magazines pioneered by Clay Felker's *New York* in the late sixties and imitated across America quite successfully. Like the original, it introduces the idea of style and glamour to political coverage à la Tom Wolfe; it caters to a sort of Yuppie South African, with an old-left hangover for social justice. Dennis Beckett, the editor and creator of *Frontline,* told me in a breathless machine-gun conversational style, almost a parody of the fast-talking New York hip reproter, that he was an "English liberal," giving heavy emphasis to the quotation marks of ironic self-distance. In true American magazine style, Beckett's creation never covers politics or cuisine, but only The New Politics or The New Cuisine. Starting with a small grant from the South African Council of Churches, the tireless and clever editor has really built a readership with his formula of best-buying tips matched with political consciousness raising and arch wisecracks about Jo'burg city life.

TRYING HARD IS NOT ENOUGH

. . . The National Statutory Council will be no more effective, or longer-lived, than any of its predecessors. Whichever black leaders serve in it will lose much of their support to those who stand on the principle of no cooperation without equality.

Mr. State President, your desire for a new South Africa is welcome but your methods of achieving it are wrong.

People on your right think you are selling them out. You can't blame them. You are selling them out. . . . People on your left think your new South Africa is apartheid with another name. You can't blame them either. That is what it is. You promise "full political rights." But you do not mean that everyone casts his vote in the same ballot for the same candidates. . . .

It is no good branding the liberation cause as "communist" "selfish" "cruel." It is natural for black people to want the same political rights as anyone else. What would you have thought of any Afrikaner who in 1910 would have settled for an "Afrikaans Chamber" or for anything else other than the same status in the same structure as the then dominant English-speaker? . . .

The magazine abounds with interviews with newsmakers who just happen to be members of the government and conservative.

An interview with the police brigadier in charge of the enforcement of emergency regulations in Soweto makes him look like Chinese Gordon standing off the fanatics in Khartoum, but it still lets him hang himself (with "English liberals") by quoting him in full: "The African National Congress is, of course, dominated and controlled by the South African Communist Party. The Commander in Chief of the ANC military wing, Umkhonto we Sizwe, is Joe Slovo, a colonel in the KGB." The interviewer, Patrick Laurence, allows himself to remark that "not everyone would agree with [Brigadier Jan Coetzee's] emphatic interpretation of contemporary events." Joe Slovo, who is white, is a choice candidate of the Afrikaners for the evil mastermind, since they don't want to admit that the blacks are "smart enough" to revolt, a twisted bit of self-condemning racist logic. Although there is no public evidence that Slovo is a member of the KGB, he is in fact the chief of staff for Umkhonto we Sizwe and was, until exiled, the head of the South African Communist Party.[23]

Another American magazine format is the forum, a sort of television roundtable in print. Beckett ran one on the release of Nelson Mandela and included Progs (Progressive Federal Party) and blacks as well as Nats in the lineup. Everything has a desperately jaunty air of trendy friendly controversy. Brigadier Coetzee's troglodytic remarks are titled "Reflections from the Hot Seat," and the Mandela forum is called "After Pollsmoor [Mandela's prison]." I do not harp on these stylistic points to either patronize or condemn *Frontline,* which is a brave endeavor in a difficult spot, but to show how our own style of gushing reportage could as easily adapt to something like apartheid as it has to Star Wars or Contra Aid or a few billion for more space shuttle service, this time reserved for military purposes exclusively, in order to encourage the private sector to innovate. The South Africans do not have a monopoly on preposterous lines of presentation for public issues.

The developing rifts in the National Party, with the right (*verkrampte,* literally, "cramped," "narrow") becoming the Conservative Party and the left (*verligte,* literally, "enlightened") becoming something now called *oor-beligtes* (literally, "over-enlightened"), are covered by *Frontline* under the rubric of (you guessed it) "The New Nats." There was still room for a chat with John Wiley, the minister for foreign affairs, titled, "Thoughts of a Conservative Politician." Here is a sample of conservative thoughts on press freedom: "Press criticism has probably done a lot to improve the SABC, and keep it up to the mark. But I cannot understand why the SABC does not return the compliment, and draw attention to the biases and weaknesses of the press, on a daily or weekly basis. This could result in better, more thoughtful newspapers. Perhaps, if newspapers were exposed to the sort of criticism they are so good at handing out, the industry would be stronger, with fewer newspapers closing."

Mr. Wiley was not giving SAC proper credit for its efforts along the lines he suggested.

Nationalist Nanny

The South African Broadcasting Company, which has a monopoly of television and a virtual monopoly in radio, does provide the Nationalist Party with the kind of mobilizing support, *consensus politics*, that it furiously misses in the English press. There are some minor inroads on the monopoly of this government agency, significantly under the umbrella of Pik Botha's Foreign Ministry, such as the growth of VCRs among the affluent and some militant groups, the signal spillage of homeland television from Swazi-TV and Bop-TV (Swaziland and Bophuthatswana) despite jamming, and growing listenership among the few commercial broadcasting outlets, like Capital Broadcasting and Radio 702. Nevertheless, SABC remains securely unrivaled in reaching the homes of supporters as well as sworn enemies of the regime. In a country where television did not make an appearance until 1976, where daily newspaper circulation for the entire country of about thirty million is only about one and a quarter million and where overall literacy is at 60.5 percent, radio remains a very important talk and cultural medium beyond wallpaper mood music or the internationally inescapable rock around the clock. Almost a third of the country tunes in on an average day. Television is catching up fast: almost eight out of ten whites are before the screen on an average night, and an estimated one in ten blacks looks on nationwide. Since television is rare for rural blacks, the township figure is undoubtedly higher.

SABC television is both the past and the possible future of American television. It is not up to American speed in smoothness of video editing and remote intercutting with studio anchoring, which gives it an amateurish and nostalgic look. But it is certainly beyond the current dreams of broadcasting conglomerates in this country in concocting its own mediaworld of images and stereotypes that make attention to the real world of events unnecessary. Filled with talking heads, most of them heads of government departments, SABC did not bother to cover the townships during the current troubles, although it does buy the occasional footage from United Press International Television News or VISNEWS of black-on-black violence. Allister Sparks never once ran across an SABC-TV crew in months and months of covering the unrest and violence in the state of emergency from September 1984 to December 1985. After a day of thrown rocks, split heads, burning tires, and the threat of burning people in the Alexandra area, very close to white Johannesburg, viewers of SABC that night saw a school ceremony of little girls dressed in white receiving their awards and certificates, blocks away from the violence.

From the American news vantage, this was ridiculous if not treacherous; from the SABC point of view, it was responsible and correct. Life goes on, and the rituals of continuity deserve to be showcased by the national medium because it is the national consciousness. Not a few observers can liken this to the BBC's not only broadcasting but sponsoring concerts of classical music during London lunch hours at the height of the blitz, carrying on with that stiff-upper-lip spirit the Brits used to have and the world still admires. More critical and contemporary judgment, however, sees these reassuring images of continuity as a reprehensible cover-up of a shameful condition that cries out for public attention in order to be remedied. Americans do not have to go back to Vietnam for the parallel. In the same summer of 1986, the mainstream media went mad assigning reporters to cover the Statue of Liberty Centennial Festival, complete with battleships and Frank Sinatra, while their coverage of such diverse but crucial issues as aid to the Contras in Nicaragua and the budget for the manned space program was reduced to terse summaries of opposing politicians and critics that always assumed the state of the question as posed by the establishment.

In the United States, this style is the amalgam of several influences, from bottom-line marketing decisions about advertising milieu to corporate ownership bias toward uncritical support of the nation's biggest buyer and spender, the Pentagon. In South Africa, marketing and corporate bias can be and are held subservient to the direct interest of the ruling party, for a consensus politics of a more barefaced type, but one not totally alien to our own media-government symbiosis.

Director-general Riaan Eksteen's admission of this policy was rather more comprehensible than the organizational evasions lavished by a predecessor, Jan Schutte, on the Steyn Commission, when Schutte told it that the SABC was "neutral toward party politics, but committed toward the general national interest," which he then proceeded to identify with the policies of the National Party.[24] The policy was clarified when the SABC broadcast its view of the role of the media, and thus of its own role, with admirable frankness while the stringent proposals of the Steyn Commission to muzzle the press were before Parliament:

What is required of the press is that it exercise its freedom with responsibility . . . refraining from publishing ascertainable factual lies designed to undermine the security of the State, incite racial hatred, or to disturb the peace internally and externally. . . . [A] propaganda war using techniques of racial incitement does exist. . . . The issue is complicated by the fact that South Africa, while observing the norms generally applicable to a modern Western state, has in common with the rest of Africa a large unsophisticated population.[25]

As shall emerge more clearly when we deal with the cultural and artistic censorship exercised through the Directorate of Publications by the police, military, and others, the premise is that the government is *in loco parentis* for the vast majority of the population, a notion common to various censorship movements in the United States that focus on sexual material in films, on television, and in rock lyrics. In the passage just quoted, the black population, so smoothly referred to in oblique terms, is seen as a vast horde of *political* children—an irony come home to roost a decade later, when the very tough teenage enforcers of resistance to government are referred to by the blacks and liberals ironically as "the children."

The SABC provides on a daily basis the model of consensus politics that the Nationalist government has in mind for the print media. A regular radio feature, *Current Affairs,* offered this example when the South African rugby team, the Springboks, beat New Zealand in a long-standing heated rivalry, which has always been followed by that kind of fierce national loyalty characteristic of countries on the periphery (Australia's unflagging attention to the America's Cup comes to mind): "As, over the weekend, South Africans rejoiced at the splendid victory of the Springboks in New Zealand, others of the country's representatives were returning from the battlefield in Angola. Their mission, too, was splendidly accomplished. . . ."[26]

When the Muldergate scandal broke, SABC behavior was predictable and predictably lamented by *The Rand Daily Mail,* which noted that the lack of broadcast coverage of the information scandal was a scandal in itself. *Beeld,* a consensus Afrikaans journal, was ashamed of the SABC for giving time to Connie

Mulder to defend himself from accusations and proven misdeeds that they had never aired in the first place.

Andre Brink, the internationally recognized dissident Afrikaner novelist, severed all his ties with SABC, at no little cost to his domestic professional career, because of the "scandalous" treatment accorded Bishop Tutu's winning of the Nobel Peace Prize. No one in the United Democratic Front will grant interviews to SABC because of the inevitable distortions they suffer when the edited versions of their views are broadcast.[27]

Writers to *The Cape Times* have noted a similar video distortion of those not in favor with Pretoria. Samora Machel, the president of neighboring Mozambique, was portrayed by a sketch in 1980 that made him look like a "ravenous wild beast."[28] This was before the Nkomati Accord, when he became a formal ally of Pretoria, and of course before his rather mysterious death in an air crash.

These are not isolated examples. The University of Cape Town analyzed SABC news coverage for December 1983 and found that it showed twenty times more aggression in foreign contexts than at home, omitting altogether news of detentions, responses of pressure groups to detentions, forced removals of blacks, and black school boycotts.[29]

An earlier study of the 1977 campaign by the Journalism Department of Rhodes University shows that SABC devoted 80 percent of its coverage to Nationalist viewpoints, more than half of which were directly presented by the Nationalists or government officials themselves. In the 1981 campaign, a survey of the first two weeks of coverage showed that the Nationalists received 1200 percent more air time than the opposition Progressive Federal Party.[30]

This superconsensus with the administration is all the more predictable when one realizes that the top management of Broederbond loyalists is matched in the ranks by a very heavy preponderance of Afrikaners over English-speakers, even though half the programming on the "white channels" is in English. In the news division, as of 1984, no English speaker had higher rank than assistant editor, the fourth level of rank in the division and the fifth in the service.

Out of eighty-five employees in the news service for blacks, only six were blacks in this same period.[31]

The news division thus has an apartheid of its own. The first channel, TV 1, broadcast alternately in English and Afrikaans, is intended for the whites and the coloured, but it is preferred by most of the groups because of the entertainment programming, purchased American and European shows. (BBC has refused to sell to SABC because of British trade-union pressure.) TV 2 and TV 3 are broadcast in five African languages, Zulu (the most widely spoken language in the country), Xhosa, Tswana, Sotho, and Venda. The radio service broadcasts in almost twenty languages with Radio Bantu. The idea is that the blacks are tribal, you see, and would only be interested in their "own" kind of thing. Although we are confining our remarks to news coverage here, we must note in passing that the deliberate ethnic orientation of the Radio Bantu service is one of the few examples in the world of the kind of culturally indigenous content that the Third World has been pushing for in their "New Information Order" campaign— but on almost diametrically opposite grounds. From watching the programs on television myself and talking with whites and blacks, my impression is that few are interested in the solemn amateurism of the black television news, but that the blacks are even less interested in the regular "white" news programs because they are perceived to be either propaganda or irrelevant.

Reuel Khoza, the founder of South Africa's first black marketing group, feels that English would certainly be the medium preferred by advertisers for reaching blacks; but the government is not so much interested in reaching as fragmenting, he says.[32]

Editor Joe Latakgomo of *The Sowetan* felt this policy would fail: "[A]fter more than ten years of Radio Bantu we have not been turned into bantu zombies or meek government stooges. We have already seen Chief Mantanzima, Chief Sebe, and Chief Buthelezi [Bantustan leaders] with their opening salvos on TV 2. We are likely to see all the other people who are considered 'safe' in the eyes of the government."[33]

By mid-1986, the policy's failure was to be seen in the form of the new Channel 4, which is avowedly "multiracial," with a number of American sitcoms featuring blacks—*Bill Cosby, The Jeffersons, Fame.* Professor Keyan Tomaselli, who has been cynically observing SABC for years, notes that the motive may well be primarily economic, since advertisers can reach more people on this channel. Since this was true before, and was so noted by Mr. Khoza, it may only be the economic squeeze brought about by the sanctions and the reputed thirteen cents per head cost of the redundant apartheid services that prompted the move, an uncharacteristic motive for Afrikaner media management. In any event, SABC has at the same time collapsed the magazine (documentary) and news departments into one public affairs division, offering even less controversial material, despite an intermittently sizzling interview with the redoubtable Helen Suzman, who has been a sort of one-woman parliamentary opposition (with the Progressive Federal Party) for over a generation. Pat Rogers, more along the lines of an American Meet-the-Press type than the civil news servants, has returned to the magazine after being hounded out of the unit some years ago.

Nevertheless, Rogers, who also serves as the broadcast critic of *The Star,* bemoans the continuing decay of the English documentary unit at SABC. He recalled that producer Stu Pringle wanted to air a program on the school unrest in Soweto just before the violent outbreaks of 1976 but was blocked by management. Kevin Harris, another former TV producer for SABC, was fired for airing his program on Baragwanath Hospital without the cuts management had demanded. Harris, now a pleasantly aggressive free-lance producer, is well known for *This We Can Do for Justice and Peace,* a video he produced with the support of the South African Council of Churches, and one of the earliest visual panegyrics to Desmond Tutu. The program has been aired all over the world, including the United States, where it won an Emmy for the Public Broadcasting Service. Harris was able to get SABC to air the piece uncut by appealing to the Publications Appeal Board, which passed it despite SABC's own demand for thirteen separate cuts.

With the SABC style of bland conformity still triumphing after recent cosmetic changes, there is one new development that can make SABC a direct enforcer of consensus politics among the print media, especially now that *The Rand Daily Mail* is gone and *The Star* is trying desperately, in the sardonic view of Raymond Louw, not to appear to be the government's principal critic. The new development is the coming of cable and the blurring of the difference between print and electronic media. In South Africa this means subscription television owned by a consortium called M-Net, made up of Nasionale Pers, Perskor, SAAN, and Argus, with 18 percent shares each, and *The Natal Witness* and *Daily Dispatch* with less than 2 percent each. In July 1985, shortly after *The Mail* closed for "economic" reasons during the "Year of the Chop," despite the second highest daily circulation in the country, SAAN, the parent of *The Mail,* and her partners cut a deal with SABC. They relinquished 30 percent of their M-Net shares for 30 percent of the advertising revenue from TV 4. Part of the deal was that any news and public affairs programming put on the new M-Net would be provided exclusively by SABC. So now Nasionale Pers owns black papers, and English journalists are permitting a government agency to program news on a medium they own. There are unconfirmed rumors that the closing of *The Rand Daily Mail* may somehow have been connected with this.[34]

Events like these, and the Media Council's taking Eksteen to task for avoiding controversy, make one suspect that the Broederbond leadership of SABC is to the right of P. W. Botha and is beginning to see itself as the national conscience as well as consciousness, that it knows the true belief better than the relatively liberal Cape wing of the National Party, which is in increasingly tenuous control. While it ignores challenges to the Nationalists from the left, it has given courage to the Afrikaner Weerstandsbeweging, an ultrarightist group similar to the American Nazi Party, complete with swastikalike symbols and military shoulder belts.

This latest development seems to fit with an earlier not so minor flap. In 1978, it was politely urged that the closing prayer on SABC-TV be occasionally offered by a rabbi. The official answer was: "South Africa being a Christian nation, only members of Christian denominations are invited to take part in regular religious programmes." For good measure, Koot Vorster, brother of the former prime minister and moderator of the Dutch Reformed Church, said it would not be right for Jews who have gone against Christ to give the epilogue. Archbishop Denis Hurley, the Catholic primate, remarked that if anything had gone against Christ it was the policies of the government.[35]

"Consensus politics," then, takes on a meaning of totalitarian uniformity alien not only to the tenuously maintained independence of the mainstream opposition press, but also to the gradient accommodations of Realpolitik characteristic of P. W. Botha's wing of the National Party and certainly to the more complete compromises seen as inevitable by the so-called New Nats. In this context, made all the more vivid by the emergency-state threats and draconian actions taken against the opposition press, it comes as a surprise to the foreign visitor that many blacks despise the mainstream opposition press because they see it as merely arguing about the relative comfort of the manacles and chains imposed on them by apartheid. They are particularly harsh on the black journalists who have been working for the white owners on such mainstream black papers as *The Sowetan*, even though many of these black journalists have gone to jail and have been beaten and harassed in innumerable ways by the government in the pursuit of their vocation. Journalism and the press have their own internal apartheid, and that requires closer examination.

NOTES

1. Cf. *New York Times*, August 3, 1986, p. 23.
2. Admiral John M. Poindexter, national security adviser to President

Ronald Reagan, launched a deliberate disinformation campaign (lying for policy purposes and seeking to enlist media gullibility as an agent for administration objectives) with regard to Libya's terrorist plans. Cf. "White House and Its News; Disclosures on Libya Raise Credibility Issue," by Bernard Weinraub, *New York Times*, Oct. 3, 1986, p. A6. Different aspects of this trend are discussed in: Kim Willenson, "Frolic in Honduras: The Pentagon Press Pool SNAFU," *Washington Journalism Review*, July 1985, pp. 17–19.; Peter Braestrup, "Duty, Honor, Country," *The Quill*, September 1985, pp. 15–21; W. A. Henry, "American Institutions and the Media: A Preliminary Report," Gannett Center for Media Studies, November 1985, pp. 19–22; Winant Sidle, Chairman Joint Chiefs of Staff Commission on Press Coverage of Military Operations. "Report of the JCS Commission, *etc.,*" 1985; Jay Peterzell, "Can the CIA Spook the Press?" *Columbia Journalism Review*, September–October 1986, pp. 29–34.

3. Alan Cowell, "Pretoria Imposes Harsh New Rules," *New York Times*, December 12, 1986, pp. A1, A8–9.

4. "South Africa Tightens Curbs on Newspapers," Reuters Wire, Jan. 9, 1987; Nigel Wrench, reporting by satellite on National Public Radio *Morning Edition* for January 9, 1987.

5. *Wall Street Journal*, August 5, 1986, p. 1.

6. *The Manchester Guardian*, June 23, 1986, p. 7.

7. *Washington Post*, March 1, 1986.

8. *Wall Street Journal*, art. cit.

9. Author interview with Committee to Protect Journalists, December 14, 1985.

10. *Los Angeles Times*, December 9, 1985.

11. *Weekly Mail*, December 20–26, 1985, p. 9. For one interpretation of the closing of the *RDM*, see J. North, "Death of a Daily," *The New Republic*, September 9, 1985, p. 12.

12. *Washington Post*, June 22, 1986, p. A26.

13. *Weekly Mail*, March 21–27, 1986, p. 18.

14. South African Institute of Race Relations (SAIRR), *Survey of Race Relations in South Africa*, 1984, p. 892.

15. *Citizen*, August 17, 1979.

16. *Cape Times*, May 2, 1979.

17. *Bulletin One*, Department of Journalism, Rhodes University, October 1979.

18. *Die Afrikaanse Patriot* was the first Afrikaans paper, the journal of the forerunner of the Broederbond, *Die Genootskap van Regtes Afrikaners* [Society of True Afrikaners]. The society was founded in Paarl in 1875, and the journal followed the next year.

19. H. Lindsay Smith, *Behind the Press in South Africa* (Cape Town: Stewart, 1945), p. 163.

20. William A. Hachten and C. Anthony Giffard, *The Press and Apartheid: Repression and Propaganda in South Africa* (Madison, Wisc.; University of Wisconsin Press, 1984), p. 48.

21. SAIRR, op. cit., p. 885.

22. Michael Massing, "Letter from South Africa," *Columbia Journalism Review*, January–February, 1987, p. 39.

23. Oliver Tambo, the head of the ANC, has admitted that a number of communists are in its top echelons, but assures Western journalists that their first loyalty is to the ANC. Cf. Daniel Seligman, "Keeping Up," *Fortune,* April 14, 1986, p. 114.

24. *Star,* February 25, 1981, p. 3. Quoted by Hachten and Giffard, op. cit., p. 214.

25. Transcript, *Africa Survey,* SABC English for Abroad, Johannesburg, March 13, 1977, at 4 PM GMT.

26. Ibid., August 31, 1981.

27. *Loc. cit.*

28. Letter to the Editor, *Cape Times,* March 25, 1980.

29. SAIRR, op. cit., p. 894.

30. Hachten and Giffard, op. cit., pp. 218–19.

31. SAIRR, op. cit., p. 895.

32. *London Morning Star,* January 4, 1982.

33. *Sowetan,* January 4, 1982.

34. Keyan and Ruth Tomaselli, "Change and Continuity at the SABC, *South Africa Indicator: Political Monitor* 3, no. 3 (Summer 1986): 19–20.

35. Entire episode is narrated in Hachten and Giffard, op. cit., p. 212.

CHAPTER THREE

The Black Alternative

Mainstream Black Journalism

The face that Joe Latakgomo, the embattled editor of *The Sowetan,* presents to the American visitor is one of worn dignity with a touch of humor and a sense of irony. Mr. Latakgomo edits the one remaining black paper of large circulation that addresses serious political issues. But it is owned by the Argus Company, a white, inevitably capitalist, firm, and thus not to be trusted. Mr. Latakgomo, who has been detained a number of times, served as assistant editor on the predecessor of *The Sowetan, The Post.* Before that he served as deputy to Percy Qoboza, editor of *The World* and *Weekend World,* the paper that preceded both. The government shut down both those papers even though no violation of law was ever proven against either of them. Now Mr. Latakgomo, having had two large-circulation newspapers where he served with distinction shot out from under him and with vivid memories of detentions and police harassment, is under pressure again.

This is what he wrote as an editorial in 1982, when the final Steyn Report accused the black press—meaning his paper and some few others—of fomenting discontent and lacking loyalty:

We do not believe any of these statements to have been true, either for the *World, Weekend World, Post, Sunday Post* or now for *The Sowetan.* What those newspapers did was precisely what this same commission suggests the Afrikaans press did not do: The Afrikaans press failed, the report says, to adequately report on the hopes and frustrations of the black community. We reported on those hopes and frustrations. We did not call on the government to pull down shacks and leave people in the cold. They came and we reported it. We did not create community councils such as that which received a disastrously low poll in Soweto. The government did and we reported it. We did not detain people without trial, ban them, deport them. The government did and we reported it. We did not fail to provide housing for people. The government did and we reported it. We did not make racist statements at public meetings. Some government people did, and we reported them. . . . Who creates the climate for labour unrest, for school unrest? Why did hundreds of kids flee from the country of their birth to take up arms? The government created all this.

We will report it.

The government suggests there are a great deal of "moderates" who are "embarrassed" by our newspapers. We would suggest that both the government and the commission are out of touch with the situation. We know the hatred. We know the bitterness that this system creates. We are part and parcel of it. We feel it; we sleep it.

I am convinced that nobody will be able to run a black newspaper which serves as a mirror of society without threats from the government. There are too many government-created ills which cannot simply be washed away. The government must stop deluding itself that there are thousands of "moderate" blacks who would buy an alternative paper which would dish out the news à la TV 2 and 3.

Mr. Latakgomo's view is borne out by the statistics. Although the laws regulating the press are theoretically color-blind, their administration is most certainly not. Even before the state of emergency, when no one could keep up with the more than eight thousand general detentions (officially admitted by the administration under parliamentary pressure), the number of detentions and arrests among black journalists, relative to all other journalists, was markedly greater. Up to early 1987 no Afrikaner journalist had ever been detained. From 1976 to 1981, the period immediately before Mr. Latakgomo's editorial, fifty black journalists were detained for up to five hundred days; ten were detained more than once; ten were banned; and one was arrested, tried, and sentenced to seven years on Robben Island, the South African Devil's Island. In the same period, white journalists suffered one detention, one banning, and one six-year jail sentence. When one realizes that, during the period analyzed, there were fewer than two hundred and fifty mainstream black journalists, but over thirty-five hundred white journalists, the disparity in applied pressure is unmistakably enormous.[1]

These detentions can be very rough. The Committee to Protect Journalists was told by one former detainee that she was tortured by being kept awake from a Tuesday through a Saturday, forced to stand for hours, beaten, kept in an isolated cell crawling with vermin.[2]

An indirect but very real chilling effect on press freedom brought about by detentions is that detained journalists continue to be paid during their incarcerations, a decent and loyal practice of the white ownership, but one that places financial strain and penalties on the hiring of black reporters at equal pay for equal work. Joe Latakgomo, speaking as an executive of the Argus Publishing Co., notes that he has had six senior staff banned and three jailed and that this places a "restriction on employing others."

During the emergency of 1986 Zwelakhe Sisulu was abducted

by what was feared to be a death squad, men in ski masks who hustled him roughly from his home and sped away in a car whose license plate was deliberately obscured.[3] Sisulu, the son of Walter, the famous compatriot of Nelson Mandela who has shared Mandela's fate since the sixties, and of the oft-detained Albertina, co-president of the United Democratic Front, is a black editor and past president of the Media Workers Association of South Africa (MWASA), the black journalists' union. His predecessors in that office have all been detained with that double mark against them: black journalists and black labor activists, for MWASA has been in the forefront of antiapartheid activity. During his three-week detention, when his whereabouts were unknown, Sisulu was interrogated about his journal, *New Nation,* and told that it had been shut down. When he was released, due to a world outcry about his disappearance, he was surprised and gratified to learn that the paper was still being published. After only a brief respite, Sisulu was once again detained, allegedly because State President Botha had had a stormy meeting with the sponsors of *New Nation,* the Conference of Catholic Bishops. The report quoted Botha and the new Minister of Law and Order (formerly Deputy Defense Minister) Adrian Vlok as characterizing the paper as both "dangerous" and "full of lies."

Donald Woods, the exiled white former editor of the independent *Daily Dispatch,* was treated to the same kind of harassment by the police, although he was banned, not detained, until his escape from South Africa. Woods's home was the subject of shotgun blasts in the middle of the night, and his child was severely burned by an irritant powder deliberately placed in the family's laundry. In his biography Woods makes it clear he felt the Security Police were going beyond the call of duty to make their point. The wedge the crisis has driven between white and black journalists is underlined by the fact that the Writers Association of South Africa (WASA), the prior incarnation of Sisulu's MWASA, had in 1978 formally declared Woods, a close friend of Steve Biko, his biographer, and consultant on the Richard Attenborough film, about Biko *Cry Freedom,* "irrelevant to the Black struggle and to Black journalism."[4]

Regrettable as it seems, this movement of black separatism among those who are trying to do away with distinctions of race is not only understandable in terms of our own American black separatists, who do not wish dependence on whites for liberation any more than in any other area of life, but also in terms of the special circumstances of South African media history. The blacks did indeed have a press of their own, earlier in this century and back into the nineteenth. Now the mainstream black press is owned by whites and for the most part is operated by them; not only Argus and SAAN, the white opposition conglomerates, but Nasionale Pers and Perskor, the Afrikaner chains, own the black press and play the part of management to black labor.

In the early seventies, apartheid rules made it impossible for blacks to belong to the white journalism guild, the South African Society of Journalists (SASJ), and the few blacks in the business decided to start their own group, in sync with the burgeoning labor unrest among blacks in general. When the rules were changed to let them in, the blacks, for other reasons, many of them tied to the black separatism of Steven Biko's Black Consciousness Movement and Pan Africanism, decided to go ahead and form their own Union of Black Journalists, which in turn became the Writers Association of South Africa (WASA), which still later broadened its base (there being relatively few black journalists compared to SASJ) to include the many blacks working in the media in a variety of other functions and so become the Media Workers of South Africa (MWASA). The separatism hardened during a strike at the white-owned black paper, *The Cape Herald,* in 1980, which began almost the next day after MWASA was formed. Although the strict economic demands of the union were met, a sympathy walkout across the country, the new union asserting its muscle, left a bitter taste. Unimpeachably oppositionist whites like editor Benjamin Pogrund of *The Rand Daily Mail* and Raymond Louw, a former *Mail* editor who was general manager of SAAN at the time, felt that Zwelakhe Sisulu, the MWASA president, was trying to stretch the black journalists' cause to embrace the entire political apartheid struggle in order to establish himself as a black leader. "We were ready to settle on the first day," Louw says, "but we could not get the national leadership [of MWASA] to even show up to discuss the issues."[5]

If these were Sisulu's intentions, it is the heritage of the black press as well as his own parentage that makes it not only understandable, but reasonable.

The black critique of the white press does not make much of the distinction between the English oppositionist press and the Afrikaans establishment press. Both are tied together as one big business enmeshed in the interests of the ruling classes, whatever the editorial pages say. Many of the blacks who voice this view are members of MWASA. They claim that the so-called oppositionist press accepts the status quo as a given, which needs to be adjusted in order to achieve social justice, whereas the system, one of their own words for apartheid, is corrupt and evil to the core.

You do not reason with the rapist so that he will be more gentle next time. This critique parallels the American New Left critique of the mass media in the United States, the corporate giants of page, stage, and screen who in one division make weapons for the Pentagon and in another division produce network news, who argue about the wisdom of isolated weapon systems or nuclear plants, but do not question the fundamental policies that will always generate new examples to argue about. And the United States, of course, has had and still has a black press of its own, one that might have been closed down during the Second World War (as it partially was during the First) for being less than enthusiastic about black men dying "to preserve the democracy of Jim Crow."[6] For the Nationalist regime, therefore, black journalists and their press constitute a particularly dangerous form of revolutionary activism, just as the black press of the teens and twenties did for U.S. Attorney General Mitchell Palmer.

In contrast to the general historical trend of the black press in the United States, the earlier black press of South Africa was considerably freer, and economically more viable, than the contemporary endangered species.

Black political journalism began in 1884 with the Xhosa-English *Imvo Zabantsundu* [African Opinion] in King Willam's Town. John Tengo Jabavu started it for the tiny black professional class, newly alert politically, who were seeing the future in the introduction of "anti-Native" legislation by the British rulers and their surrogates. With time, the strong independence of the paper eroded. In 1897, *Izwe la Bantu* [Voice of the People] and, in 1903, John Dube's *Ilanga Lase Natal* [The Natal Sun] picked up the torch; *The APO* of 1909, Dr. Abdul Abdurrahaman's paper for the African People's Organization, sounded the first strong voice, this of the coloured, for equality with whites and not just something called decent treatment from the masters. Three years later, the South African Native National Congress, meeting in Bloemfontein, created a new journal, *Abantu-Batho* (abantu is "people" in Zulu and Xhosa; *batho* is "people" in Sotho and Tswana); it was printed in English as well as the four major African languages. From 1916 until its decline in the twenties, *Abantu-Batho* championed protests against white domination and pushed for a breaking down of tribal barriers to black unity. In 1938 *Inkundla Ya Bantu* [Bantu Forum] achieved a high circulation for the time, 7,000, reporting ANC politics, but generally taking a nonradical line until its demise in 1951. Socialist and Communist papers had a special appeal for blacks. *South African Worker* published more than half its articles in Zulu, Xhosa, and Sotho and was most influential in the twenties, as was its descendant, *Inkululeko* [Freedom], in the forties. The Defiance campaign of the early fifties was fueled heavily by *The Cape Guardian*, a multiracial communist paper with direct appeal to the black population. Banned, the paper kept reappearing under a variety of guises, from *New Age* to *Spark*. A smaller journal of the early fifties, Robert Sobukwe's *The Africanist*, was the seed of his Pan Africanist Congress, a separatist movement that broke away from the ANC.[7]

In the minds of the Afrikaner and English working class alike, the black journalist thus became identified with agitation, not only for racial equality, but also for the communist cause. This confusion served as excellent soil for the cultivation of hysterical red-baiting and for the facile identification of indigenous demands for social reform with Soviet masterplots for world domination.

Today there is no independent black press. All papers of this type were crushed by the government in the sixties. Beginning in the seventies, racially mixed groups on predominantly white liberal campuses, particularly Witwatersrand in Johannesburg and the University of Cape Town, began putting out socially conscious journals of their own, much influenced by the Black Consciousness Movement of Steve Biko, who briefly edited his own publication, and the Pan Africanist Congress. The Soweto uprising of 1976 and government intolerance have made of these papers a fluid and changing world, with issues appearing and disappearing, titles changing, editors and reporters fleeing or deserting or changing places and names. While this blunting and dispersion was going on among struggling community periodicals, so to speak, the mainstream press was also changing.

An illustration of this change is the current role of *Imvo Zabantsundu*, now owned by Perskor and a vehicle for government propaganda aimed at blacks, and that of *Ilanga Lase Natal,* which was founded by the first president of what later became the ANC, but gradually turned into an apolitical newsheet aimed at black consumers that was sold to the Zulu political party, Inkatha, in 1987. *Abantu-Batho*, started by Dube with Sol Plaatje, the first general secretary of the ANC, could not survive the depressed thirties, and was later revived, in name only, by a white liberal, Bertram Paver, who started the Bantu Press Co. based on his vision that the blacks would become consumers of the mass production their numbers were making possible in South Africa. Paver got into the black press almost by accident, since he was primarily trying to establish national distribution for goods like beer and bicycles. He realized a national advertising medium was necessary, and, starting with *Bantu World* in 1932, his Bantu Press devoured *Imvo, Ilanga,* and other black papers such as *Ikwezi le Afrika* [Morning Star of Africa] and *Mochochono* [The Comet]. Although Paver's main purpose was commercial, he was not unaware that the growing literacy among blacks could prove dangerous and that there was a need "for the development and sane guidance of Bantu opinion and [said guidance should be] expressed in the native press."[8]

Soon acquired by the Argus Publishing Company, *Bantu World* evolved into a sex-sin-soccer rag with headlines that have stuck in the memory of former South African journalist Roland Stanbridge: "Sex Hungry Granny Rapes Young Guys in Graveyard." This dreck from the sixties, the decade of black silence after Sharpeville, was gradually left behind in the seventies by the new *World,* under the influence of Biko and other forces of Black Consciousness. Community grievances and police brutality began to shoulder aside the "triple S," and black editor Percy Qoboza, who was to go on later to a Niemann Fellowship at Harvard, began to criticize the regime in a consistent manner. Stanbridge recalls, however, that in 1978 former *World* subeditor Graeme Addison, now a professor of journalism at Rhodes University, felt the new paper, although thoroughly reformist, did not go so far as the earlier independent black papers:

. . . the breed of black consciousness peddled by Qoboza in his popular *Percy's Pitch* column and also in editorials was a far cry from the socialism implicit in much black thinking. *World* spoke for the moderate wing of the black consciousness movement which stressed themes of moral and educational uplift, human dignity, freedom of speech, an economic square deal for blacks under free enterprise, and common South African nationhood for all races. . . . As a white-owned paper in the Argus group it did not dare take a radical line.[9]

Ironically, it was through the Soweto troubles that *The World* came to prominence in journalism, since it became too dangerous for white journalists to enter black townships and they had not developed contacts with black leaders in any event. As Allister Sparks put it when he was still editor of *The Mail* in 1979:

A visitor from another planet, going through these pages [of the white mainstream press before the Second World War] day after day, year after year, would get the impression that South Africa was a country populated almost exclusively by 3,000,000 whites. . . . Blacks did not exist, except as nameless units of the labor force and as constituting a vague and amorphous Native problem.[10]

It was the combination of an event, the Sowetan uprising of 1976, and a trend, the gradual growth of black readership (by 1980 more than half the readership of English newspapers was black, Indian, or of mixed race), that pushed *The World* into prominence. Percy Qoboza, it must not be forgotten, had both the grit and the talent to turn these circumstances into opportunity. Under different black leadership, the first mainstream black-edited paper might not have come so rapidly to the forefront of South African journalism. "Percy's Pitch" was well-timed, and cannot be dismissed as a form of Uncle Tomism, especially in the light of subsequent events. By the middle of 1977, daily circulation was about 200,000; making *The World* the largest daily in South Africa.

At this time, in response to some of the demands of the alternative radical critics of the mainstream, *The World* introduced an educational supplement called "People's College." Alternative magazines, like *The Reader,* as we shall see, picked up this function. According to Stanbridge, the supplement was of high quality. The main thrust of the paper, though, was criticism of police actions in the townships; it singled out Justice Minister James Kruger as primarily responsible for police brutality. On July 29, 1977, Qoboza was summoned to Kruger's office and told that his paper would "be taken off the streets" if it continued to "encourage disorderly conduct." Qoboza's reply was the editorial page:

Not a single complaint has brought us before the Press Council and not one article or comment has necessitated us being brought before court and yet we are now threatened with supreme action by the Minister of Justice. It can only mean that we as a newspaper have not done anything wrong legally or broken any part of our ethics which we hold supreme and that therefore the action envisaged by the Minister of Justice is another practical demonstration, and evidence, that this country is steadily moving toward authoritarian rule where dissent is equated with treason.

Kruger later told a *Rapport* interviewer that Qoboza had stepped beyond the bounds of press freedom. John Vorster, the head of the government, who was to resign over the Muldergate scandal two years later, read Qoboza editorials to a mass meeting of the National Party, which ignited the chant: Ban them! Ban Them! When Biko died and suspicions grew about the circumstances of his death, Kruger made crude jokes about Biko; they were reported worldwide, and disgraced the regime. Qoboza harped on the theme that Kruger was the cause of racial troubles, not the press, which merely reported what he had done.

On October 16, 1977, Kruger publicly described Qoboza as a "fat, fully grown lout" to a National Party meeting. Qoboza publicly demanded an apology. On the nineteenth the Vorster government closed down *The World* and *Weekend World* permanently and Percy Qoboza and his news editor, Aggrey Klaaste, were taken into custody under the Terrorism Act. It was also at this time that Donald Woods, editor of East London's *Daily Dispatch,* was banned for five years, and the Union of Black Journalists and almost a score of other organizations were declared illegal. The papers were closed because, in the opinion of the state president, they were a danger to state security and public order. For months before this period, three of *The World*'s top reporters, Joe Thloloe, Willie Bokala, and Moffett Zungu had been detained without charge; the paper ran their names every day with a demand that they be charged or released. When the paper closed, they had already endured detentions of 233, 126, and 66 days, respectively. Thloloe and Bokala were eventually released, but later detained again. Zungu was given a nine-year sentence.

Survival Strategies

In the same month that *The World* was shut down, an experiment in a wholly black-owned newspaper was begun. It was called *The Voice* and was launched with high hopes. It had significant support from German church groups and was affiliated with the South African Council of Churches. At one time or another, Dr. Nthato Motlana, Steve Biko, Bishop Desmond Tutu, and Chief Gatsha Buthelezi's Inkatha were involved in the planning stages and in early production. Perhaps this was the trouble. Subsequent events have shown that these different black figures and their forces are at times incompatible, with different agenda for the removal of apartheid and with variant visions of what is to come after apartheid. (See Chapter Six.) The subtitles carried on the masthead of *The Voice* almost tell the whole story: first "An Ecumenical Newspaper"; then, "Voice of the Voiceless"; finally, and pathetically, "The Only Sunday Paper Owned by Blacks." Harried by the political climate of the time, frantic to replace *The World* but not properly organized to do so, the paper converted from a monthly to a weekly publication schedule too quickly. Some inside observers also felt that the staff's close ties to the Black Consciousness Movement as found in the Rand leadership of MWASA, the black media union, and the Azanian Peoples Organization (AZAPO), a controversial black group trying to preserve Black Consciousness, when the central thrust of black activism was moving more toward ANC and UDF initiatives, alienated potential readers in the Rand area. In its final stages the paper resembled one of the white-owned "extras" (for-blacks-only supplements of major papers) with a dash of political consciousness. Beauty queens and music promos might share a page with Andries Treurnicht's "Conservative Party Racist" and "Madame Maripondo Says Her Powers Are from God." Ultimately, the venture went bankrupt for lack of readership, despite heavy subsidies from those who wished passionately for it to succeed.

When *The World* was closed, it had a circulation double that of *The Mail*, and it carried a lot of advertising; its closing was a blow to the revenues of the Argus Publishing Co. Taking a leaf from the independent black press's book on living under government oppression, the company moved an existing paper, *The* (Natal) *Post*, from the south, where it was aimed at the local Indian population, to the old offices of the defunct *World*. When Qoboza was released from six months of solitary confinement, never having been charged, he walked right back into his old office as editor once again. Many of the old hands from former days were back as well, now putting out a paper called *The Post* and *The Sunday Post*. Granted the logic of the radical dismissal of the mainstream opposition, this and other actions of the opposition companies cannot be explained away as mere pursuit of the profit motive. Critical articles and scathing editorials certainly cause more trouble than they generate sales, where sex-sin-soccer have worked just fine. The companies do put out so-called "extras," like *The Star*, that milk this method of boosting sales. But it must be remembered that over half the readership of all the English papers is already black, and the black share is growing. When *The Mail* closed, its readers did disperse among the official replacement, *Business Day*, the unofficial *Weekly Mail*, and *The Star*.

If Argus were solely concerned with profits, its repeated resurrections of highly critical papers and its repeated rehiring of black journalists decidedly *non grata* to Pretoria would be a baffling mystery. Lacking any hard evidence on secret motivations, I can only accept the daylight truth that at some real level democratic convictions about the political responsibility of a free press were and are operative.

One can make the point against Argus that its method is to limit its responsibilities by containing its conscience, as it were, in a sort of expendable cartridge, like a crusading black paper thus sparing the rest of the operation from excessive burdens of righteousness. In the United States, mutatis mutandis, the commercial broadcasters and large corporations lend support to the endeavors of the Public Broadcast System for quality entertainment and probing public affairs programming because PBS is a convenient charity that demonstrates not only their good intentions but also the futility of such programming as a business proposition, and thus they are absolved from serious support for news divisions, documentary production, and quality entertainment. Executives that I know praise PBS and like to watch it, but they refer to it affectionately as the *Private* Broadcasting System because so few people, in broadcast marketing terms, attend to its presentations.

So the Argus Company, in reappointing Qoboza, not only was going with a newsstand winner, it was also asking for trouble. *The Post* became *The World* revisited—with predictable results.

In February 1980, Police Minister Louis le Grange gave public notice to *The Post* before a National Party meeting that it was abusing press freedom and was being watched closely. Dr. Nthato Motlana, head of the Committee of Ten in Soweto, an alternate antigovernment leadership cadre designed to undermine the rubber-stamp authority of the local Bantu Council, an idea pushed hard by *The World,* dismissed Le Grange's remarks as paranoid. *The Post* was not intimidated; Qoboza celebrated Robert Mugabe's political capture of the former white-run Zimbabwe and inaugurated a write-in campaign to free Nelson Mandela from Robben Island. Le Grange again publicly called such activities and editorials "venomous." Qoboza replied in the paper that they would continue to support bodies relevant to the black populace, just as the Afrikaans papers supported the National Party. "We will continue exposing the injustices to which our people are subjected," he concluded.

It was at this time that the MWASA strike at *The Cape Herald* was taking place, and the nationwide sympathy walkout hit *The Post* as well, which had to suspend normal publication. Another law now automatically fell into place for the exasperated National government. A newspaper, to maintain its registration, has to publish more frequently than once every five weeks. Argus was aware of this requirement and made sure to publish one sheet regularly to be filed with the government. The government announced on December 23, 1980, the day the strike ended, that *The Post* had lost its registration, despite Argus's maneuver. The paper, which had reached an estimated 907,000 readers with its 112,000 circulation, was never to appear again.

Under that name.

Enter *The Sowetan,* a handout Argus used to carry advertisements in the township. Now priced, it moved its editorial offices to the old *Post* building. Joe Latakgomo, Qoboza's assistant and replacement when he had been to Harvard on a Niemann Fellowship, became editor, with the predictable and admirable attitude we have seen. Qoboza later became editor of *The Golden City Press,* which he gradually transformed into a paler version of his old paper, but at some cost. Having lost money, the *City Press* was sold to Nasionale Pers, the Afrikaans company supportive of Botha's Cape wing of the Nationalists.

Pressed by the general outcry against the blatant technical legalism used to close an embarrassing gadfly, the government finally gave reasons why they had shut down *The Post.* Kobus Coetzee, deputy minister of justice, claimed that the paper had published the entire Freedom Charter, the Magna Carta of the banned ANC, had served as a vehicle for ANC propaganda, and had even lent its editorial office as a place for briefing ANC terrorists before they left the country. When the Argus Company demanded that these charges be brought in court, the government declined, citing the need to protect secret sources.

In my view, the mainstream black press need not apologize for being mainstream, to wit, being part of a large company owned by whites, if they have a record comparable to *The World-Post-Sowetan.* Of course, this kind of record is rare, and the black extras are for the most part apolitical vehicles for advertising, much as *Bantu World* began.

Black Yellow Pages

The black extras came on the scene in the wake of Sharpeville and the suppression of so many independent black publications. As the eighties began, they were doing very well. *Star Africa,* from the publisher of *The Sowetan,* was selling in the mid-twenties. Even *The Mail* had an extra that sold in the fifties. The now-defunct *Sunday Times* had an extra that was 30 percent of its total sales of almost half a million. WASA, the black journalists' union, has called for the elimination of black extras on the grounds that they are racist. *Nux,* a student publication in Natal, examined *Echo,* the extra for the *Natal Witness,* and found that one half of the copy consisted of advertisements. The remaining newshole had less than 2 percent dedicated to politics, all the rest of the copy dealing with sports, beauty contests, awards, and crime.

As the radical critique has it, to be nonpolitical is to make a political choice. Nonetheless, the extras are relatively innocuous compared to the many publications aimed at blacks that are owned or influenced directly by the government for sheer propaganda.

Bona, owned by Afrikaner interests, reaches close to two million blacks in English, Sotho, Xhosa, and Zulu. It is high on pictures and photographs, low on copy, a typical sample of which is: "The Venda people are such a happy nation: always singing and dancing, their music filling the air. They are glad to be alive and living in their beautiful land. . . . These people are preparing for their independence in such a way that their independence can only be a success." The same magazine carried simple stories of the origin of Bantu Radio, a service of the SABC (broadcasting in seventeen separate languages) that emphasizes the tribal differences among the blacks by dealing with traditional crafts, arts, and festivals—a parody of the indigenous culture wrap that so many Third World countries say they wish they could provide in lieu of Anglo-American masscult. (One of the tapes provided for headphone wearers on South African Airways conveys the same kind of anthropological wonder that the black man is so marvelously [and therefore irremediably] "other.") *Bona* had a little story by an alleged black freedom fighter from Namibia, where the leftist revolutionaries, SWAPO, the South West Africa Peoples Organization, are fighting South African troops and their surrogates for the independence the United Nations has long been promised. The comic strip character, Kuaima, is faced with a huge man who smells of whisky and menacingly demands that he join SWAPO: " 'SWAPO,' thought Kuaima, 'the South West African People's Organization. A political power group dedicated to violence and communism. . . . [who] cared nothing for the feeling of the people.' Kuaima knew there was only one answer he could give: 'My fight is for my people's freedom. Not for their enslavement! I will join SWAPO never!' "

Hit is another magazine of the same type, but funded directly through the Muldergate slush fund in its origins and bankrolled in some measure by John McGoff, the North American Nationalist sympathizer who tried to buy *The Washington Star* for the National Party government. An article glorifying a career in the South African police would be typical fare. Another crude propaganda attempt, printed by a McGoff subsidiary, Xanap, near Pretoria, was *Mighty Man,* a black Captain Marvel, who did superhero combat with rotten communists and ANC saboteurs. The Sowetan teenagers for whom it was intended either laughed at or trashed this failed effort. *Pace* was also started by the South

African government to give capitalism a better name in the town ships. It has been condemned by MWASA. *Pace* was involved in Muldergate, although it still claims to be independent and is in fact a very successful magazine, just behind *Drum*, the former snappy, sexy magazine that circulated all over Southern Africa during the fifties. *Drum* published top black writers like the late Can Themba, a sort of Hemingway-Orwell of the townships, but the suppression of the sixties dispersed *Drum*'s writers. Jim Bailey, the "William Randolph Hearst of South Africa" finally sold it in 1984 to Nasionale Pers (along with Qoboza's *City Press*).

At the other end of the spectrum are the many—in fact count-less—underground publications that are either contraband in themselves or the work of banned organizations and for that reason illegal, whatever the content. These very mixed and varied sheets, newsletters, magazines, and pamphlets can be considered along with other contraband material when we look at the cen-sorship apparatus as it deals with the world outside the jour-nalistic press that is exempt from the Publications Act. Suffice it to say here that mere possession of a "radically undesirable" object is grounds for a prison sentence. Or worse. A hapless man named Ahmed Timol was apprehended in October 1971 with four hundred copies of the South African Communist Party journal *Inkululeko* in his car trunk: he died during interrogation pro-cedures.

There does remain another category of publication that rejects the values of both the mainstream press and of the government yet strives to abolish apartheid in a way that, though legal, is nonethe-less part of a more fundamental reordering of society, a reordering in which conservative and liberal, reactionary and radical, may become irrelevant. This is the so-called alternative press, a ka-leidoscopic collection of all kinds of material, including videotape and improvisatory theater, which has affinities with the so-called American underground press of countercultural provenance from the sixties, with ties to some of the utopian community move-ments of the nineteenth century. By their very nature, these ini-tiatives are evanescent.

Grassroot Alternatives

Rhodes University in Grahamstown has the only journalism de-partment in the educational system that is open to blacks. The department of this multiracial but essentially white English-speaking school is almost swamped by the number of applicants it gets from all over the country. One reason is that journalism is seen as a way of working and being socially reformist at the same time; another is that according to the rules of the South African educational game, blacks must go to a black school unless the subject of their choice, for which they must be qualified, is only available in a white college or university. By a sort of reverse Catch-22, the government, which does not wish to see the black schools turning out journalists who will only make trouble later, has set up a situation where any black who wants to be a journalist will meet his counterparts from all over the country at Grahamstown, including, of course, young white hopefuls as well, such as Tony Heard's daughter. Les Switzer, Shaun Johnson, John Grogan, Graeme Addison, Tim Couzens, and many other sharp critics of both journalism and apartheid have all passed through Rhodes's ranchlike campus, which dominates the small Grahamstown, a shallow green dish of population on a bare pale plain.

A student journal called *Bulletin Two* (*Bulletin One* was banned earlier) has set out the radical critique of what they call the liberal press. It is a critique familiar to students of neo-Marxism from Berkeley to Leicester to Frankfurt; and it became familiar to practicing journalists from the UNESCO report on the New Information Order, which takes Western media to task for cultural imperialism and other forms of domination. The student critique undermines two claims it attributes to the liberal press, what I have been calling the mainstream opposition. The first claim is that the liberal press is a staunch opponent of the National Party regime and particularly of its policy of apartheid. The second claim is that on principle the liberal press is a neutral reporter of events of significance, restricting its opinions to the properly labeled editorial page or to bylined columns.

Let us begin with the second claim. Neutrality is impossible, according to the critique. One always has a point of view, and it is best to declare at the outset what that outlook is and then proceed with one's report. The pretense to objectivity merely confuses the issue. While granting that individual reporters and editors are acting in good faith, honestly believing that they are being objective, the critique maintains that the structure of the news as a commodity precludes objectivity because it comes with preset categories that are themselves judgments of value. To use their own example, a meeting of one thousand students may be reported, but the content of the meeting will be given short shrift because it is not news. Obversely, the report of a member of

Parliament to his constituency, however small, will be reported in full. Arguments among government officials or captains of industry will be reported as news, but disagreements among groups of blacks will be reported as "unrest" without any reference to the point in dispute. To step outside the terminology of the report, it may be helpful to use the sociological concept of legitimacy. "News" and "news judgment" are decisions about what is of valid general interest and thus worthy of reportage. But the categories of the business and the division of the paper into departments, like "sports," "lifestyles," "politics," and so forth, carry with them implicit choices of legitimacy, which are in accord, to return to the terminology of the critique, with middle-class capitalist values. This explains the vacuity of the second claim.

As to the first claim, the students say yes, the liberal press is opposed to apartheid, but as a tactic, a format, a finite policy. The press does not dispute the claims of the ruling class, of which it is a part, to exploit labor. It is quibbling about a particular means to that end, like clergy of different churches arguing over tea about how best to save souls. The argument can be heated, even bitter. But it is never fundamental. In the language of the critique, it is merely a factional fight within the ruling class.

In the light of the very special meaning the Nationalist regime gives to "consensus politics" it is interesting that the student critique uses the same term to lump the English liberal press with the Afrikaans press, because they share the same basic social contract.

By using the term "student critique," I do not mean to patronize the position, but merely to locate it accurately on campus, where it is held most strongly. South African students in general, journalism students in particular, and especially those at the very active and oppositionist Rhodes University are not spoiled theatrical radicals who never let study or protest interfere with rock concerts. Since the early seventies, they have been politically active on behalf of blacks and labor unions, providing them with information and dedicating their student publications to hard-nosed reporting of apartheid's atrocities, for which they have paid with bannings and security police invasions of their offices and homes. American television viewers were perhaps surprised to see on television the vicious beating of University of Cape Town students by police with lethal whips—something they thought was reserved for unruly blacks in violent townships. The history of strenuous opposition to the regime on the part of the English campuses fueled police energy far more powerfully than similar but weaker grudges did in the police riot in Chicago in 1968.

Throughout the seventies up to today, one of the very best ways to learn about state repression has been to read *Saspu National,* the nationally distributed paper of the South African Student Press Union, and *Saspu Focus,* their quarterly, both of which have been frequently banned. About the size of *Time* and running some thirty pages, *Saspu Focus* has consistently published news of forced removals, political prisoners, oppositionist organizations like SACC and UDF, protests, police brutality, living conditions in the townships, homelands, and squatter camps, with special concentration on trade unions and labor movements, with whom NUSAS, the white National Union of South African Students, has had a special affinity since the early seventies.

When *The World* was closed down, so were *Crux, Z,* and *Crisis;* in subsequent years, *Spark, National Students,* and *Varsity* were permanently shut down. These closings, accompanied by police raids on campus, prompted *The Cape Times* to remark sarcastically that there must be a dangerous espionage ring masquerading as students or else the police might be thought to be busy with pointless intimidation. By 1979 only one student had ever been charged, and this only for publishing a banned publication—a case which the student won. (He was Sean Moroney, now editor of the London-based *African Business.*)

When pressed, the regime offered various reasons for the bannings:

Z: "Marxist, Communist, Far-Leftist *[sic];* encouragement of a Communist dictatorship [Frelimo in Mozambique] which has threatened South Africa with terrorist attacks; allegations of torture and brutality against the guardians of law and order."

Crisis: "The statement that the homelands act as 'child extermination camps' . . . [is] an outrageous accusation against the authorities who, whatever their shortcomings might be, are at least making a sincere effort to provide health services for the black people, vastly superior to their own traditional methods."

Bulletin One: ". . . anti-society, anti-White, leftist propaganda . . . to establish an integrated Black-White society, socialist in structure and presumably under Black domination."

Undeniably, the students have paid their dues and have every right to apply the familiar formula to the South African press. But though their cause is just, it does not make their reasoning right. And ultimately, I believe, it is divisive for the antiapartheid cause, which if anything must surely tolerate differences among its own ranks.

One can easily concede that many editors and reporters in the liberal press are naive about what they are doing or are stubborn know-nothings or arrogant dogmatists of "professional news judgment." Nevertheless, a surprising number of working journalists, like Joe Latakgomo, the present editor of *The Sowetan,* or Allister Sparks, formerly of *The Rand Daily Mail,* or Rene DeVilliers, the retired Prog parliamentarian and former president of the South African Institute of Race Relations who also happened to edit the allegedly compromised *Star,* or scores of others, really do have night thoughts, wonder about what they are doing, seek elusive truths, labor to change constricting formats and crushing marketing directives, and try to stay alive and sane.

The most serious limitation on what I prefer to call mainstream media is a technical one. Since the invention of the printing press, there has been a constant trend toward turning all means of communication into more capital-intensive operations. Clever machines at each level of production and distribution, from word processors to satellite transmissions, replace human beings using art and craft. The machines are expensive, and to recoup costs the owner's income must be higher, which necessitates greater outreach, higher ratings, broader readerships. Objectivity was introduced not so much as an ethical ideal but as a marketing necessity to extend readership beyond the narrow coterie of an avowedly partisan press. And, of course, "objectivity" is not the philosophical concept of absolute neutrality; it is a policy decision taken to avoid offending large blocks of readers. If few or none will be offended, then "hippies" or "fascists" can be trashed with abandon: they don't buy enough of the goods advertised. Further, the demand for broader outreach obliterates the small distinctions of close-knit community and forces the medium to create an artificial catalogue of "media community issues and people," what in a parallel context of analysis have been called celebrities and pseudo-events. "News" thus becomes a highly artificial commodity, a processed stream of artificial ingredients bearing the same relation to reality as junk food to fresh farm produce. Blacks in South Africa reading about the efforts of Harry Belafonte to help starving Ethiopia are no less part of this process than whites reading about Nancy Reagan's well-publicized appearances on behalf of drug-abuse treatment and prevention. Starvation and drug abuse are real, and may be vividly experienced by large segments of the public, but as members of the media audience, these selfsame segments are spared any scrutiny of things close to home or any guidance or help as to what they can do about their own versions of these problems. The mainstream media, which now are in a global net of international media issues and faces, can only present the themes of "Aid for the Starving" or "The Terror and Tragedy of Drug Abuse." The world is a stage, but only well-known, reliable celebrities can be players on it. Given this technoeconomic configuration, it is a wonder that local papers exist, let alone that they provide occasional vigorous and aggressive reportage of truly local real issues, be it in Cape Town or New Jersey.

There are a few brave and smart people in the world who try to stem this tide with truly local community reporting, who ask questions not only of sources but of readers, and who do not ever hope to become rich or famous in trying to serve genuinely useful information to communities that are often in the dark about issues vital to them but barraged with repetitive and unilluminating headlines about superpower conflicts or UN resolutions. Despite or because of the added political repression of this kind of endeavor, South Africa seems to have more than its share of such people.

Rashid Syria is one of them. He works in a mainstream journalistic job, but donates a a considerable piece of his time to a truly remarkable community journalism initiative in the Cape area called *Grassroots Community Newsletter*.

When he is asked about this project, Syria, a quiet man of mixed race, does not so much talk about journalism as he does about community. We must have finished a pot of tea before he began talking about the production and distribution (both difficult) of the actual paper. Before that, he wished to emphasize that no one was really in charge; that the paper sprang from community needs among the black and so-called coloured of the Cape; that a large annual meeting took place when all important decisions for the coming year were made; that monthly, weekly, daily meetings were scheduled over the five-week production schedule so that the content, even the style of the stories, could be democratically decided. As a professional journalist, he must have found this tedious and needless, I suggested. Far from it, he replied, with level insistence. It was the whole meaning of the project, a *prensa chica*, a "little press," derived from the consciousness-raising community work in South America inspired by Paolo Freire. In fact, legally, *Grassroots* was run not by a company, nor even by a trust, as originally intended, but by an association called Grassroots.

Significantly, the project began in 1980 with a grant from WASA, the antecedent to MWASA, and a very specific charter: to articulate the views and aspirations of workers and communities; to assist grassroots organizations in developing communications skills; to produce a publication that would be a catalyst for community organization with how-to articles; to provide basic survival information on health care, legal rights, social services, labor relations; finally, to promote the concept of alternative media by example. Subsequently, church groups have made up the constant budget shortfalls of the organization, which relies on donated space and labor. Advertising revenue is meager and, in any event, is curtailed by a strict policy of limiting ads to 30 percent of total copy and of not accepting any from sources at odds with community values. Occasional issues have been banned, but the newsletter holds on, sticking very closely to the original mandate, and serving as a model to other community newsletters around the country, like *Eye,* in the Pretoria area; *Ukusa* [Dawn] in Durban; *Speak,* in Johannesburg; and, in Port Elizabeth on the eastern Cape, *Umthonyama,* the Xhosa word for the first cattle dung to fall in a corral, the cultural equivalent of "grassroots." Syria is hopeful and enthusiastic, although he admits that even now the paper is still looked on as a "coloured paper" by many of the blacks in Nyanga and Guguletu where they have tried to solicit subscribers—which in this context means community members, not just passive readers about life elsewhere.

What kind of stories do they cover? This, Syria informs one, is the wrong kind of question to ask of an alternative publication. They do not cover stories. They approach community needs and seek to galvanize community action for common solutions. For instance, when a community survey discovered that seventy percent of the Mitchell's Plain community paid their electricity bills late and were penalized an additional R400,000 annually, *Grassroots* did not send a reporter to get the scoop on the survey and maybe a reaction from the city council, which collects the bills. They had a common meeting with the Electricity Petition Committee to plot out a common strategy of mobilizing publicity to get the penalty system changed.

This is beyond advocacy journalism, and maybe it should not be called journalism at all, but it is what is needed in South Africa, and so far it is working. It must be stressed that community newsletters, although action oriented, are not political in the sense that the United Democratic Front or the Progressive Labor Party are—groups with national agendas for the Botha regime to adopt or to fight. Rather, they deal with the everyday nitty-gritty problems of poverty and survival under apartheid. In this they cannot escape the Scylla and Charybdis of Botha's "confrontational" label or the radical critique that accuses them of accepting the system while adjusting the details.

How were the electricity bill details adjusted? After the full committee of the association approved of the final article, it was printed under a cartoon showing a light bulb in the city council filled with cash: "The Big Lights Ripoff!" But this was not the end. Volunteers were assembled to distribute the paper door-to-door in Mitchell's Plain and invite readers to the community meeting on the problem announced in the story. Three thousand people turned up for the meeting, and two days later they marched on city council offices. The penalties were revoked. Grassroots, the association, won by means of its alternate medium, *Grassroots.*

In English, the linqua franca among all the blacks and so-called coloured (who speak Afrikaans, although the young are abondoning it), the newsletter runs about sixteen pages. They are filled with articles on what to do if your child gets worms, the need for a local hospital, how to improve reading skills, how to claim maternity pay, your rights when under arrest, your rights when laid off from work, and so forth. The look is deliberately unsophisticated, and many cartoons and illustrations are used. Starting with a 5,000 press run, *Grassroots* now prints over 30,000 copies and reaches an estimated quarter of a million members of over seventy affiliated black groups: residential associations, trade unions, women's organizations, and school and professional clubs. On average, fifteen groups are represented at the frequent editorial meetings, and about fifty volunteers help put out the paper in Athlone township. Rashid acknowledges that it is hard to keep the enthusiasm of volunteers up, and at times only a few very dedicated people do 90 percent of the work. He also admits that the association and its project could not survive without the church support and private donations that make up about 60 percent of their budget, not counting the great value of free labor from overworked and tired people. Four full-time staff are paid a minimal salary with checks that at times bounce. By 1982 the minimum cost per issue was R7000. The newsletter has been banned twice, and members of the association have been hounded by the police. Johnny Issel, who had been previously banned, was banned again after he began working for *Grassroots* and for that reason. When he got a job with the church social service agency CUPS, he was warned he could go to jail for violating his banning order because he was working for an organization which published. (CUPS publishes an occasional newsletter for the clergy.)

Despite these pressures and the lack of any prosperous company ownership behind them such as the mainstream press at times enjoys, the members of the Grassroots Association are humbly defiant. Their editorials have more than once said, "We will not be silenced," directly after bannings and harassments.

In 1983, after the success of *Grassroots,* Rashid Syria and Mansoor Jaffer, a fellow journalist from that project, started another community newspaper, *Saamstaan* (Afrikaans for "stand together"), with the financial help of Roman Catholics in Holland. The government has continually harassed them with health inspections of their premises, with threats to close them down, detentions under the Internal Security Act, mysterious office fires, and large fines levied for trivial errors of fact under the Police Act.

Working for the church is a frequent employment of alternate media people since the churches, particularly the South African Council of Churches, have funded a large number of antiapartheid and community self-help media projects. As we have seen, they have contributed to the secular *Frontline* and *Grassroots;* they commissioned Kevin Harris to do a 16-mm film (since converted to video) soon after his dismissal from SABC; they were the principal funders of the failed *Voice.* We will be taking a closer look at the churches later, but there is one further major secular effort at alternate publishing which originally began as a specifically Christian project: Ravan Press.

The press got started in the early seventies, around the same time as the beginning of the Black Consciousness Movement and the radical politicization of the student press. It sprang directly from a Christian venture called SPRO-CAS (the Study Project on Christianity in an Apartheid Society), and its founder members were all members of the Christian Institute, a militantly religious but nonchurch group put together by Beyers Naude, the crusading minister who abandoned his high position in the Dutch Reformed Church rather than collaborate with apartheid. He was consequently banned for many years with the added stigma of the political apostate, only to emerge in the eighties to take over SACC from Bishop Tutu, when the latter was promoted to the episcopacy of Johannesburg. In fact, all the founders, Naude, Danie van Zyl, and Peter Randall, were banned and had to relinquish all official ties to Ravan Press, which has been ably and bravely run by Mike Kirkwood since 1978. Having said this, however, one is reminded by Mike (as one was told by Syria about his own alternate press activities) that no one is in charge; that it is a team effort with policy decisions arrived at democratically, through a system of committees: editorial, financial, sales, administrative.

This sort of thing pops up so frequently when dealing with the opposition outside the mainstream that at first I thought it was a sort of underground ploy so that the police would not know whom to arrest. I now see that it is the result of a confluence of conflicting pressures. Certainly the fact that any head that sticks up too high may be chopped off makes the committee system a practical tactic for continuity and offers marginal protection from greater persecution for the most dedicated. Still, after talking and meeting with these folk for so long, I believe the communal flavor of their efforts is derived from a very special rejection of the core of apartheid, the us-vs.-them mentality and the master-servant relationship in all of its manifestations. It is also obviously influenced by the ecumenical movement among the churches, where committee work is a necessity, a burden, a curse, and a blessing. But one cannot construe this remarkable communal family spirit as a narrowly Christian phenomenon, since so many of the anti-apartheid efforts, like Grassroots, are multifaith and secular as well as multiracial.

So when I asked Mike Kirkwood to tell me about Ravan Press, he gave me a committee report on what they were about. The basic aim, though now secular, has been constant from the beginning: to publish work that on the one hand challenges the apartheid ideology and on the other promotes a democratic and classless South Africa. Ravan, like so many university and church oppositionist groups, identifies apartheid with class and thus with capitalism.

Unalterably opposed to totalitarianism, whether its mask be communist or fascist, the alternative media people see apartheid as the historical result of capitalism, the exploitation of cheap labor so that great wealth can be accumulated. Ironically, by harping constantly on the communist menace and by unremitting emphasis on the relative health of the South African economy under the apartheid regime, the Nationalists have convinced a great number of those religiously opposed to officially atheistic regimes that there is truth in the Marxist analysis of South African history. This of course places the liberal white businessman, who really does wish to give equal pay for equal work, and who sees capital formation and industrialization as the cure for social ills by enlarging the pie for everyone, in a difficult position. And it is one more reason for those in alternative media to distrust the mainstream business-and-advertising-supported oppositionist press.

In keeping with the collectivist style of alternative media like *Grassroots,* Ravan seeks to be a clearinghouse of publishing ideas for an army of other organizations, not just for bright individuals. To this end, they have established an array of advisory committees outside the press on various topics that represent readerships as constituencies rather than merely as customers. Kirkwood gives the example of the adult literacy committee made up of elected representatives from three organizations who work in this area: USWE (Using spoken and Written English), Learn and Teach, and ELP (the English Language Project). This sytem not only addresses the problem of project design and the publishing program in an antimarketing manner that still manages to meet real needs, but it also helps toward solving the great distribution problem that any alternative medium has (as nonmainstream publications and even independently produced commercial movies have in the United States). There are just not that many bookstores and outlets for books and paperbacks in South Africa, and one cannot realistically expect the readership Ravan seeks to be habitués of the bookstores that exist. So the organizations become distributors for books aimed at the interests of their constituents. For instance, the Ravan Worker Series of short booklets on specific labor problems is being published in conjunction with various appropriate unions: The Metal and Allied Workers Union was involved in *The Sun Shall Rise for the Workers* by Mandlenkosi Makhoba of that union; Petrus Tom's *My Life Struggle* was issued in affiliation with the Congress of Trade Unions, of which Tom is a member. On another scale, Ravan handles the business management and distribution for the scholarly *South African Journal on Human Rights,* and is the producer of *South African Review* and *Working Papers in South African Studies,* each the result of university and research institute input.

For years Ravan has been distributing *Staffrider* magazine, a collection of writings by black authors, mostly young, who try to convey the experience of apartheid not merely as a political statement but as a cry of literature about the human condition. Flowing from this has been the Staffrider Series of paperbacks showcasing the work of such outstanding African authors as Es'kia Mphahlele, Modike Dikobe, and Njabulo Ndebele, whose *Fools and Other Stories* (No. 19 in the series) won the 1984 Noma Award for publishing in Africa. Internationally known South African writers Nadine Gordimer, J. M. Coetzee, and Christopher Hope have also published with Ravan.

Children's books and historical studies published in conjunction with the University of Witwatersrand History Workshop, like *The House of Phalo* (about the Xhosa when they were independent), *The Destruction of the Zulu Kingdom, The Colonisation of Southern Tswana, Khoikoi and the Founding of White South Africa,* and a number of others, contribute toward a wresting of historical myth from white mainstream perspectives as well as from the Afrikaner mythmakers' covenant concoction (God gave them South Africa) that Professor Leonard Thompson, the distinguished director of the Yale-Wesleyan Southern African Research Program, has so meticulously dissected.[11]

Ravan, true to its origins, still publishes books that are distinctly religious, such as the works of Rev. Allan Boesak, the UDF leader, and books of inquiry and discussion in the area of liberation theology. And today, with their banning orders lifted, both Peter Randall and Beyers Naude are on the Ravan board of trustees, as are Archbishop Tutu and Father Smangalisu Mkatchwa, the secretary of the Catholic Conference of Bishops (the organization through which the Catholics, who are not formal members of the SACC, collaborate with its members).

Appropriate Technology

The communal attitudes found among so many of the alternative media people are especially present in the nonprint area, because all opposition here takes on the alternative form. Because of the virtual government monopoly over broadcasting, a medium which lends itself readily to centralized control, there is no such thing as mainstream oppositionist television or radio. For the same reasons, nonprint alternative media perforce take the form of Super-8 and 16-mm film, convertible to videotape, or are shot on tape to begin with. When the SACC commissioned Kevin Harris to produce a film about Desmond Tutu and Peter Storey, he shot it in 16-mm before converting it to video. Early in the seventies, when the white National Union of South African Students was beginning to show social consciousness in its publications, they produced a Super-8 film about a protest at Witwatersrand University, *Wits Protest.* In the early eighties, Mark Kaplan filmed the boycott of the Indian Council Election in Athlone near the Cape, and was attacked by the police. (Kaplan is now back in Zimbabwe.) A number of protest documentaries in 16-mm have been made since the middle seventies. *FOSATU: Building Worker Unity; Allan Boesak: Choosing for Justice; Grandfather, Your Right Foot is Missing; Last Supper in Hortsley Street* (about the forced removals and the destruction of District Six in Cape Town), and *Crossroads,* all made in the 1980s, are also available on videotape.

The Second Carnegie Inquiry into Poverty and Development in South Africa bankrolled eight film/videos all over the country, among them *The Tot System, I am Clifford Abrahams,* and *Reserve 4.* Although the tape of *Crossroads* is banned, I was easily able to see it in Cape Town. These films and videos are hard to come by outside of South Africa and of course are not available to the casual person within South Africa, both because of the law and because of the difficulty, once again, of distribution outside the mainstream. Internationally available film/videos like the powerful *Witness to Apartheid* and the International Defense and Aid Fund for Southern Africa's *Anvil and the Hammer, Isitwalandwe: The Story of the South African Freedom Charter,* and *The Sun Will Rise* (prizewinner at the Moscow and Amiens film festivals for 1983) are becoming more common as part of the world movement against apartheid.

Indigenous alternative film/media production and distribution are more modest affairs and follow the model of the print alternative media. They can only survive because of free or very cheap volunteer labor, church funding, and university technical backup. Super-8 film was the early medium of choice, since it was relatively cheap and easy to use. Sixteen millimeter film, when it could be afforded and speed of shooting was not so essential, was also prevalent. But, of course, film is a difficult medium for protest. It is awkward to distribute and, unlike print, requires exhibition facilities that attract the wrong kind of attention. Video is growing as a means of distribution and exhibition, because it is so much easier to show to people. And it is much easier to shoot as well, if one has the budget for the latest and lightest equipment, especially the compact and unobtrusive Video-8. The videocassette, indistinguishable from a flood of innocuous nonpolitical product and not requiring literacy, is a medium of protest with overwhelming potential. It is used to flout the strict rules of the Saudi regime on broadcast material; it is being used in China and other places of suffocatingly prescribed cultural programming. Everyone remembers the powerful effect of the less forceful audiocassette on the Shah's regime in Iran, when sermons of the charismatic Ayatollah, transcribed from the telephone, fueled bloody rebellion.

Not unlike Grassroots, the Community Video Resource Association, founded in 1977 with a grant from the United Church of Canada and kept going by SACC and the Anglo-American-De-Beers Chairman's Fund, does not go beyond immediate community affairs and is used to build and serve specific and local constituencies. In 1980, James Polley of the University of Cape

Town Film Education Unit told me, it provided "videoletters" for striking workers to send back to their families, mostly in the Transkei and Ciskei homelands hundreds of miles away. John van Zyl of Witwatersrand University's theater and film department, spoke in his turn of the use of Super-8 all over the Third World to capture the customs and oral cultures that are fast dying out because of industrialization. His unit received equipment and technical assistance from the Center for Direct Cinema at France's University of Nanterre for his students to film local black life in Johannesburg and in the homelands. This work is remarkably similar in spirit to Ravan's efforts to tell black history from a black perspective. Bernard Spong, a minister who heads the Interchurch Media Programme for the South African Council of Churches, gives aid and education to a number of groups, whether church affiliated or not, in Super-8 production and in slide and photographic recording of life under apartheid. Spong was raided by the Security Police a number of times in 1985 and 1986, and his material was damaged or confiscated. No charges were ever filed, but a point had been made. And, of course, the police find the films and photographs and tapes of the alternative media people excellent sources of evidence in their political prosecutions: During the government investigation of SACC, excerpts from Kevin Harris's film and some ten others were used by the Security Police as evidence of subversion. Community Video and Afrascope have also been raided for the purpose, it is believed, of gathering evidence against sixteen United Democratic Front Executive Board members who are on trial for treason.[12] Americans will recall the "mass media trial" of Dr. Benjamin Spock, Rev. William Sloane Coffin, and others ("the Boston Five") who opposed the Vietnam War: the FBI posed as reporters at press conferences to use the defendants' public statements as evidence of conspiracy, and the Justice Department used tapes of televised newscasts and subpenaed cameramen to verify the footage. Among other controversies, the trial sparked the bitter argument about the privileged status of tape outtakes (material discarded from the final broadcast version) and reporters' private notes. The South African Police, with no First Amendment to worry about, would be the envy of the prosecutors of that scandalous trial.[13] During the states of emergency of the mid-eighties, the police have also confiscated videotape from foreign news crews.

As might be expected, Rhodes University has an excellent film and video department. Keyan Tomaselli, a professor of indefatigable critical energy with enough aggressive drive for a swarm of gadflies, has worked in the Rhodes department, has studied for his doctorate with Van Zyl of Wits, and now is directing a new Contemporary Cultural Studies Unit at the University of Natal in Durban. A former chairman of the South African Film and Television Technician's Association, Tomaselli, often assisted by his wife, has written, lectured, and, in my silenced presence, talked volubly on the entire question of alternative film/video in South Africa. Not untypically, he sees virtue in what others see as a lack—the problem of distribution. Tomaselli feels that video, by its nature, should quickly respond to local needs and not be conceived of as some megaproject to inflame the nation. (Some South Africans call this "trigger video," a Madison Avenue phrase if I ever heard one.) Again, like the journalists of *Grassroots,* the alternative video producers see themselves first as political organizers.

Tomaselli provides a telling case in point: video was used in 1984, after the fashion of corporate training programs, to train activists to dissuade voters from supporting the tricameral proposal of the Botha administration. The activists were shown how to ring doorbells and deal with strangers, much as salesmen are trained with demonstration tapes. The trainees then viewed their own rehearsals at the task in front of groups charged with pointing out mistakes and urging better methods.

Media Populism

Opposition to the apartheid regime expresses itself, therefore, in both the mainstream press and a variety of alternative media forms. Outside the mainstream, or so-called liberal English press, opposition to apartheid is inextricably linked with dissatisfaction over modern industrial life. In fact, for many among the alternative media, apartheid is understood not as springing directly from primitive racist attitudes, but as a logical, if extreme, component of the modern capitalist system of managing labor. Europe and America, where modern industrialization is most advanced, have managed to use labor pools among less-developed countries (labor platforms) through the global reach of multinational corporations. For the most part, these laborers are paid very low wages and also happen to be people of color. Oceans enforce a global apartheid that is reinforced by immigration quotas. When work must be done locally, America exploits illegal aliens and Europe uses guest workers; both these classes have exactly the same status, barring the petty apartheid of separate public facilities that the Botha regime is phasing out anyway, that the South African regime imposes on the native black population. It is the proximity and crudeness of the system that offends the West; they conveniently ignore its striking structural similarity to their own systems.

Simplistic as the comparison is, it is remarkably in tune with George Frederickson's scholarly study of the origins of white supremacy (the form of racism that is almost exclusively meant when the term "racism" is employed, if only because it is more successful than the majority of forms of domination practiced, cruelly but inefficiently, throughout large parts of the Third World, with the possible exception of the repression of women). Frederickson found that racism, with its dogmatism about the inherent inferiority of the exploited and their need for guidance and uplift from barbarism, was invented by the British to justify their exploitation of the Irish in the face of Christian doctrine on the equality of all men and women. The British doctrine was conveniently exported and adopted by plantation owners in the American South and by farmers and mine magnates in South Africa, both at one time part of the British Empire.[14] As we shall later see, this functional view of apartheid at least partially explains the seemingly suicidal insistence on economic sanctions that will certainly damage the entire South African system, particularly those at the bottom. Before that, however, we must examine the way the regime seeks to control through the Directorate of Publications *all* expression beyond the press and alternative news media.

NOTES

1. William A. Hachten and C. Anthony Giffard, *The Press and Apartheid: Repression and Propaganda in South Africa* (Madison, Wisc.: University of Wisconsin Press, 1984), p. 134.

2. Committee to Protect Journalists, *South Africa and Zimbabwe: The Freest Press in Africa?* March 1983, p. 18.

3. *Washington Post,* June 27, 1986, p. 19.

4. Hachten & Giffard, op. cit., p. 139.

5. Ibid., pp. 139–41.

6. Patrick S. Washburn, *A Question of Sedition: The Federal Government's Investigation of the Black Press During World War II* (New York: Oxford University Press, 1986).

7. Shaun Johnson, "Barometers of the Liberation Movement: A History of South Africa's Alternative Press," *Media Development* 22, no. 3 (1985): 18–21. Mr. Johnson has graciously provided me with many of his unpublished notes on the alternate press in South Africa. He is currently

earning a doctorate in the history of the black press at Oxford University, where he is a Rhodes scholar. As a journalism student at Rhodes University in Grahamstown, he studied under Tim J. Couzens, an expert in black journalism history. Les Switzer, who, with his wife, Donna, has published the definitive bibliography on the subject, *The Black Press in South Africa and Lesotho* (G. K. Hall, 1979), was professor of journalism at Rhodes before coming to the United States. Johnson shared his reminiscences with me on the founding and early history of *SASPU National,* the journal of the South African Student's Press Union, of which he is past president.

8. Tim J. Couzens, "History of the Black Press in South Africa, 1836–1960," Yale-Wesleyan Southern African Research Program, n.d., p. 25.

9. Professor Roland Stanbridge, now professor of journalism at the Journalisthogskolan I in Stockholm, has generously shared much of his research and many of his recollections with me.

10. Hachten & Giffard, op. cit., p. 144.

11. Leonard Thompson, *The Political Mythology of Apartheid* (New Haven: Yale University Press, 1985).

12. Keyan Tomaselli, "Progressive Film and Video in South Africa," *Media Development* 22, no. 3 (Summer 1985): 16.

13. Four of the five were found guilty of conspiracy to obstruct military conscription (a serious offense carrying maximum penalties of twenty years) in varying degrees. On appeal, the review court ordered a new trial because of technical violations of procedure. The trial took place in 1968; the decision on appeal came some years later, when Vietnam was a place that everybody, hawk and dove, was trying to forget; so the government decided not to pursue the matter any further.

14. George M. Frederickson, *White Supremacy* (New York: Oxford University Press, 1981).

CHAPTER FOUR

The Bureaucracy of Censorship

Reasoning the Need

Witwatersrand University, or "Wits," is one of the two principal English-speaking universities in South Africa. Like its counterpart, Cape Town University, it has long been a center of dissent and an occasional focus of protest demonstration against the Nationalist government. Neither university has a journalism department, but each has film and drama departments that engage in protest theater and documentary production in film or video, forms of dissent in that they call attention to injustice and record grievances. Both universities have research and teaching interests that can be construed as forms of criticism insofar as they examine public policy and its practical impact. In Cape Town, a learned focus of such critique and record is SALDRU, the South African Labour Development Research Unit, affiliated with the Carnegie Endownment in the Unitd States and headed by the distinguished social scientist, Francis Wilson (whose wife, Lindy, is a television producer locally celebrated for her banned video, *Crossroads*).

At Wits, the focus of this kind of criticism, ánd of its nature more sharply oppositionist, is the Centre for Applied Legal Studies (CALS), vigorously captained by John Dugard, the single towering legal critic of the government's policies. Dugard is not the kind of flamboyant crusader Americans tend to associate with antiestablishment lawyers like Ralph Nader; he is soft-spoken, but he speaks with great intensity, conviction, and concentration—a characteristic of his style of writing and form of advocacy. Some figures of opposition, here or elsewhere in the international gulag of human-rights violations, give the impression of quixotic defiance, of unreal hopes in a practical world of realpolitik. Dugard impressed me as though he were a momentary visitor to a barbaric pit from a high bright plateau of established norms of civilization, soberly astonished at the sheer ignorance of oppressive measures. Just as the light of world media attention has forced the regime to try to dress up its acts in a wáy it imagines is attractive, so Dugard's relentless dragging of a world context of civil judgment into local government policy has forced officials to seek justifying arguments for their actions. He has brought to the attention of the World Court the abuse of standards of citizenship as affected by apartheid; he has sought to implement a "training program" for South African judges and magistrates in sentencing so that fairness will be "understood." In May 1985 CALS launched *The South African Journal of Human Rights,* which seeks to apply internationally recognized legal standards to South African law enforcement and policy formulation. The *Journal* has analyzed with cold detachment the system of detention without trial, political asylum, a doctor's ethical responsibilities in treating prisoners, and, with special force, the standards used in censoring expression and curtailing its free exercise.

Ironically, it was the Publications Act of 1974 that gave Dugard the impetus to introduce standards of judgment for the notoriously capricious censors, compelling them to the attempt, at least, of appearing consistent. Such use was far from the minds of the devisers of the act, who wished to remove censorship decisions from the embarrassment of judicial review. The previous enabling act of censorship left it subject to repeal by the Supreme Court. The new act leaves censorship only remotely reversible in individual instances where an appeal is made to a Publications Appeal Board, a body within the purview of the censorship apparat, and whose decision is final. Further, anyone can institute censorship proceedings against any publication; indeed, against anything, for T-shirts and rings, bumper stickers and songs can be declared "undesirable" by anonymous committees acting on the complaint of anonymous individuals or of the state. But only those who have standing can institute an appeal, and standing is generally accorded only to those who have a financial interest in the banned object or censored publication. I registered surprise that Dugard's own book, *Human Rights and the South African Legal Order* had not been banned or censored. He nodded and told me that it was assumed that nobody likely to read his book would be affected by it. The censorship apparat, he went on, operated on two assumptions: likely readership and putative respect for vigorous political debate. He was a preacher to the saved, by the lights of the government; disgruntled blacks who might get revolutionary ideas would hardly be influenced by the likes of Dugard. Once more, as with the control and suppression of newspapers, one had an example of the curious combination of respect and contempt for intellectual standards.

There was also the familiar notion of the state as the protector of political children. Dugard reminded me that in the act itself the language stated: ". . . in the application of this Act the constant endeavour of the population of the Republic of South Africa to uphold a Christian view of life shall be recognized." In fact, he went on, although the average person might have the idea that the committees were busy looking at pornography or antireligious tracts to preserve a Calvinist orthodoxy, political dissent was the major concern.[1] And if religious matters were dealt with, it was mostly as they interacted with political behavior. He passed over a thick sheaf of papers with the title, "Publications Amendment Bill." Constant refinements. "You might want to take a look at that. But it might be more interesting if you were to go to a Publications Appeal Board hearing. As it happens, we are arguing a case there in a couple of days. Interested?"

Nicholas Haysom of CALS would be arguing the case, it turned out, and he was kind enough to drive me the forty minutes or so to the hearing in Pretoria, along a modern freeway crowded with South African soldiers hitchhiking. "They wear uniforms on weekend leave, and it is considered patriotic to give them a lift. I suppose it also is a way of 'showing the flag.' Most of them are reluctant conscripts anyway, quite young."

Haysom was in his mid-thirties, tall, blond, with an engaging smile and a quiet, confident manner. As we got closer to Pretoria, he began pointing out landmarks. The vast modernistic stone structure of the University of South Africa, which maintains an immense correspondence degree program, commanded a high ridge overlooking the curve of the highway. After a few weeks I felt that the same architect had designed the city halls, universities, and other recent institutional buildings of the country in a sort of Stalinist motif that would have been right at home on the stark slabs of the Albany Mall. As we got closer to the center of Pretoria, we passed a building that reminded me of the insane asylums erected in New York State in the fifties, with characteristically intimidating steel security windows. A mental hospital? Haysom smiled. It was the prison where he had been held last year for six months. In solitary. He was never charged. The last week he was allowed a small transistor radio. Haysom related this in a matter-of-fact manner that rerinded one of Dugard ticking off the latest string of bureaucratic brutalities. I told him I could never endure solitary, even for a much shorter period. Laconically, he said one can endure all sorts of things in the event that would be paralyzing in mental prospect. His hardest experience, unanticipated, was managing to be sociable once he was released: it was hard to be with people again. He had mentioned to the lieutenant who released him that his detention must have been a mistake. "Probably," the policeman flatly concurred.

Pretoria, unlike Johannesburg, fairly bristled with uniforms in the administrative area where the appeal would be made. August is in the middle of the southern winter, but there was a darkness about the corridors, the coffee shop, the elevator, and, finally, the hearing chamber that seemed metaphysical.

As we had come up in the elevator, the young assistant-district-attorney type who would argue against the appeal joined us by chance. An earnest and polite Afrikaner who appeared to be about six or seven years Haysom's junior, he asked if Haysom didn't object to his arguing in Afrikaans. No objection. There were some attempts at small talk, and then we entered the chamber.

With two other members of the public, I sat at a long table behind the two attorneys, who faced a high, wide tribunal. Five men walked in quietly; four of them appeared to be very elderly. All, of course, were white.

Haysom began his plea. The case, I was later to learn, was very typical.

An issue of a black magazine, *The Reader,* had been banned in March. It was *Time*-sized, twenty-four pages, no advertisements, glossy paper; all text was broken up with photography, art work, boxes, large heads, and subheads; it was cheap, about an American quarter. There were eight principal articles: "We Came to Play Cricket, We Are Not Politicians"; "Jomo's Dream Comes True"; "The Gangster Who Became a Poet Don Mattera"; "Blacks Say No to Botha's Plan"; "Mapondera the Bandit"; "The Fight for Reserve Four"; "Labour News"; "Adopted Schools—Good or Bad?"

Although completely secular, the magazine was published by the South African Committee for Higher Education (SACHED), whose board contained a number of clergy, including Desmond Tutu, and whose finances were dependent on overseas donations from interdenominational church groups, such as the ones that supported *Voice.* SACHED was formed to fight ignorance among the black population that came about through poor education and information. It published another magazine explicitly for children, *Upbeat,* with a paid circulation of 15,000; a further 85,000 unpaid copies were distributed in schools throughout southern Africa, including Namibia and Zimbabwe. Both magazines were designed to improve the reading skills of its readers, to give them positive images of blacks who were winners and go-getters, and to raise their political awareness. *The Reader* was aimed at adults from twenty-five to forty-five who worked in the cities and who had had a minimum of four years of primary school. At the time of the ban, the magazine had a paid circulation of about 1,500, a further circulation through SACHED outlets of about 3,000, and a projected readership of about 20,000, mostly in the townships surrounding Jo'burg and Pretoria. Neither in form nor content was this an alternative medium, since it was not community-based; it was intended for a mass audience, using slick copy and reliance on the celebrity syndrome to catch attention. It also had a professional staff on salary. Yet income was only about 8 percent of the total budget, which came from the SACHED Trust, a creature of church-related donations.

Some anonymous person, a private citizen or a government official, had seen fit to call the March issue to the attention of the Directorate of Publications, which in turn was required to appoint an anonymous committee to look at the offending material and come up with a verdict. The verdict was a banning of the issue and the threat of a ban on future issues. (In the case of a periodical, a committee may not only ban a particular issue but also suspend or halt any future publication of any subsequent issue.) Why? If no appeal had been made—and for the last period for which statistics are available, July 1982 to June 1983, fewer than 200 of 1,790 cases were appealed—we would never know, for no reasons are given unless an appeal is made by persons with standing. An appeal gets the reasoning, if not the identity, of the committee on the record. We do know that panels of ten, approved by the minister of home affairs, all anonymous, are the source from which the Directorate of Publications draws committees of four.

It is up to the committee to decide whether anything submitted to it is "undesirable" or "radically undesirable." It is a serious crime even to possess something radically undesirable. What are the criteria for undesirability as defined by the Publications Act?

For the purposes of this Act, any publication or object, film, public entertainment or intended public entertainment shall be deemed to be undesirable if it or any part of it—
A. is indecent or obscene or is offensive or harmful to public morals;
B. is blasphemous or is offensive to the religious convictions or feelings of any section of the inhabitants of the Republic;
C. brings any section of the inhabitants of the Republic into ridicule or contempt;
D. is harmful to the relations between any sections of the inhabitants of the Republic;
E. is prejudicial to the safety of the State, the general welfare or the peace and good order;
F. discloses with reference to any judicial proceedings—
I. any matter which is indecent or obscene or is offensive or harmful to public morals;

II. any indecent or obscene medical, surgical or physiological details the disclosure of which is likely to be offensive or harmful to public morals [the Steve Biko clause].

The committee described the magazine as a well-known monthly concerned with "non-white social matters, family, sport, art, and a little political *[sic]*." Their overall objection was that "several pieces show a tendency to grievance mongering and miss the broader view showing both sides of the undesirable situations which are described." The committee gave three examples of the "tendency" which they admitted were not of a sufficient degree to warrant banning, if they were the only offenders: the interview with the West Indian cricket captain, which raised political issues; an article on the demolition of shacks and consequent disruption of family life that was "graphic"; and an article that reported conflict between two black groups (AZAPO and the UDF) but that advocated the UDF and the Freedom Charter [the original manifesto of the banned ANC that is in itself no more inflammatory than the American Declaration of Independence].

The main objection and chief exemplar of the offending "tendency" was the article on Don Matterra, "The Gangster Who Became a Poet," a well-known black columnist. Haysom's task was to show that this article could not be taken as an example of any of the clauses that describe undesirability in the Publications Act. Before we listen to him, let's freeze the frame in the dark hearing chamber and try to understand what *undesirability* and *tendency* are all about, for these concepts are at the heart of all attempts at censorship in societies that profess to honor the notion of freedom of expression, as do South Africa's and our own.

Abandoned Heritage

The Anglo-Saxon legal tradition we share with South Africa reveals a long history of struggle between the power of the Crown and then of Parliament and the rights of individuals simply to be left alone and to be themselves. Free expression is at the heart of those rights.

It is one of the great ironies of history that freedom and its repression spring from the European experience of Christendom and Christianity, the former demanding conformity of minds and hearts and the latter unceasingly trumpeting the sacredness of the individual and the inviolability of private conscience. For centuries wars were religious wars, conflicts of conviction and inner truths having devastating outer consequences, a situation we seem to be returning to (now in the age of Star Wars) in Poland, Iran, Ireland, Israel, Pakistan, and Indonesia. Ever so painfully, in fits and starts, the notion that the state had no power over belief and could only presume to control behavior (and that within limits) gained political ground, reaching a high pitch at the time of the American Revolution and the drafting of the American Constitution, enshrined in the Bill of Rights.

Ever since, law has drawn a delicate distinction between the beliefs of individual conscience and behavior having public consequences. Speech has been seen as the external, and only tangible, manifestation of conscience and thus, in the language of First Amendment jurisprudence, is "protected [from state power]." During the chronic protests of the nineteen-sixties, the general public became aware of a stretching of the concept of speech to cover what common sense might well consider conduct, which is subject to state control: the burning of draft cards, the pouring of blood on public records. In more recent years this notion has been carried into the realm of sexual behavior, for centuries seen as an area of conduct with profound public consequences, now presented as a private affair between (or among) consenting adults, with no public interest affected. In these classes of cases, "speech" and "privacy" are being extended as concepts to reduce the established area of state control over conduct. The development has met with sharp conservative opposition, tinged with moral outrage. On the other hand, libertarians feel outrage at the long-established and tolerated stretching of conduct to include areas of speech and conscience, so that the state can once again ignore the distinction between belief and behavior and seek to control both.

The key to this draconian direction is the concept of "tendency." If behavior may be controlled, but speech may not, then one must establish a link between behavior that must be controlled, like rape or revolution, and words quite literally to that effect. Words that lead to rape or some other illegal sexual behavior can thus be outlawed as pornographic or obscene; words that lead to revolution or some other form of violent opposition to established authority can thus be punished as seditious libel. It is damnably difficult to prove a causal connection between words spoken and deeds done, aside from the cliché situation of shouting "Fire!" in a crowded theater. It is even more difficult to show such a possible connection between words expressed and deeds that *might* have followed but did not. "Tendency" provides a conveniently vague link that is not quite causal.

The prevailing cultural and political climate has its seasons of particular fears and taboos. In Victorian England, the obscene was legally held to be that which "tends to deprave and corrupt" those who are subject to such influences: a maddening bit of circular reasoning to the post-Freudian crowd, but an obvious platitude to the paterfamilias who feared his upstairs maid would be dallying during working hours. During the McCarthy era all sorts of books and films and magazines were seen to be part of the communist conspiracy. If the behavior is sufficiently feared, then even the most remote connection becomes an alarming tendency. Nuclear plants require more elaborate safeguards than gasoline stations. Justice Holmes is famous for defining the kind of tendency that can be legally punished as a "clear and present danger," but the fear of treason some felt during the Schenk case, for which he wrote the opinion, led Holmes himself to consider impassioned urging to resist the draft as a perfectly clear and threatening danger to the state, because it happened during wartime.

For some, the United States is and will continue to be in an unending cold war against international communism. This mentality of total warfare is manifest in the rhetoric of "wars" against poverty, drugs, racial prejudice, illiteracy, and drunken driving. An all-out effort against a devastating threat can brook no weakening; it is war.

The South African Publications Act is a classic case of this siege mentality. It is being applied in a universe of discourse where "total onslaught" is the ruling explicit cliché for the political position of the state. All sorts of speech, in this emergency situation, become potential bombs that must be disarmed. "Tendency" here is defined as the "undesirable," pointing to a connection between speech and just about any actual or possible defect in South African society. One seems to be falling into a philosophical black hole when one reads the Publications Act. Not only are things legally punishable if they are connected with clearly illegal behavior, they are punishable if they point to any socially embarrassing reality. The message is the crime. Sticking one's head in the sand is a patriotic duty. Everything not forbidden is compulsory.

Whereas until recently the American direction has been to require "tendency" to be a very tight connection of an obviously causal nature to clearly illegal behavior, the South African practice has been to expand "tendency" into any connection with anything not desired by the regime, even if it is legal! This turns

The Bureaucracy of Censorship

the history of free expression on its head, not only stripping speech of its shield of protection from state power, but relegating it to the most controlled and repressed type of behavior. Quite literally, one can be punished for saying anything that might cause ill feeling between different groups, even if the utterance does not in fact cause any ill feeling and even though ill feeling itself is hardly illegal. Lewis Carroll, meet Franz Kafka.

Nicholas Haysom had his hands full that dark August morning in Pretoria.

Through the Looking Glass

"The Gangster Who Became a Poet Don Mattera" was declared undesirable because Mattera himself, the committee stated, was wild and intense and some of his verse "which is quoted is directly inflammatory and does not encourage the objective state of mind necessary for the removal of existing grievous wrongs." The article creates a "cumulative effect in the magazine which is undesirable."

The most extreme statements in the short simple article:

> There is nothing as evil as being banned. . . . In the end I could not take any more of it. I broke the banning order many times. . . . I will not rest until my leaders on Robben Island and in other jails are free. Both Black and White leaders. I am now 48 years old. My only wish is to see South Africans of all races coming together and solving their problems. Otherwise there will be a violent revolution. And it is very close.

Haysom began his argument by pointing out that the committee had accepted most of the magazine as providing articles that were "informative and relevant to social events." He emphasized that the general scope of the magazine was relevant and not undesirable. He was attempting to do what John Dugard and his aides have been pushing for years: to hold the censorship apparatus to standards developed in the American system. As followers of American film and book censorship cases will recognize, only the total drift and substance of a work can make it "pornographic." Objectionable and isolated parts cannot condemn the whole. But the Publications Act of South Africa explicitly states that anything can be undesirable if any part of it is undesirable. Nevertheless, Haysom pushed bravely on to defend as completely harmless the three articles mentioned above that had offended the committee in a lesser fashion. Haysom then proceeded to go through the Gangster Poet piece showing that most of it was harmless biographical detail. He gently reminded the board that no poetry of Mattera's was in fact quoted, as the committee reported. Haysom returned to his main argument that the overall quality of the magazine was nonpolitical and generally edifying. He concluded by didactically listing the general principles which the Appeals Board had claimed to be guided by.

Where did Haysom get these principles? From the laboriously collected *Publications Appeal Board Digest of Decisions,* compiled by and available only from his own Centre for Applied Legal Studies. These principles were deliberately injected into the texts of a number of decisions mostly penned by the *verligte* chairman of the board (not present on this occasion) with the explicit purpose of guiding the anonymous committees in their deliberations. The committees had a deserved reputation for carelessness (the inaccuracy about the quoted poetry is not untypical) as well as unprincipled caprice. It was the strategy of appellants, taking Dugard's lead, to pretend that these informal guidelines had some sort of force as legal precedent under the further pretense that this administrative tribunal was a court of law. Before this point can be examined, the attorney for the state must be given a hearing.

In Afrikaans, which I do not understand, but which was translated for me by a companion, the young advocate rejected Haysom's point that the magazine was harmless and apolitical. He turned the attention of the board and Haysom to a piece that was not even mentioned by the original committee report: "Mapondera the Bandit." Told in the deliberate elementary school reader style of *The Reader,* the story blandly narrated the lifelong battle of a Shona chief in what is now Zimbabwe against the British, casting him in a romantic Robin Hood role. The young attorney claimed that this story glorified rebellion and placed white men in the role of brutal oppressors. Again, "one side of the story."

Haysom and the Afrikaner debated this for some time and were interrupted by puzzled questions from the bench. My interpreter explained, with some amusement, that the elderly gentlemen had been trying to follow the argument by looking at a different article in the magazine.

The substance of the proceedings was not amusing, however. First, the raising of a new objection to the magazine during the appeal, an unheard-of practice in any legal review, which can only deal with the points raised by the initial action, is perfectly in order before the Publications Appeal Board, which hears each case, as it were, *de novo.* Second, Haysom was forced to play the game of "proving" that the magazine was "harmless," which is both an impossibility in logic and an insult to the power of ideas, however humble. Third, the whole affair brought home the terrible waste of brains and lives that censorship spreads through society. Milan Kundera, in his bitter, wry way, has pointed out that the state security apparatus has guaranteed even the most boring Czech writer an attentive audience. This was John Milton's objection, in essence, to censorship: it would be impractical, since it would require subtle minds and careful work that would be ground down by the monumental triviality of the enterprise.[2] So, in fact, the least subtle are attracted to the censoring function, which by fiat makes them critics whose opinions are crucial. But Milton forgot about those outside the apparat, subtle or not, who must out of conviction plod their weary way through a gulag of the imagination, lending dignity to a preposterous project peopled by mental midgets. Great issues, unfortunately, may turn on small cases and poor arguments.

For this reason, many authors and filmmakers will not submit to the indignity of an appeal. There are some who even condemn CAL's strenuous efforts to wrench and wring the conceptual blob of the appeals process into some sort of consistent and thus accountable system. Fikile Bam, the outstanding black lawyer of the Legal Resources Centre and the Lawyers for Human Rights, who has been imprisoned and exiled for his efforts, raises the same kind of question about poverty law and other legal methods of redress of grievances that perforce must recognize the system in order to use its mechanisms. Bam, who is an impressive physical presence of great inner strength, sees the irony of his career, in a sense "joining them" in order to "fight them," but he feels that in the wait for the great wheel of historical justification to turn, too many bodies will be broken if they are not helped now. Dugard, Haysom, and other human and civil rights activist advocates like Halton Cheadle, Gilbert Marcus, Geoffrey Budlender, Godfrey Pitje, Jules Browde, and scores of others feel the same way. They have championed the cause, no less because it has been forced on them.

Although, clearly, censorship is a numbing instance of the banality of evil, accounts of its historical embodiments drive home John Milton's original insight and may make its continued or expanded use less inevitable out of sheer embarrassment. Nicholas Haysom, in his patient and exhaustive plea before this bizarre tribunal, was thus part of an army meticulously chipping away at a fundamentally weak, if momentarily powerful, structure. In each point that he made about the obligations and constraints that should be incumbent on the anonymous committees, he cited chapter and verse from previous rulings of the board he was addressing, but no precedent antedated the appointment of the current chairman, law professor Jacobus (Kobus) van Rooyen, who sincerely desired the board to follow logical principles and who saw a number of useful rules of thumb in American Supreme Court rulings on both pornography and seditious libel cases. I was to meet Professor Van Rooyen a year later in New York, but at the time I was in that hearing chamber with Haysom I had no idea he was the unlikely source of many of the restrictive precedents that Haysom was reminding the board they should bear in mind as they ruled on *The Reader*'s "undesirability." The guidelines would sound familiar to anyone who followed the *Ulysses, Roth, Miller, Whitney, Gitlow,* and other landmark First Amendment cases in United States law. It gave one a sense of pride and hope as Haysom went through what some might consider a futile exercise.

The board is on record as being guided by its own precedents. According to precedent (which Haysom cited for each point I am summarizing in more narrative form), it is not up to publications control to approve of works as desirable, but only to decide on their undesirability as defined by the act, which would have to be absolutely necessary because the likely effect of the work on its probable readership would constitute an actual threat against an interest explicitly protected by the act. The American "clear and present danger" test had been admitted by the board, Haysom went on, as a relevant guideline in determining undesirability. No common knowledge, commonplace views, or matters of published news could possibly constitute such a danger. This was particulary true in political matters, which required widely divergent views vigorously put forward as a basis for a free society and for Parliament itself. The board was in no position to judge the *truth* of any proposition, and no moral, social, or political issue should ever be regarded as above criticism. To this end, the board had in the past made it quite clear that advocacy of the voting franchise for all South Africans, of thoroughgoing antiapartheid measures (short of violence), and of the Freedom Charter were by no means undesirable. Further, the board had tolerated criticism that was avowedly "sharp, emotive, one-sided, and intemperate" as well as "provocative," although it had found incitement to violence or illegal actions, the ruling out of peaceful change as a possibility, and the exacerbation of racial hostility undesirable. By all these standards, Haysom concluded, the article on Don Mattera found undesirable by the committee was in fact not undesirable in terms of the Publications Act, not least for the reason that the views expressed were trite and commonplace.

Van Rooyen is a tall, handsome, and muscular Afrikaner, with a boyish demeanor. When we met later in New York, he was quite proud of his broadening influence on the administration of the Publications Act, through the guidelines he has written and through the explicit statements of prinicple that he has carefully placed into rulings he has made. He is delighted with the efforts of CALS and others to keep the committees in line with these guidlines. He has absolutely no doubts about the necessity of the act and the need to control dangerous revolutionary tracts and (something that was on his mind since visiting New York for the first time) degrading pornography. He solicitously asked me how one raises chidlren in the outrageously sexual atmosphere of New York. Van Rooyen came across as a sort of authoritarian Candide, the mirror image of Dugard, sadly shocked at the depths to which New York (and presumably other Sodoms of America, like Los Angeles or Las Vegas or Miami) had been brought by an abandonment of public enforcement of moral standards and respect for the human person—so well provided for by his own laws, which he admitted were at times administered in a brutish or ignorant manner. Like so many *verligten* I had met, he was sold on the system while admitting any number of dreadful instances of human rights violations as "aberrations," or "temporary short-comings," that would be ultimately erased. South Africa was a very new country and one had to look to the rest of Africa, not to America or England, for standards of comparison. On this scale, South Africa came off as a genuine, if flawed and inchoate, democracy. As John Henry Newman had pronounced in a different context of loyalty, "A thousand difficulties do not make one doubt."

He told me that no work of any merit had been banned since 1980, and indicated that a number of highly critical works by black authors like the Nigerian Ayi Kweh Armah *(Why Are We So Blest?)* or the South African Sipho Sepamla *(A Ride on the Whirlwind)* were passed by the censors. He did admit that distribution controls relating to time and place, or age, were applied, and he approved of such restrictions. John Updike's *Rabbit is Rich,* for instance, was only available in hardcover and was not sold to minors. As he sees it, since 1980 (he assumed the chair in 1978): "[W]ithout stifling development in literature and drama and without hampering political debate, the Act achieves its purpose in combatting pornography, blasphemous material, and truly undermining material."

Nadine Gordimer takes issue with the view and the man.[3]

One of the signs of the new relaxation supposedly come with Van Rooyen was the unbanning of Nadine Gordimer's *Burger's Daughter* at the instigation of the directorate itself, followed two weeks later by the same dispensation for Andre Brink's *Dry White Season*. The establishment press greeted these acts as marks of magnanimity. Brink pointed out that the same week his work was released Mtutuzeli Matshoba's short story collection *Call Me Not a Man* was banned for one of the stories, "A Glimpse of Slavery." Gordimer called attention to the reasons for the banning: the objectionable nature of the events reported and intended for a black audience, even though the work might be a literary creation. When Van Rooyen was appointed, he announced that he would not give any public statements about his views of censorship. Evidently, though, he would not consider "A Glimpse of Slavery" a work of merit, in the phrase he used with me. This is what galls Gordimer. His predecessor was an out-an-out bigot who said, (1) "[B]lacks are an inarticulate people . . . not interested in censorship," and (2) "Of blacks I have no knowledge at all." But Van Rooyen strikes Gordimer as an autocrat who believes there is an official cultural norm. If his version of the norm differs here and there from that of the committees it is of small moment. "[H]e is so convinced of his approach to his job that he is not prepared to discuss it, let alone admit any necessity to defend it."

So writers with international reputations, white writers who no longer feel on their own books the restraints that lesser known writers and all black writers still feel, reject Van Rooyen's claims out of hand. After an exhaustive study of board decisions, law professor Mary Cheh of George Washington University has authoritatively concluded that in fact the Publication Appeal Board does not in any way follow American guidelines such as the clear-and-present danger test and that it does not seek to be consistent even with its own precedents, despite all those efforts of CALS.[4]

But even if the *board* did follow the rule and the precedents, it would still not affect the committee system greatly, for the committees are not under the control of the board and, in the light of studies of bannings and board pronouncements, not perceptibly influenced by the guidelines Van Rooyen has been painstakingly injecting and CALS has been doggedly using in appeals.[5]

Gilbert Marcus notes the following about the mysterious committees: they do not have any black members, the identities of members are never revealed, their deliberations are totally secret, and there is a special political committee.[6] Although Van Rooyen made sure to remind me that since 1980 a panel of specialist experts was available to advise committees (presumably to indicate the presence of masterpieces or the works of recognized international geniuses to committee members who might not be aware of these qualities), Andre Brink finds this a travesty, and indicated that in the supposedly magic year of 1980 his own *Looking on Darkness* had its ban reinforced on the advice of a literary committee, none of whom spoke English as a first language (Brink, an Afrikaans novelist, writes in both languages).[7]

Marcus, Haysom, Stanbridge, and others are fond of quoting the judges' description of the publications committees in the Moroney case (the former student editor now exiled in London and editing *African Business*):

[A publications committee is] an extrajudicial body operating in an administrative capacity, whose members need have no legal training, before whom the appellant has no right of audience, who in their deliberations are not required to have regard to the rules of justice designed to achieve a fair trial, whose proceedings are not conducted in public and who are not required to afford any reason for their decisions.[8]

Blackballed

As we have seen in the cases of *The Reader*, the black alternative media, and black authors and journalists, there is certainly a double standard in the application of all communications control legislation (as in most other legislation) based on race. The Publications Act, since it deals with every form of expression, has a particularly strong effect on black media and black languages. If an African writes in one of the African languages, the fate of his book or play or script is in the hands of language boards which must approve books for schools. If the work is not deemed suitable for schools, it is virtually dead; no one will publish it, for there will be no readers, no audience available. For this reason, more and more black writers are turning to English, to ensure a chance at a broader public and in the quixotic hope of a better committee hearing if they are denounced to the directorate; but above all, they seek a chance to be published abroad if banned at home.[9] Ironically, the apparat is forcing global fame on some writers by denying them readers at home (one more parallel with Russia that the regime would like to ignore).

In this light, it is an added irony that the British antiapartheid movement supports a ban on exporting books to South Africa, although they see nothing wrong in meeting orders for specific books. This parallels the labor union–induced BBC ban on exports to South Africa. Most British publishers see themselves as contributing to black education (Oxford University Press, Longman, Hodder & Staughton, Macmillan—all publish textbooks in Xhosa, Zulu, Tswana) or as fighting apartheid by letting in the light of outside knowledge. Nonetheless, Oxford University Press was willing to publish its *Oxford History of South Africa* there in 1971 with the section on African nationalism expurgated. Outside of texts, their readership is mainly white, and the heavy taxes on books go to the apartheid regime, of course.[10]

In an address to the South African English Academy, Es'kia Mphahlele, professor of African literature at Wits, said: "[T]he Black man here has vested interests in English as a unifying force. Through it Africa can be restored to him and, together with French, English provides a pan-African forum, widens his constituency."[11]

The Silver Jubilee Conference of the English Academy, a prestigious nongovernmental body for ESSAs, that is, English-Speaking South Africans, was addressed by Njabulo S. Ndebele, Lesotho University professor of English, Afro-American and African literature. Ndebele, whose *Fools* won the 1986 Noma Award, Africa's major book prize, stated that English was not an "innocent language"—since the "functional acquisition of English . . . further enforce(s) the instrumentalisation of people as units of labour." Jeremy Cronin, an officeholder in the UDF underground, called for a new South African type of English (as did Ndebele) incorporating funeral oratory, toyi-toyi dancing (jogging in place with upraised fists), worker plays.[12]

Repeated efforts of black writers to be published have been continually slapped down by the Directorate of Publications. Publishers, in this climate, are reluctant to take a chance on publishing books with such high odds of being banned: the financial loss is considerable. When a small press just for blacks, Skotaville, tried to publish a magazine for black writers, *The Classic,* the first issue was banned. We have already seen that in the same week when Van Rooyen's board unbanned Brink, it confirmed the banning of a black writer. About the same time another black collection of short stories, this one an anthology edited by Mothabi Mutloatsee, *Forced Landing,* was unbanned on appeal. Huffing and puffing about literary values, which were not found to be outstanding in the collection, the board treated the public to its reasons for permitting the reading of the collection:

> Though there is much in the anthology that is a matter of opinion, there is much that provides the reader with insight into the tribulations, more especially, of urban Blacks: the danger of overcrowded trains, the terrorism that train gangs indulge in, the problems of urban hostels, the alcoholism to which shebeens contribute, and indirectly, commercial exploitation. Another point in favor of the publication is that although disparagement of Whites appears to be a common element in many of the stories, criticism of Blacks by Blacks is a compensatory feature in others. Self-censure, however, is less evident in the anthology than the condemnation of Whites.[13]

Both the form and content of this published judgment tell us much about the mentality of the censors. A work of fiction is disparaged for containing matters of opinion and is found acceptable on the grounds that its content is sufficiently critical of elements of black life that whites need not take any responsibility for. What has literature got to do with any of this? Think of all those matters of opinion, even basic assumptions now known to be scientifically false, that burden *Hamlet*. There is a dangerous tendency to blame the rottenness of an entire country on the moral life of its royalty, who are presented in a very cynical, even sick. light. Still, the carousing of the common soldiers is a mitigating factor; and the role of foreign trade and German philosophy in causing societal breakdown are given some, if scant, attention. On the whole, an acceptable work.

To my mind, the condescending paternalistic tone, which has the gall to *permit* what is an inalienable right, more clearly reveals the evil of any system of censorship than outright intemperate intolerance; it partakes of an imbecilic dignity and a Laputan logic that ten Swifts could not sufficiently satirize. One is mindful of the chilling scene in the great Hungarian film, *Mephisto,* when the entire audience at the opera house rises to its feet and turns in smug sycophancy to the high central box of the Goebbels-Hitler figure as he *congratulates* the gifted actor who has sold his soul to the regime. It is a world in which art and literature, as well as trash and pornography, have no meaning in themselves but only an imputed worth based on political power, the sole criterion of beauty and truth. And this is the great educative value of the Directorate of Publications to attentive libertarians everywhere: its naked arrogance. The corporate agenda in American and other politically free societies that reduces all news operations, scientific inquiry, and artistic endeavor to some type of product which must ultimately be judged by the criteria of a so-called bottom line, for its profit or its defense value, plays *Brave New World* to the directorate's *Nineteen Eighty-Four.*

Staffrider, the black literary magazine put out by Ravan Press, has been banned any number of times by frightened or outraged committees. The directorate has appealed against its own committees in some of these instances. Listen to the board:

> The fact is that the Black masses, even the illiterate, have heard at gatherings like funerals the things that have been re-uttered here, and finding *Staffrider* undesirable on such grounds would be like locking the stable door after the horse has bolted. Whites are likely to gain more than to lose by being given access to black thinking through this kind of medium. What is published in *Staffrider* has been written for the literate by the literate and for the converted by the converted. . . . Exaggerated political invective, however, is almost an art form amongst Third World Nations. . . . Western man, who believes in under- rather than overstatement, is often unnecessarily perturbed at these verbal onslaughts which, through their very exaggeration, lose a measure of their effectiveness.

It is instructive in the same vein to turn to the decisions that Van Rooyen had called to my attention as enlightened. First, the unbanning of *A Ride on the Whirlwind* by Sipho Sepamla, which dealt with the 1976 Soweto uprising:

> [The novel is] a work with literary pretension—even if it does not succeed as a work of art or great literature. . . . [R]evolutionaries find their inspiration in publications of a more direct and inciting nature.

In the companion appeal by the directorate against its own committees, the Nigerian novelist Ayi Kweh Armah had two works (referred to by Van Rooyen as well) unbanned. The significant departure here was that a panel of *black* experts was called in to advise the board, among them the distinguished Es'kia Mphahlele, whom the board quoted in their unbanning of *Two Thousand Seasons:*

> We have no justification to infer a one-to-one relationship between events, characters, ideas in a literary work and life experiences. People do not wait for a novelist or poet or playwright to play around with images and symbols to incite them to strike or march in the streets and revolt. There are more immediate and direct forces to impel them to act against authorities. Moreover, a novel like Armah's is too complex to push readers into the streets to burn and kill. It would not be read by a large population.

The words of the professor of African literature are carefully chosen. It is clear he believes there are ample grounds for violence in the townships without any prompting from literature. He also makes the obvious point for any student of literature that it is from life, out of experience, but not life or experience itself. Yet there is a trace of a tone here that seems to echo the yahoo assumptions of the bureaucracy that he must deal with in a good cause. The notion is that this book, and books, are really *divorced* from life and are harmless, impotent, not worth worrying about, eunuchs in the palace. The worrisome note here is that what is adopted as a tried-and-true tactic may become a too easily assumed anti-intellectual tenet. In a censorship system, toleration is won at the price of indifference.

Mphahlele and other defenders of freedom are naturally led to welcome indifference because South Africa's system is so hysterically high-pitched and compulsively comprehensive. The infinitely inflatable notions of "tendency" and "undesirability" have empowered something called the *Publications* Act to forbid and control far more than mere publications, embracing any undesirable *object*. And the act covers far more than the act of publishing, it goes on to enable punishment of printers, distributors, and editors as well as authors—and even warehousers. Haysom told me that the banning of a publication is retroactive, so that a seller or a shipper of a book (or anything else declared undesirable) that was perfectly legal for them to have acquired in the past become violators of the law. If one wears in public a T-shirt whose slogan has been banned (as in the case of "The Front Line," with a picture of a clenched fist), one is subject to penalty for "distributing" the slogan.[14] Ignorance of the banning, although successfully used on some appeals, is in general no excuse. One can only certainly ascertain an object's undesirability through reading the *Government Gazette* or by being informed by an official, usually as one is arrested. Since objects once banned can be restored to legality on appeal, and since objects cleared or unnoticed by directorate committees can at any subsequent time be subject to a finding of undersirability, one would need a high-tech information system to stay abreast of undesirability's current contours and thus remain free of liability for criminal prosecution.

All this is bad enough for people in the book, film, play, record, art, and T-shirt business, but there is a further category of undesirability that brings to mind Milton's prescient insight that the banning of books, if allowed, logically leads to the banning of everything that might carry the same threat the books are deemed to bear. "Why not forbid Morris Dancing?" Milton asked rhetorically.[15] "Great idea," would have been the astonishing answer of the devisers of the category of "radical undesirability."

The Longest Arm

One is punished for having in one's house, or car, or attic, or tree, for that matter, anything deemed "radically undesirable." The enforcement of this law, outside of states of emergency when no pretense at legal procedure is attempted, has made a hash of the many protections of human rights painstakingly incorporated into Anglo-Saxon judicial practice. In our system, intention and deliberation are generally looked for before one is found guilty. Yet in South Africa, "witting possession" does not require "a continuous and conscious awareness that one has the relevant object under one's control. No one possesses so jealously."[16] Thus a defendant was found in violation of the Publications Act for having in an old cardboard box a forbidden publication placed there years before. But in another case a bookish counselor, with hundreds of books and pamphlets in an untidy room, was exonerated because no one could prove he knew all that he had.[17]

It was assumed that the defendant would know all that the directorate had to say about anything he knew that he had, if you follow. Yet this would be extremely difficult, as we have already seen. Haysom and Marcus, of CALS, point out that on any given "object" there are at least eight possibilities, involving decisions, declarations, prohibitions, withdrawals. Pending an appeal, there may be a suspension of the committee's ruling—or there may not be. Appeals can be made against findings of permissibility or of undesirability. After two years, a fresh process can be inaugurated against or in favor of any given object. Haysom and Marcus note that in at least one case a person was found in contravention of the act because the judge thought a publication had been banned to a degree and in a manner that in fact was not the case.[18] Another judge (Van den Heever) put the view of the opposition succinctly:

What we are dealing with under the Publications Act for present purposes is not a reasonable constant set of rules designed to govern a specific facet of modern life in the interests of society or ecology or foreign exchange; but a series of *ad hoc* decisions, not only revocable but often revoked, as to the undesirability of individual publications from among the deluge published daily, where such decisions when unrevoked do not necessarily and inevitably lead to a further *ad hoc* decision prohibiting the very possession of what one may not, as having been found undesirable, disseminate.

. . . It cannot seriously be contended that the activities of reading about, or possessing publications on "political" topics or "erotic" topics or "contentious" topics are activities that the State intends to control. Were that so, parliamentarians, artists, theologians, poets, scientists, lawyers, everyone bar the readers of the merely blandly beautiful, would be too busy studying *Government Gazettes* to have time for their studies.[19]

The continuing and constant committee persecution of *SASPU Focus*, the student magazine circulated all over the country with in-depth coverage of forced removals, detentions, township troubles, homeland poverty, and other hallmarks of life under apartheid given less prominence in the establishment press, coalesces all the worst feature of Publication Act administration.

Because of the cost to them and the dangers to their distributors, *SASPU Focus* is distributed, as are many of the Ravan Press publications, by members of organizations, among students, trade unions, churches, and black communities. Two union members in Queenstown were arrested and sentenced to a fine of R76 or twenty-five days in jail for distributing an edition of the magazine that had been found radically undesirable but that was under appeal.

Why was it so seriously objected to?

The reasons were two. First, there were continual approbative references to the Freedom Charter, the manifesto of the banned ANC. In the Laputan logic of the system, the Freedom Charter itself is not banned, because the board has pointed out to the overzealous committees that it is merely an affirmation of basic human rights. But the *use* to which the Charter may be put, ah, that is another matter.[20] It may not be linked with violence or the "glorification" of the ANC. *SASPU Focus* placed the charter in the context of a photograph of a large number of black students, with the caption "In the Footsteps of Soweto." The accompanying text said in part: "The 1976 uprising changed the course of history. It announced a new era of mass resistance . . . and mass repression." Leaders of the uprising, Sechaba Montsitsi and "Prof" Morobe, were called "national heroes," and were interviewed in depth as proud Robben Island "graduates."

The reasons the committee gave for declaring the magazine illegal, even as a possession, were set aside by the Publication Appeal Board. But then they came up with their ówn reasons for banning it, as Gilbert Marcus recounts the case.[21]

SASPU Focus had an article on the executions of three ANC

members, Simon Mogoerane, Jerry Mosololi, and Marcus Mo-
taung, convicted in 1982 of violent attacks on three police stations, a power station, and a railway terminus, in the course of
which lives were lost. The article sympathized with the men and
recounted approvingly the international campaign for clemency in
their behalf. The board called particular attention to a paragraph
which attributed these words to yet a fourth prisoner, Solomon
Mahlangu, as he stood before the gallows: "My blood will nourish
the tree that will bear the fruits of freedom." These words,
whether spoken or not, are almost exactly the words spoken by a
great hero of the Afrikaners, Jopie Fourie, before his firing squad
when Jan Smuts was head of the government under British rule.
As Marcus points out, to this day for many Afrikaners, Fourie is
the patriot and Smuts the traitor. This attribution apparently
struck the board as seditiously inflammatory in the case of a black
man asking for what the white man had, as if their grievance—oh,
sacrilege—were comparable.

It may be recalled that Fourie's execution led directly to the
founding of *De Burger* (later *Die Burger*) so that Afrikaner opinions and grievances would have a vehicle for self-expression. It is
hard to say whether the board's decision would have been more or
less outrageous if made with conscious reference to the historical
irony.

NOTES

1. Andre du Toit of Stellenbosch University confirmed this to me two
weeks later and subsequently published a detailed analysis of directorate
statistics in which he conclusively demonstrated that more than half of all
submissions to censorship committees are political; that about half of all
submissions are made by the police and the security police; that political
submissions are judged by a special committee of a permanent nature;
and that two-thirds of all political submissions are banned for possession
(even having one is a crime). Cf. Andre du Toit, "The Rationale of
Controlling Political Publications," *Censorship*, ed. Theo Coggin, (Johannesburg, South African Institute for Race Relations, 1983), pp. 80–129;
esp. p. 92.

2. John Milton, "Areopagitica," in *Complete Poetry and Selected
Prose of John Milton* (New York: Random House, The Modern Library,
1950), pp. 677–724.

3. Nadine Gordimer, "New Forms of Strategy—No Change of
Heart," *Critical Arts; A Journal for Media Studies*, 1, no. 2 (June 1980):
27–33.

4. Mary M. Cheh, "Systems and Slogans: The American Clear and
Present Danger Doctrine and South African Publications Control,"
South African Journal on Human Rights 2, pt. 1 (March 1986); 29–48.

5. Cheh, op. cit.; Gilbert Marcus, "An Examination of the Restric-

tions Imposed on the Press and Other Publications Which Appear in Practice to Affect Members of the Black Group More Severely Than Other Groups," Human Sciences Research Council, University of Witwatersrand, p. 7; Louise Silver, *A Guide to Political Censorship in South Africa,* Occasional Papers no. 6, Centre for Applied Legal Studies, University of Witwatersrand, 1984, pp. 3–16.

6. Gilbert Marcus, op. cit., p. 8.

7. Andre Brink, "Censorship and Literature," *Censorship,* ed. Theo Coggin (Johannesburg: South African Institute of Race Relations, 1983), p. 44.

8. *S* v *Moroney* 1978 (4) SA 389 (A) at 403.

9. Marcus, op. cit., p. 9.

10. Jane Dibblin, "The British Publishers Tale," *New Statesman,* September 26, 1986, pp. 24–25.

11. Ibid., p. 10.

12. Mike Kirkwood, ". . . and the South African," *New Statesman,* September 26, 1986, pp. 25–6.

13. This and subsequent quotations from board decisions are taken from Marcus, op. cit., pp. 15–18.

14. Nicholas Haysom and Gilbert Marcus, " 'Undesirability' and Criminal Liability under the Publications Act 42 of 1974," *South African Journal on Human Rights,* 1. pt. 1 (May 1985): 37.

15. John Milton, op. cit., pp. 696 ff.

16. Haysom and Marcus, op. cit., p. 38.

17. Ibid., p. 39.

18. Ibid., n. 87.

19. Ibid., pp. 43–44, quoting S v Cleminshaw at 690.

20. Louise Silver, op. cit., pp. 213 ff.

21. Gilbert Marcus, "*S* v *Simoko* 1985 (2) SA 263 (E): A Black and White View of South Africa," Centre for Applied Legal Studies, University of Witwatersrand, 1986. Unpaginated.

CHAPTER FIVE

Showing Up and Closing Down

High Tech and the Censor

John Milton's classic *Areopagitica,* whose catalogue of arguments against censorship is central to the libertarian canon, was prompted by the parliamentary proposal to introduce a Licensing Act, which would in effect require prior permission for any publication. The newfangled printing press was revolutionizing the reach and power of the written word in a time when belief and behavior, religion and politics, were tightly intermeshed. Parliament, like the Tudor rulers before them, sought to control this very effective instrument. For the most part they succeeded; Milton's great effort was a literary success and became an almost scriptural text for libertarians, but he lost his cause, and, as often noted, he actually became a censor under Cromwell. In the long term, however, the English nation gradually rejected the notion of the state imposing a *prior restraint* on publications.[1]

The framers of the First Amendment to the U.S. Constitution were construed as having the same attitude: speech was protected primarily from the power of the state to restrain expression prior to publication.[2]

But when the newfangled motion picture camera so multiplied disrespectful images of foolish police and pompous judges for new and unassimilated immigrants, who did not need to speak English to be influenced by this silent medium, there was a clamor for licensing in thousands of local jurisdictions. In due course prior censorship was enacted in hundreds of municipalities and in the major cities of America. As the scattered film operations coalesced into a centralized Hollywood, with a few major studios accounting for virtually all films distributed throughout the entire country, there was a movement to centralize control as a prior restraint at the source. The result was the Production Code, whose lines guided filmmakers from initial screenplay to final cut.[3]

Today the American film industry still has a Production Code, much watered-down, and voluntary. Although in place because of federal and local government pressure, it has evolved into a marketing device to avoid the crippling boycotts of interest groups and to provide a convenient (and mechanistic) indicator of a film's offensiveness. Few movies can get broad distribution without code compliance.

With the arrival of new technologies of broadcasting sound and images, the notion of prior restraint returned again, tempered somewhat by First Amendment considerations. Now broadcasters (station owners) have to obtain a license from the federal government and comply with technical regulations. Although most of the rules deal with the mechanics of engineering standards and facility management, there are nonetheless some rules as to content. Obscenity, pronography, political debate, religious programming, all these traditionally censored areas are subject to at least time-manner-place restrictions.

As with print and film before them, time has eased the stringency of content concerns in broadcasting. Following precedent, the latest technological innovations in message distribution— video and tape, particularly as vehicles for hard-rock music—are perceived as the current clear and present danger.

The latest arts, songs and music, were also among the earliest to be enlisted in the antiapartheid struggle. "Nkosi Sikele i' Afrika" (God Bless Africa), written by a schoolteacher, Enoch Sontonga, as a prayer for the continent, was first used politically on January 8, 1912, by the Native National Congress, the forerunner of the ANC, at the instigation of Sol Plaatje, the first general secretary of the organization and a writer. He was the first to record the song. On August 9, 1956, after a year of defiance and resistance to the government's extension of passbook requirements to women, 20,000 women gathered before the main government offices in Pretoria (the Union Building), raised their fists silently for thirty minutes, and then sang "Nkosi Sikele i'Afrika." It ends every ANC meeting, and is sung at demonstrations and meetings throughout South Africa today.

After Sharpeville, Africa borrowed many protest songs from the admired American culture of freedom folk songs. Perhaps it comes as no surprise that the Nationalist regime has banned "We Shall Overcome." The SABC has decreed that "If I Had a Hammer," "Blowin' in the Wind," "The Times They Are A-changin" and other chestnuts of the Vietnam War period are subversive communist songs.

Today, there are few meetings of protest that do not use songs, songs African and songs English. Jessica Sherman, a rabbi's daughter and music teacher, is known now as the "songbird of the United Democratic Front." An example of an African song (banned) that she has sung is (in translation) "Here is Koeberg in flames / We are Going Forward / The Boys of Umkhonto were here yesterday. . . ." (Koeberg is the site of an atomic reactor, and Umkhonto we Sizwe is the militant wing of the ANC).

Now, given high-tech means of reproduction and distribution, protest songs are more of a threat than ever. They exemplify the thesis-antithesis of political repression and technical innovation.

At each stage there is a similar technopolitical structure: A new means of multiplying copies and distributing them to broader and wider categories of consumers, in a format that requires less cultural assimilation for comprehension or enjoyment, strikes fear in the hearts of the ruling elites, who then devise defensive restraints (censorship, licensing, and content and format regulations imposed by state power or market monopoly). In time, the new technology does become a major factor in shifting the social order and its cultural preferences, until it is threatened in turn by a new medium, which then provokes a new cycle of repressive controls.[4]

In South Africa, long before the Nationalist Party began its long reign of growing controls over publications, the government exercised prior restraint over films. After a number of early ad hoc prohibitions of specific films, notably a film of the Johnson-Jeffries interracial prizefight, the government of the Cape Province passed the Public Control Ordinance, which prohibited any film that might bring any section of the public into ridicule or contempt (language later applied to every conceivable form of communication in the Publications Act). This beginning came in 1916, just one year after the U.S. Supreme Court failed to recognize films as a form of speech and thus in principle entitled to First Amendment protection.[5] In 1931, just before the American filmmakers put together the self-regulating Production Code to stave off direct government control, the South African Entertainments Act required prior censorship of all foreign films (the vast bulk of all films available for South Africans). In 1963, three years before the Motion Picture Association drastically liberalized the American Production Code, the South African Publications and Entertainments Act required prior censorship of all films, foreign and domestic, and regulated separate exhibition controls for different races. As mentioned, *Gandhi* was shown to segregated audiences. The 1974 Publications Act now in force over all expression and "objects" requires prior clearance for all public performances, plays, and films.

Television, the latest and most broadly accessible medium, whose huge appetite for costly productions entails the purchase of much programming from abroad, was delayed until the late seventies and, as with radio, is directly controlled by the state. Amendments to the Publications Act have at times required even the state-owned-and-operated SABC to submit to prior screening by the Directorate of Publications.

As in our own system, then, more recent and popular media are more carefully controlled: there is that structural similarity. But South Africa was compelled by the fundamental unfreedom of, first, slavery, then a form of serfdom, and now the modern apartheid system to stifle all threats, particularly the honest voice of common humanity so often at the heart of literature and sensitive documentary.

Beyond this structural reason for the particularly strong control of prior restraint on film and video, there is the further reason that, in a small and peripheral country (relatively speaking) like South Africa, film and video are in fact ineluctable agents of foreign cultural domination: other values are intrinsic parts of the imported package even when unintended. Long ago G. K. Chesterton wrote that the British detective story was perfect propaganda for democratic values: native readers might be concerned primarily with who done it, but those in less free lands could not help but notice the civil procedures of the police and the assumption of innocence until guilt is proven. Closed societies like Stalinist Russia and Maoist China relentlessly exploited their size and centrality in tirelessly issuing an endless stream of indigenous statecult through their own wholly controlled media systems.

British comedies, American Westerns, German dramas may well come from societies where racism is no stranger, yet they all bring backgrounds which challenge the official arrangements of apartheid and its bigoted premises. The story is told that under Stalin the Russian government took delight in showing newsreels of American race riots (of the 1930s and 1940s) until it was realized that the audiences were chiefly impressed by the quality of clothing and especially the shoes worn by the blacks fleeing the oppressive capitalist police. Pogroms and police beatings were not novelties to these audiences.

Beyond the broad appeal and global reach characteristic of any new media technology, film and video pose an added threat: they are experienced in groups, sometimes very large and purposeful groups. They thus have an immediate political dimension, as does theater, beyond the force of the book.

As we shall see, the uneasy combination of contempt and respect for ideas or art that the censor (and sometimes his critics) brings to the printed word vanishes when he looks at moving pictures, which are universally assumed to be a powerful tool of both truth and propaganda.

Reading is essentially a private affair, even though millions may ultimately be affected by the contents of a book. Christianity and Islam, granted their dependence on scripture and texts, only gained their power to expand and change the world through the word preached before congregations. *Fides ex auditu:* Faith comes from listening. South Africa has always placed tight controls on political meetings, and in times of unrest has gone so far as to ban all public meetings, for the state recognizes that the public spoken word is a force to be reckoned with. Those removed from the South African situation are either puzzled or outraged by the violence often attached to funerals and by the stern police restrictions on funeral services. This is because the occasion of the funeral is one of the few in which there is an opportunity for public gathering and preaching. Since the mourned may well be victims of police violence, the occasion presents itself as ideal for criticism and denunciation of the state. Religion is very important for Afrikaners, and has long served as an instrument for controlling the behavior of the underclass. The police are thus loath to directly crack down on church services as such (although they have done so in isolated instances and under recent emergency conditions have not hesitated to arrest entire congregations).

Public performances are not accorded even such grudging immunity. Films and live theater are thus singled out for special attention. Oppositional films have the advantage of being portable items that can be shown over and over again and perhaps even exported and televised eventually to millions. They have the disadvantage of relatively high costs and high visibility to the authorities during production. Protest theater has the advantage of requiring little more than a room or an open space and imaginative writers and performers. Film has chiefly been the vehicle of the white critics of apartheid, who have the money, sophistication, and access to film equipment. Protest theater is overwhelmingly the vehicle of township blacks. Given the ever vigilant censorship apparat, it is amazing how many fine examples of both have been produced and are still being exhibited.

Screening the Opposition

Oppositional films are perforce low-budget affairs, for the most part. Their funding comes from such sources as the National Union of South African Students *(Wits Protest),* the South African Council of Churches *(This We Can Do for Justice and*

Peace), the Federation of South African Trade Unions *(Building Worker Unity).* The Danish antiapartheid movement directly funded *The Other South Africa,* but local organizations funding films are very often (like those mentioned here) recipients of significant foreign funds. More established artistic figures who are also critical of apartheid, like Athol Fugard, are often funded by such sources as the BBC and the Ford Foundation, which in fact supported his *Lesson from Aloes* and *Marigolds in August.* Ironically, the state pays for a number of protest films, since major producers of opposition documentaries are the various university departments of media, communications, or theater, especially at Wits, Cape Town, and Rhodes. The state does not incur great cost; the films are mostly Super-8 productions (now moving into home video equipment), and their production may also be allowed to some extent because of the mixed attitude of respect and contempt for the ineffectual intellectual. *Diagonal Street* and *Rhythm and Dues* are examples of such films.[6]

Let's take a look at four films locally produced, critical of the apartheid order, noticed by the censorship apparat, and available for theater or television distribution in the United States. They are two documentaries, *Witness to Apartheid* and *Other Voices of South Africa,* and two short dramas based on Nadine Gordimer stories, *City Lovers* and *Country Lovers.* In fact, all the films have been shown on the American Public Broadcasting System

The first film is a cinema verité documentary produced and directed in 1985 by the American Sharon Sopher and co-produced and co-directed by South African Kevin Harris, whom we have seen before in his adventures with the SABC (for his unauthorized airing of a hospital documentary). The "researcher" for the film was Peter Davis, once celebrated (and dismissed, some believe) for his *CBS Reports: The Selling of the Pentagon.* In the late seventies, Davis had produced in partial association with the United Nations an effective trilogy of documentary and assembled file footage attacking the Nationalist regime: *The White Laager, Generations of Resistance,* and *The Nuclear File.* Not untypically, the film *Witness to Apartheid,* a production of Developing News, Inc., in association with Channel 4 Television of the United Kingdom, has a host of sponsors, dominated by the Christian churches, Catholic and Protestant, altogether eleven organizations, from the World Council of Churches and the Episcopal Church to Christian Aid. The Corporation for Public Broadcasting, Oxfam, and other secular entities also contribued to the film's impressively broad support.

Witness to Apartheid gets its title from the premise and procedure of the film: let South Africans in touch with apartheid look straight into the camera and tell us what they think and how they feel. Although the film opens with the grim, almost mute, testimony of a brutally battered black boy, a plurality of the witnesses are white, many of them doctors who must treat victims of police brutality. To make the doctors' point, the film often displays these victims, all black, in gruesome detail. The version of *Witness* that I saw has a 1986 postscript by Sharon Sopher, who indicated that a number of the witnesses used in the film were subsequently detained by the police.

The film was shot in 1985 during the first of the recent series of states of emergency. One of the film's key scenes shows Sopher interviewing two blacks, a father and son. The man's youngest son had been shot dead in front of his brother while they were playing in a schoolyard. The killer was a white man, who they suspected was a policeman in mufti. In their account, the police made no attempt to investigate the murder, and they were never informed officially that the killing had even occurred. The older brother just happened to be there and survived. Suddenly, the South African army appears and surrounds the house where Sopher is conducting the interview. Remarkable footage of this event is followed by artist's impressions of the army's interruption of the filming and their removing the film crew to a military compound for questioning.

The crew was released in short order when Sharon Sopher was found to be an American, and quite obviously, the film was not confiscated. Sopher said that the officer in charge did not want "an international incident." There is no indication that any other interview was interrupted by the authorities.

Witness to Apartheid was predictably banned by Pretoria, an action that of course did not stop the film from receiving major international exposure and acclaim, including an Oscar nomination. This notice ultimately persuaded Pretoria to "lift" the domestic ban, while still retaining restrictions as to the age of audience and place of exhibition. Such a cosmetic ploy enraged Sharon Sopher, who sarcastically commented on the barring of children from screenings: "If the South African government is so concerned about children, why then does it have at least 2,500 children currently detained in prison?"

Bishop Desmond Tutu (now, at this writing, archbishop of Cape Town and Episcopal primate of South Africa) is accorded the place of prominence. His face is shown in particularly tight close-up as he recounts his futile attempts to bring about the dismantling of apartheid through peaceful means. Bishop Tutu has a great sense of presence, in pulpit or on screen, and has the ability to convey meanings without seeming to endorse them. In this sequence, his interview is intercut with shots of black teenagers peacefully, but most exuberantly, demonstrating at a funeral for some of their schoolmates who were allegedly killed by police. The South African blacks have a very powerful musical vocabulary, and all their demonstrations are to strong rhythmic chants, emphasized by a sort of bouncing graceful jog, with clenched fists in the air. This is not considered violent, and in fact is not, but the sight of uniformly moving and chanting angry blacks, sometimes in the thousands, has panicked not a few whites in the past. Although the small crowd of teenagers shown in the clip of the schoolyard demonstration does contain a few younger children, looking to be about twelve or so, most are what Americans would call teenagers as tall as the average adult, but less filled out. Other shots, of young blacks in a police van and in a courtroom, show quite young children. Throughout the interview, and in all subsequent parts of the film, all these young blacks are called "children" or "schoolchildren."

Bishop Tutu appears on the scene, conferring with police and students, obviously in the role of peacemaker and at possible risk to his physical well-being. His voice patiently drones on, with a certain pained and self-ironical admission of defeat. He tells Sopher that a young boy asked him what he, the bishop, had accomplished with his conciliatory methods. Tutu admits it is absolutely nothing and then quotes the boy as saying that he will show what can be accomplished with a few rocks. There is a pause of tolerant understanding—no further part of the conversation is reported. After the scene of the demonstration, still within the Tutu interview frame, three black teenage boys are shown reverently saying this prayer:

Our Father, Who are in heaven, hallowed be Thy Name, Thy *Freedom* come, Thy will be done, *in South Africa as in Lusaka,*[7] give us *the weapons for our daily military training* and forgive *the South Africans, our leaders,* and lead us not *to apartheid . . .*

The film does not allude to the widely publicized fact that Archbishop Tutu met with the leadership of the African National Congress in the Spring of 1986 and urged them to renounce the armed struggle. Oliver Tambo replied that this would require drastic action on the part of Pretoria, including the release of Nelson Mandela and other black leaders.

In the industrial Port Elizabeth area, Mkhuseli Jack, the boyish and cheerful organizer of the black boycott of white merchants, is a witness. He had already been detained and threatened anonymously with death at the time of the filming. The white and Indian merchants briefly interviewed all indicate, flatly, that the boycott is successful, and one blames the government for not listening to black grievances before it came to this.

Further black witnesses are young members of the Congress of South African Students, their faces in darkness to protect them from reprisal. One of them explicitly states that their freedom will only be won from "the barrel of a gun." Curtis Nkondo of the United Democratic Front, who had been charged with high treason by the time of the filming, quietly states that all the blacks seek is simple justice. "You cannot have peace with injustice." And then there is the interrupted interview with the grief-stricken father and son, who both feel that they will never be free.

Other blacks speak with their wounds and scars visible as different white and Indian doctors clinically describe the types of injuries caused by the dreaded sjambok, lead bullets, rubber bullets (which look something like large hockey pucks), and projected tear-gas canisters. In brief action footage of police in the townships, some firing shotguns at distant, indistinct (in the film) figures, the voices of the doctors indicate that it appears the police often shoot to kill.

There are other white witnesses. Mark "Cheeky" Watson, a friend of Mkhuseli Jack, and a soccer coach of black players, is shown wandering through the utterly bombed-out shell of his formerly sumptuous home in the white area of Port Elizabeth. He was subsequently arrested by the police on the charge of burning his own house down. (Presumably for propaganda purposes!) Johan Fourie, an Afrikaner advertising executive in Jo'burg, donates his time and car to drive injured victims of detention and violence to medical facilities. He describes himself as horrified when, as an adult, he finally realized at what price his affluent lifestyle had been purchased. Subsequent to release of the film, he left South Africa for good.

No South African official presents his or her viewpoint in the film, and there is no statement that they were sought out and refused to be interviewed. But a number of casual pedestrians in Johannesburg are asked if they have ever visited the townships. None of the persons shown in the final cut of the film has been to the townships, and give as explanation that they had no inclination or reason to do so. If I read the indirect point of the filmmaker, this is seen to be shameful or hypocritical or in some other way reprehensible. A special distaste is reserved for those who have black servants but have never been to the wretched township hovels of those who serve them. This seemed a gratuitous and distracting target. A number of whites do in fact care very tenderly for their servants, who after all make up a very small proportion of the blacks under apartheid. I have no more precise knowledge of just how many are in this category than Ms. Sopher has of those who are callous and cruel. And it would seem that the matrons of Scarsdale do not often visit Harlem or Mount Vernon, where many of their domestic workers commute from, even though such a trip would be comparatively much easier than from Sandton, say, to Soweto.

One white Afrikaner woman, grocery bag in arm and seemingly interrupted suddenly in mid-course (unlike any of the "witnesses"), is treated to a rather long series of provocative open-enders, such as, "What do you think is going to happen?" In sum, she believes that P. W. Botha, who was far too easy on rebellious blacks, possibly for the sake of the interfering foreign press, would be forced to call in troops and have what she called a "wipe-out."

With the exception of Mark Watson, who was not presented as such, no white or black businessmen are shown. No hope of any kind of reconciliation is offered. Jopie Fourie, the mild and kind Afrikaner, is fled and gone. Desmond Tutu, the Nobel Peace laureate, has thrown in the towel. We are left with blacks praying for guns and whites confident of a wipe-out.

South Africa is in a desperate situation, and I have no way of knowing what the actual state of affairs will be when this book is published, but surely interviews with people like Father Smangalisu Mkatchwa (who was in detention at the time) or the venerable Beyers Naude or Progressive members of parliament might have tempered what can only be called a filmic invocation of a just war, a war that the just might well lose.

Other Voices of South Africa, a Telco Production out of Los Angeles, aims deliberately to counter such extreme views of an admittedly explosive situation. In Johannesburg, Cape Town, Durban, and even the hottest bed of dissent, Port Elizabeth, the camera shows broad expanses of sunny and dramatic landscapes, people going about their business, daily life. There is rare footage of a well-to-do black neighborhood, easily comparable to the upper ten percent of American suburbs.

Although important figures like Helen Suzman, the perennial Prog of Parliament, and Rex Gibson, the assistant editor of *The Star,* are interviewed, most interviewees are common people, often in groups: English-speaking students and their teachers, a white high school principal, Afrikaner soldiers, comfortable

Jo'burg Afrikaners at a family gathering, Indians on the beach, black children in an attentive class, a Soweto family at home. Although none of these people sees a time of linked black and white hands dancing across a flowery meadow, they do not see violence as totally inevitable, although this question is pointedly asked. Gibson sees a time of "initial revolution" that could perhaps be prevented if the government made a more thorough effort to grapple seriously with black grievances. When prodded, the Soweto family, in the person of the shy young adult son, sees violence as a certain part of the future. Less dramatic if no less true than *Witness, Other Voices* gets a small fraction of its exposure and presents a picture of South Africa that is not typical of what U.S. media customarily project because of their orientation to the depiction of crisis.

Witness to Apartheid is being seen all over the world, showing in graphic detail the horrors of apartheid. Needless to say, it is banned in South Africa. But perhaps needful to say, it was made in South Africa, and it was passed out of South Africa. We have no films of the gulag or of the Argentine death squads.

City Lovers, a short film directed and written by the gifted Barney Simon from a short story by Nadine Gordimer, is a different kind of assault on apartheid. Simon, a white like Gordimer, is director of the Market Theatre in Jo'burg and is most recently acclaimed for his direction and production of *Born in the RSA*, produced at New York's Lincoln Center in 1986. The heart of the story is shared by *Country Lovers*, another of Gordimer's filmed stories, with which it is often paired.

Both films deal with the effect of apartheid on sex, the effect of sex on apartheid, and the consequent crushing of possibilities for love.

Nadine Gordimer has said that in South Africa politics is character.[8] By this she means that one cannot write a novel without dealing in some way with apartheid, since novels deal with character and each South African is profoundly touched, in youth, maturity, and old age, by apartheid.

Apartheid is an almost mythic example of state power, the realm of public issues, intruding harshly into private troubles, into people's sexuality, family life, livelihood, residence, relationships, education, and career. Northern Ireland, Iran, and Israel are also places where character is often politics, since the burning public issues are so often couched in theological terms and cradled in family and nursery consciousness, but even in those places there are some apolitical havens from the constant grinding demands of the cause.

City Lovers takes place in Jo'burg. The lovers are a white West

German geologist, on an extended contract of some kind, probably with the mining industry which built Jo'burg, and a "coloured" woman. The man is in his fifties, the woman in her twenties; the man is a sophisticated cosmopolitan, a world traveler, and important enough to be interviewed on television; the woman is a checkout girl in a supermarket near his apartment. He lives alone, but often goes out to elegant dinner parties, and has a passionate love of classical music, which he plays on tape when he works outdoors, chipping rock samples, or on his record player when he works at home. She lives in a house of women—mother, kid sister, granny—in an area designated for "coloureds," in a sort of genteel poverty. Her father is on the road a lot, and we never see him. One is given the impression that the family is resigned to the modest contentment of relative peace, a roof over their heads, and enough plain food, and that they are warmly affectionate and kind. The geologist is also seen as a brilliant but kindly gentleman, a hard worker, and a tough careerist who nonetheless likes a glass of wine and the company of women.

The young girl spots him in the supermarket and realizes he was the intriguing man she had seen on television the night before. As he checks out, she strikes up an innocent flirtation with him. Later, meeting him on the street, she offers as a favor to pick up and deliver his groceries for him. He is touched and by stages invites her to be his cleaning woman. Lonesome, he draws her into conversaton and takes delight in teaching her little items about music, his work, the great world he has seen.

It seems a charming and well-worn tale, December and May in a passing sweet exchange that each knows cannot last. But this is the land of apartheid. They really cannot go out dating together anywhere. The girl, who makes excuses to her parents so she can move in as a live-in maid for a mythical married couple, is a virtual prisoner in the apartment. There is a sense of suffocation; the great world the man brings with him must remain unreal for her, a fantasy of television. She is often fatigued, because of her job and the dreadful confinement of the arrangement. He is up and about, with many interesting affairs, and he loves his work.

As might well happen in any apartment building, other people begin to suspect that the girl is not just a domestic worker for the geologist. On one occasion the man registers quiet fury that people do not mind their own business. The young woman tells him that this is South Africa; that it is illegal for them to be together, that she could never live with him openly.

One night there is a knock on the door, an imperious knock. They both freeze, but the geologist moves to let the police in while the girl, in terror, seeks a hiding place. The man is outraged by the degradation of the scene and orders her not to hide, but her terror and his worldliness win out, and she does hide. The police enter, announcing themselves as the vice squad, and they proceed to rummage brutally through clothes and bedsheets and laundry hampers, smelling underwear and linens like dogs. The geologist tries to appear calm, but the girl is discovered while he is talking with his lawyer on the phone. They are taken into custody.

At the police station both of them are subjected, separately, to stripped medical examination, the girl in gynecological stirrups as a vaginal probe is inserted. The film ends as we learn in text that no proof of intercourse could be found. They will presumably be freed. It is clear that the affair is over, a good bit earlier than either had intended. (Since the film was made, the relevant laws governing interracial marriage and sex have been in part repealed.)

Country Lovers, directed by Manie van Rensburg, is a more ambitious film. It has more active characters, covers a longer period of time, and tries to convey the feel and flavor of the Boer farm and the experience of black and white children growing up together and then, when it is time for school, being separated.

The story would be familiar to readers of Tennessee Williams or William Faulkner. A white farmboy, the heir to the property, has a black girl as a childhood playmate. In late adolescence they become lovers, and she has his child. He kills the child with poison, and is accused of the crime and brought to court. His case is postponed until he completes military service. When he returns, the charges are eventually dropped, perhaps because the Boer paterfamilias has paid off his farmhand, the father of the black girl, so that he and his entire family will leave the farm.

The film is told in flashback as the memory of the young white man, returned to the abandoned farm house after the death of his father, the proud Boer disgraced by his son's behavior. The technique strives for a sort of folk epic impact, with frequent bridge shots of the front gate opening and closing, with the little black girl in enthusiastic attendance at the very beginning and then the final closing when the young man, alone, finally leaves the abandoned farm and its way of life. The roles are those of types, even stereotypes, because of the folk nature of the tale. The tragic inevitability of the situation, rather than the particular figures in the frame, is the focus of the effort. It could easily have taken place in the American South of the past.

The Directorate of Publications spent a lot of time on these films, largely because of the producers' international distribution plans (for the most part later fulfilled).

The committee's unpublished and unpublishable report saw each film very differently.

They had nothing good to say about *Country Lovers*. It "has no real artistic merit since it is crude antiwhite propaganda which is also aesthetically flawed in many respects." The committee also felt the film lacked credibility because the background of farming was technically incorrect, "uninformed farming methods."

In addition to the incorrect farming methods, the use of North Sotho dialogue among the blacks in such a setting was also faulted on grounds of realism. But the real objection was to the portrayal of the Boer family as callous and venal. The Afrikaner pater-familias refers to the black girl's pregnancy with his son's child as "some nuisance about Joseph's daughter."

In short, this story is not *representative* of real life on the Boer farm, although white men getting black girls pregnant and then forgetting about them is not unheard of. That is the heart of the objection.

There is certainly no dismissal of the film as being merely a story, divorced from real life. Like so many Americans, the South African committee sees the film (made for television distribution) as a special and privileged slice of real life, more real than real, symbolic of a type. In the United States it is all too common for minority groups and interest groups to strenuously, and often successfully, lobby producers, exhibitors, distributors, sponsors, and government agencies to stop portrayals of fictional characters that are taken as *representative* of blacks, Jews, women, clergy, homosexuals, and others and to promote "positive" portrayals of these types. There is even a move to check the total fictional population of a given cross section of television programming to see if there is a correct match with the demographics of the real population, as though there were an obligation to mechanistically match fiction with fact. If *Death of a Salesman* were not already an established modern classic with proven "redeeming social value," retail personnel associations would no doubt dramatically insist that there are relatively few actual suicides in their midst and that most salesmen are noted for their admirably positive mental outlook.

I mention this only to point out that South Africa has legalized, in a system very similar to our own, censorship methods that aim to accomplish ends most compatible with those desired by our own disgruntled would-be critics and according to virtually the same criteria.

City Lovers was screened by the same committee. They found it "of high aesthetic quality" and faultless "from the artistic point of view." They were particularly pleased with the acting of "the well-known radio, stage, and television personality Joe Stewardson and the unknown coloured actress," and with "memorable shots of old coloured women's faces in Coronationville." Barney Simon was singled out for his "overall intelligent, understated, and discreet direction." The plot is "well-constructed" and the relationship between the white man and coloured girl "natural and uncontrived."

The committee does fault a few of the technical details about police procedure but feels these are minor. The final forced gynecological examination by the police doctor was judged by them to be shown as "civilised and sympathetic conduct" that compensates for the brutality of the vice squad. In short, "There are enough subtleties, ironies, and correctives to militate against any form of propagandistic intent."

In my own view, *Country Lovers* had a certain amateurish flavor due in large part to its low production budget; *City Lovers* is a better film. But of course my view of artistic merit and that of the committee are totally irrelevant to whether or not a film should be allowed to be made and distributed.

In looking at film censorship in the United States, a tangled history of special interest groups and genuine concern for common decency, one is first amazed and then appalled at how many of the various censors, official or self-appointed, cannot help but see themselves as critics. It certainly is a more socially acceptable role. Why be a puritanical moral policeman or an orthodox political priest when you can be a sort of Noel Coward of the correct, sniffing in amused disdain rather than banging your fist in redneck indignation? In our own legal history, "redeeming social values," the cliché that lifted meretricious pornography to the realm of artistic license, was perforce mechanistically translated in court proceedings to the testimony of a critic on the literary or artistic (in some instances, educational or scientific) value of the contested work. Whereas, in fact, the battle should be seen in terms of minimum necessary social control versus the preferred freedom of expression, it is often argued as a battle of the critics, the liberal critics frequently being forced to lie about the aesthetic good in order to tell the truth about the political good, and the conservative critics being offended by dissent.

In the light of this hypersensitivity to types and fear of inciting "wrong ideas" about what reality should officially be, it may at first come as a surprise that there is a thriving black exploitation film business, run by whites for black audiences. Written in English or Afrikaans, the films are dubbed or translated on the set into one of the African languages, usually Zulu. Typical of this type is *Strikeback*, a film shot in two weeks for under R68,000 in 1986! Oiled naked black men, muscles and eyes bulging, use flamethrowers, bite bullets, tear down trees, and overturn cars in the pursuit of some kind of vengeance or justice. "Kind of like Rambo Sambo," according to the producer of *Strikeback*, white Ronnie Isaacs, who has produced about twenty films, "not one of them depicting the [real] African way of life. . . . There's no Soweto, no witchdoctors, no huts. I don't do political."

Tonie van der Merwe, another white producer with over sixty black titles behind him, says he was motivated to make them when he observed his employees (Van der Merwe once employed six hundred blacks in his construction business) going to see American adventure movies week after week, many with radios snugly placed over their ears so they could listen to their favorite music since they neither understood the English soundtrack, nor, in common with most film critics, saw much point in the dialogue. Van der Merwe started shooting in Zulu.

Tonie van der Merwe's own comment can spare us any tedious Marxian analysis of why the regime not only permits such films, but actually includes them in its arts subsidy program. For the June 1986 issue of *Frontline,* he told Gus Silber: "When the police see five people standing in a group, they just throw teargas. But if they see a lot of crowds at the cinema, they don't worry. So everyone goes to the cinema. There's no teargas there."

Once again, the exotic setting of South Africa makes clear to Americans a system that in principle they share. As this is written, Clint Eastwood's *Heartbreak Ridge* is romanticizing, of all places, Grenada. Rambo himself, on screen and in the White House, is of course an American invention.

Staging Protest

There is not one theater in any of the townships, although there is an astonishing amount of improvised theatrical performance and a bewildering number of repertory theater groups in all the major townships, many of them of such a high professional caliber as to go on world tours. Churches, school auditoriums, factory floors, school yards, open space—all these places are used creatively and even frenetically by the Africans, among the most sociable people in the world. Bizarre confirmation of this comes from the Security Police, who recognize that solitary confinement is particularly hard on the African, who typically when he arrives in a hotel or motel leaves his door open so that everybody can wander in and out to visit. From film and television coverage, white Americans are familiar with the enthusiastic participatory nature of black church services, the congregation often shouting approval of preached points. Black theater is no exception to this conviviality and casts light back on community alternative media, like *Grassroots,* which is organized like a family, not a newspaper.

Black theater is also much closer as a genre to improvisation. Just about any script in mainstream theater is altered in rehearsal, and most playwrights will accept at least some suggested changes from actors, directors, or play doctors. But the black theater is very much a group enterprise from the initial "composition." Barney Simon, the manager-director of the Jo'burg Market Theatre, a white dissenter who often works with blacks, acknowledged this in the 1986 Lincoln Center production of *Born in the RSA:* the credits declared it a work of "Barney Simon and cast."

And if politics is character in the South African novel, then certainly politics is drama in the black theater, often called "protest theater" for that reason. I have seen about a dozen black plays and read outlines or scripts for two dozen more. Not one treated life and conflict outside the context of apartheid. Significantly, none of the "folk operas" or "variety musicals" I watched on the SABC-TV African language channels took notice of apartheid.

To date, the best-known black protest play is *Woza Albert.* It is also one of the best in quality, and it is typical in style. It is spare in production: no set and virtually no props, just two black men of stunning energy and drive, who act with every part of their muscular bodies, who sing and dance, who mime brilliantly, who go from *fortissimo* to *pianissimo* in a totally apt and controlled instant. As mentioned earlier, the premise of the piece is the Second Coming of Christ to South Africa. Since both the Nationalist Party and the antiapartheid movement have deep roots in Christianity, the resultant farce cuts deep without ever losing joyous hope or a sense of compassion even for the enemy.

Typically, as well, the performers are the collaborating playwrights, Percy Mtwa and Mbongeni Ngema, both of whom were in their twenties when they began the piece.

Ngema comes from Durban, where he began working with the Kessie Govender Stable Theatre as an actor-collaborator and soon afterward wrote his first play, *The Last Generation.* He worked with Mtwa and Barney Simon of the Market Theatre on *Woza Albert.* The American tour of this smash put Ngema in touch with the Mexican-American experimental company, El Teatro Camp-esino. Inspired by the style and purpose of this political folk theater, Ngema founded Committed Artists back in Durban. (One is reminded of *La Prensa Chica*'s influence on *Grassroots*.) With this group he wrote and directed *Asinamali* (We have No Cash), which took him back to America again as part of a tour of such plays in 1986, collectively called Woza Africa.

Mtwa began as a poet-painter in his teens under Mafa Mgwenya and at seventeen became a singer-dancer-composer with "Percy and the Maestros." While working as a clerk, he managed to win a number of dance competitions and to provide choreography and score for *Destiny Calls* and *Umthakathi, The Witch*. He helped direct *Son of Africa*. In 1979 he he was accepted into Gibson Kente's G. K. Productions, which led to a singing-dancing role in the hit *Mama and the Load*. It was while touring with this production that Mtwa met Ngema and they began their collaboration on *Woza Albert*. Mtwa subsequently became a resident director of the Market Theatre and wrote *Bopha!*, which became such a hit that it brought him back to America sharing the Woza Africa with his collaborators, Simon and Ngema, as well as a number of other companions of the South African protest theater enterprise.

There is of course harassment of protest theater. In South Africa, the audiences in the halls and other make-do spaces often have one eye on the exit, for the police can and do raid performances. Texts and performances can be banned, and sometimes restrictions are placed on the size of audiences. *Gangsters,* Maisha Maponya's rather didactic tribute to Steve Biko's heroic witness under the lawless treatment he received from the Security Police (the "Gangsters"), cannot be shown to more than ninety people at a time in South Africa, although it was allowed to come to Lincoln Center in New York. And now with the fever pitch of rebellion in the townships, fueled by the particularly aggressive cadre of "children" known as "the comrades," plays are under threat of violent disruption because they have been decreed an unseemly diversion during the time of crisis. (Christmas has not been celebrated in Soweto since 1976 for similar reasons and pressures).[9]

To put matters into further perspective, it should be pointed out that going to any theater in South Africa, even if it is for a Neil Simon standard (he is quite popular) at the massive Baxter Theatre complex on the outskirts of Cape town, is a bit more daunting than taking the underground to the West End or a taxi to Broadway. There are few theaters of any kind in South Africa and they are not found in anything like a bustling "theater district." It is virtually impossible to safely attend the theater unless one drives one's own car or has a ride. The area near Newtown, where the Market Theatre (and the much harassed Action Theatre of black Benjy Francis) is located, is sparsely populated at night and hazardous to one's health. It is a fringe area between commercial and industrial buildings, bordered by railroad yards. In general, the business districts of Jo'burg, Cape Town, and Durban at night are as inviting as downtown Detroit at midnight.

Mtwa's *Bopha!* and Maponya's *Gangsters* offer an illuminating contrast within the protest theater movement.

Bopha! goes to the central nervous system of apartheid: the police and the passbook. The story is about a middle-aged black policeman with a teenage son. The policeman is portrayed as a loving father and fundamentally good person; he does what he does because it is the only way he can make a living. He is gruffly affectionate and heaps scorn on the head of his son, who wants a better world, who despises his father's collaboration with the system, but who has no viable alternative except violent resistance against what is and a vague hope for something better later. The policeman has a younger brother who gets into trouble for not having a proper passbook. Using his influence, he gets the brother a job as a new policeman and in this way manages to get him a valid passbook.

From the beginning the brother makes a reluctant cop. He does not understand that the laws do not apply equally. He arrests a white drunk for pissing in public because he has seen his senior brother arrest a black man for using a toilet reserved for whites.

There is much humor in the piece along the old Sgt. Bilko lines: the wily subordinate cutting out a comfortable niche for himself by humoring the irrational rages and whims of his military superiors. The white senior officer is presented as a bumbling fool, a Col. Klink type. The vaudeville altercations among the brothers and the young teenager are handled with expert timing and broad wit.

The play has no set and only three players, who assume different roles by changing hats or shirts or, something of a convention in black theater, a large mustache as a sign of the white man. There is a lot of mock close-order drill and military singsong that is brilliantly satiric and popping with electric energy. In the end, the young man is arrested, his mother (always offstage) is shot by police in a confused melee, and the policeman's house is burned down by an angry mob; the reluctant brother sheds his uniform. Conquered, the policeman resigns and leaves with his son to join an antiapartheid rally. The son is jubilant, the father destroyed. He was so proud of his status as a policeman; he kept his nose clean; he helped his relatives, he was generous with his resources. But the price he paid was his soul, and he now knows it.

Bopha! combines the best of indigenous African forms with the broader theatrical traditions of the great world. Anyone can identify with each of the characters from the inside. Mtwa has put a very human face on what at times can seem an archetypal struggle against abstract hegemony and human individualism. As in life, one finds humor and farce within tragedy, and no one figure embodies all of good or evil.

Gangsters, on the other hand, seems all rage. It is based on the type of event connected with the death of Steve Biko, who died as a result of beatings and lack of medical attention at the hands of the Security Police. It is by no means an attempt to recreate a specific historical event.

Once again there are only three players: a white Security Police officer, his black assistant, and a black woman protest poet (in earlier versions, a man), whose public declamations against the inhumanities of apartheid are seen as dangerously inflammatory. The play begins with the poet among the audience, marching about with monumental indignation, screaming unrelieved rage on what seems one long sustained note of fury. The police officer is at first conciliatory with the poet. But the poet is sullen and refuses to cooperate in any way, recognizing the cool cordiality as a mask. In a rapid series of confrontations, the officer becomes more open about his hatred and hostility, finally ordering his black assistant to torture some sense into the recalcitrant detainee. This is done in darkness, after we see the black cop tie her down rather severely. When the lights come up, there is a bier-bed, with a covered sarcophagal figure. It seems the poet has died under torture. The black man is in trouble with his superior, who wishes to avoid bad publicity. After examining the body, whose condition brings the white officer to the verge of vomiting, the two policemen have an absurd dialogue in which the black man comes up with incredibly ignorant cover stories which the officer rejects. The play ends with the suggestion that the spirit of the poet has triumphed.

There is a great deal of anger in this play, but it does not seem to drive anything creative. It is a long complaint. None of the parts are characters; they are cardboard figures, particularly the poet, whose death loses meaning because of the hysterical nature of the role. Instead of a tragedy or a statement, we have a poster. That the cause is just cannot make the art good.

Of course, like theater or art or literature anywhere, South African protest theater has its share of the inadequate, although the guilty liberal or conservative reader-viewer is loath for politicoreligious motives to register a negative reaction. Jane Kramer made this point tellingly in her review of *A Chain of Voices* by Andre Brink, the Afrikaner protest novelist:

It may have taken crafty masters like Dickens and Zola to invent the guilty reader, but by now guilty reading has come into its own as an armchair ritual among the bourgeoisie, and it does not depend on crafty masters—just on a vague appetite for self-chastisement.

It is this appetite, this pleasant moral twinge, that we bring, lately, to books by white South Africans. We judge South African writers less by their quality than by the risks they take in putting the wall of their own dissidence between ourselves and the black Africa we praise and fear. We love them for being South African *for* us. They are our surrogates in resistance. And so we are undone by the bad books—books like Andre Brink's *A Chain of Voices*—they often write in earnest exploitation of their (our) just cause. We are undone by books of mediocre purity.[10]

A similar point is made in the text of *Born in the RSA,* the only play on the Woza Africa tour that dealt with both white and black in central, fully drawn roles. One of the characters, a white university student with kinky sexual tastes who turns police informer, speaks for many when he says that South Africans have become the world's celebrities, whom everyone else observes from a safe and moralistic remove, as if apartheid were a sadomasochistic scene played out in a leather bar.[11]

Like his former collaborator, Mtwa, Ngema also returned to America with a new play *Asinamali*. Not quite as inventive or involved as *Bopha!,* it is nonetheless explosive in its energy and unflagging in its pace. It takes place in prison, where five male prisoners, among them a con man, a murderer, a philanderer, tell in that powerful mime style the histories that have landed them in jail from the larger prison of apartheid. As in Mtwa's work, there is humor in sorrow, farce in tragedy.

Perhaps the average level of protest theater is exemplified by Matsemela Manaka's *Children of Asazi.* It opens on a shanty, imaginatively made of shields with small cutouts for eyes, the assemblage representing the fragile and mobile shelters of the squatter camps, such as Crossroads. The bulldozers are coming; a young couple wants to get married; a mysterious sax player wanders in and out; the young couple are revealed to be brother and sister, and just as conveniently the revelation turns out to be a mistake. It is melodrama no worse than the run-of-the-mill productions found in school halls all over the world, but there is, in the shadow of apartheid, a passionate edge which makes its very mediocrity a cry for recognition of the world its players inhabit as fully human, with the same aspirations and tastes as that of the privileged whites who can go to the theater and live their lives, of perhaps quiet desperation, without the added complications of state terrorism or persecution.

There are countless troupes and companies of players all throughout South Africa, far more per capita than in the United States or France or Germany, a sign of the family orientation and clubbability of Africans as much as their starved need for some kind of effective political participation and public venting of cruelly suppressed feelings. The Bahumutsi Drama Group, the Committed Artists, the Soyikwa Institute of African Theatre, the Earth Players, G. K. Productions, Action Theatre, Stable Theatre, Rural Theatre Workshop—the townships are teeming with all sorts and levels of theatrical energy.

A very special place in South African theater belongs to the Market Theatre Company, run by two extraordinary men, Barney Simon, the artistic director, who has produced and directed a number of black theater pieces and who has also directed some film as well (notably Gordimer's *City Lovers,* as we have seen), and Mannie Manim, the managing director, an internationally acclaimed lighting designer, who has worked in London and New York as well as all over South Africa, where he has played a leading political role in a variety of theatrical associations, from the Federated Union of Black Artists to the South African Association ot Theatre Managements.

Both men have worked all over the world and won numerous awards in and out of South Africa. Despite this high commercial and artistic success, the Market Theatre remains in the renovated market where it began, in a relatively run-down area of Jo'burg, with limited seating and primitive if ingeniously exploited technical facilities. To preserve their integrity, they have steadfastly refused any government subsidy. Both have had a long association with Athol Fugard, the dissident Afrikaner playwright (*Master Harold and the Boys, Blood Knot,* and so many others produced internationally). The Market Theatre Company is not only fully integrated, it integrates the society, black and white, during those rare moments of inspired theater when politics is seen solely in terms of human character, and it has integrated South African theater art with the world stage of international touring, the big time of Broadway and the alternative styles of El Teatro Camp-esino. Protest theater has been presented along with the international repertoire of everything from *Medea* to *The Seagull* to *'Night Mother.*

Sadly, the separatism that the increasing tensions of apartheid have brought on may force Simon to leave black theater when the government has failed to do so. Recently he turned down two blacks who wanted to work with him on a play about the militant young blacks called "the comrades," because it might have caused them problems. "In certain political circles, there are problems if you work with a white," he told *The New York Times.* "If I find myself without blacks to work with, . . . I might leave, I would stop theater, yes," he added.[12]

A black play that was conceived in real conflict to tell in court not *a* truth but the *particular* truth of a labor dispute gives a rare insight into the intimate connection between black theater and the black community. In the original conflict fifty-five black migrant workers from KwaZulu, members of the Metal and Allied Workers Union, were arrested for illegally striking at an iron foundry that did not recognize the union. In trying to build a defense for the workers, the lawyer, Halton Cheadle, had great difficulty in reconstructing exactly what happened. There had been meetings with management before the strike; there had been the style and methods of the strike itself; and, further, there had been the manner and circumstances of the actual arrest. With fifty-five defendants, he got almost fifty-five versions. In desperation, he asked one of the workers to play the part of the manager and asked others to "play" themselves in a dramatic reconstruction of the actual events.

He had tapped a torrent of pent-up expression. The workers became wildly enthusiastic in recreating the events that led to their imprisonment and showed a passion for accuracy that only came out when "rehearsals" were challenged on the most minor of details: the exact gesture of the manager at a particular point, the precise words used, and so forth. Once the final agreed version was audiotaped, Cheadle took the recordings to Ari Sitas of the Junction Avenue Theatre Workshop. The company then went to the workers and tried to impose the structure of art on the documentary narrative they had produced. The workers balked: That's not the way it happened, they would shout, and then proceed to demonstrate facial expressions, gestures, words.[13]

Finally, after the trial was over (the strikers received six-month suspended sentences), a play was produced, *Ilanga Le So Phonela Abasebenzi,* played by the workers themselves at first and then gradually by the actors from the company. A grievance was being transformed into art, and art was being used to communicate a grievance—the essense of protest theater. Once again, one is reminded of *Grassroots,* the community newsletter that went to the local street committees and helped them to organize the protest against rate increases that the paper was covering. To adapt a famous phrase, community media, alternative media, protest theater not only portray life or report life, they aim to change life.

Not a few protest pieces have had a similar origin in fact and have a directly and deliberately didactic point.

Although not sparked by a specific incident, the workers at Sarmcol-BTR have a play, *The Long March,* which dramatizes their struggle against their multinational. Though originally created in Zulu with some English, it was staged at the Hague in English at a time to coincide with the hearing there against BTR for breaking the Common Market (EEC) Code of Conduct. More English had been added, with inevitable Zulu spins on it, as the play made its way there via the Transvaal, where black Sotho speakers were better served by English, the lingua franca of the blacks.

Another example of a consciously didactic play is provided by Don Mattera, the bone of contention in *The Reader* censorship case argued by Nicholas Haysom. Mattera has written a children's play, *Kagiso Sechaba,* for the Open School Street and Community Theatre Programme, an organization which produces a number of didactic and avowedly propagandistic presentations, such as *One Time Brother,* designed to fight the government's campaign for the new constitution (and banned by the government). It is thus often wrong-headed to apply Jane Kramer's criteria to all antiapartheid works, because they do not seek classification as high or elite art (as Andre Brink's aforementioned work did in the eyes of Kramer and the critics and readers she rebuked). In the proper context, a poster is more suitable than a painting.

The theater of protest thus occupies a pivotal place in the apartheid media wars. It is indigenous to the black communities, not a quaint throwback to tribal rituals that were born long before apartheid and modernization; it runs a long gamut from didactic melodrama to situation comedy with a social bite. In this context, apartheid is only the latest local form within which the human tragedy, shared by Oedipus, Faust, and Hamlet, is being played out.

Protest theater is thus in direct conflict with SABC masscult, the modernizing media machine that aims to depoliticize the masses it supposedly serves. SABC news, as we have seen, is bland and reassuring. It either gives the government line on matters of concern or deals with the whimsical and the trivial, like the parking problem in downtown Jo'burg, a main feature that was given a sort of pseudo-Morley Safer turn on *Midweek* during a time of significant unrest. Religious programming treats religion as a strictly personal affair with inner peace as its primary purpose—usually achieved through creative resignation to the status quo. And the bulk of programming, entertainment, consists of a preponderance of American television imports.

One is at first surprised that the flamboyantly defiant Eddie Murphy's *Beverly Hills Cop* is passed through the system and the SABC has bought as regular shows *Miami Vice, Tenspeed and Brownshoe, The A-Team,* where black men are the equals, in fashions, ineptitude, and mindless brutality, of white men. *The Jeffersons* and *The Cosby Show,* with their bland and lovable domestic situations, are less of a surprise; such blacks are conventionally successful Americans, and the South African blacks who cooperate with the regime and buy into the system have a dim hope of perhaps "making it" and becoming bourgeois home-owners (under a recent dispensation) in affluent sections of Soweto or Mamelodi.

The key is "likely viewer," a cardinal consideration with the Directorate of Publications. Eddie Murphy is a cop, and black South African cops are not likely to imitate his style with whites. In all cases, the blacks are seen as integral parts of the enforcement system. As for the whites who look at the program, they may well see a potential in blacks that they might have ignored or not thought possible. But it is a potential to become cooperating members of a white regime; not rivals, and certainly not revolutionaries.

The rest of SABC fare is not very different from mass media entertainment in the United States or England, or the world in general, which is becoming homogenized into one large mass media market, with James Bond chasing bad guys all over the world before audiences all over the world. One great advantage of American serials is their tendency, as in the old *Mod Squad, Hawaii Five-O,* and the current *Miami Vice,* to have multiracial casts in multiracial locations. Bop-TV, which is independent of the SABC if not of the South African government, interestingly offers about the same kind of fare: *Dynasty, Moonlighting, Diff'rent Strokes.* The SABC "black" channels, in African languages, resemble early American television, chock full of variety shows and taped studio drama with folk themes. Despised by radicals and ignored in any case by most blacks, it is, ironically, an attempt to pursue authentic indigenous art forms free of Western masscult. The apartheid system encourages this to keep the blacks apart from inclusion in the First World side of South Africa; outside of South Africa, Third World nationalists seek to encourage local cultural programming to keep from losing their identities in the tidal wave of Western masscult.

Black protest theater, unlike masscult, is local and traditional, but at the same time, unlike tribal folk culture, it is timely and political. It is community-based, like the community newsletter *Grassroots*. Having learned from some of the alternative media of professional consciousness-raising of South American provenance, the much repressed yet still flourishing antiapartheid media can give lessons in community building to any number of American communities, so dependent on the distant and antiseptic media services of corporate communications conglomerates or public relations experts who speak for elected officials.

NOTES

1. Donald Thomas, *A Long Time Burning: The History of Literary Censorship in England* (London: Routledge & Kegan Paul, 1969), p. 13.

2. Zechariah Chafee, Jr., *Free Speech in the United States* (Cambridge, Mass.: Harvard University Press, 1967), pp. 3–36.

3. Murray Schumach, *The Face on the Cutting Room Floor: The Story of Movie and Television Censorship* (New York: William Morrow & Co., 1964), pp. 81–116.

4. John M. Phelan, *Disenchantment: Meaning and Morality in the Media* (New York: Hastings House, 1980), pp. 107–146.

5. *Mutual Film Corporation* v. *Industrial Commission of Ohio*, 236 U.S. 230 (1915) at 244.

6. Keyan Tomaselli, "Oppositional Filmmaking in South Africa," *Fuse*, November–December 1982, pp. 190–94.

7. Lusaka is the headquarters-in-exile of the African National Congress.

8. Nadine Gordimer to Alan Ross in "A Writer in South Africa," *London Magazine*, May 2, 1965, pp. 22–23.

9. Alan Cowell, "South African Dramas Echo Cries of the Beloved Country," *New York Times*, August 31, 1986, pp. 1, 19.

10. Jane Kramer, "In the Garrison," *New York Review of Books*, December 2, 1982, pp. 8–12.

11. Critic Frank Rich: "*Born in the RSA* is that rare political drama with the power to make participants out of history's voyeurs." (*New York Times*, October 3, 1986, p. 3.)

12. Alan Cowell, op. cit., p. 19.

13. Halton Cheadle told his story to Keyan Tomaselli for *Critical Arts* 2, no. 1 (1981): 24–28. I later met Cheadle at Yale and learned of his intimate connection with John Dugard and the founding of the Centre for Applied Studies. Like Haysom and many of the others I have met in his line of work, Cheadle is aggressively cheerful and impressively upbeat in his assessment of the future for a just South Africa, after a transitional period of turmoil.

CHAPTER SIX

Church-State Apartheid

Since 1948, when the National Party took over, South Africa has become more and more of a police state. In the middle eighties, with the imposition of virtual martial law through various types of states of emergency and the particularly stern controls exercised over the media, South Africa is more of a Poland with palm trees than ever before. It is like Poland in one other respect as well: opposition to the virtual one-party rule is fueled and maintained by the Christian churches, which are aided in no small measure by their counterparts overseas. Unlike Poland's, however, South Africa's oppositionist Christian churches are not monolithic and hierarchical, like the church from which the present Roman Catholic Pope emerged. Furthermore, the National Party, unlike the officially atheist Communist Party, is deeply allied with some local South African versions of the Dutch Reformed Church. Further, South Africa is officially, even officiously, a "Christian nation."

In a very real sense, Christianity is on both sides of the apartheid controversy. True, the World Council of Churches and an overwhelming number of national and world churches have officially condemned apartheid. True, a major focus of opposition in South Africa is the South African Council of Churches, which draws almost 100 percent of its budget from overseas contributions of sister churches, particularly from German and Dutch Lutherans, who have the angered parent's attitude toward the Afrikaner Christians whose churches have in the past supported apartheid.[1] In fact, the necessarily simple drama presented in the American media of the forces of evil, Afrikaner Teutonic Knights with crosses and swastikas, against the children of light, the African National Congress and Desmond Tutu, distorts both Christianity and South African politics. Christianity has survived the millennia because of its remarkable ability to adjust and compromise and to absorb apparent contradiction, even as it is a force for uncompromising demands for justice and human rights, perhaps its basic paradox. Although moral worlds apart, both the Grand Inquisitor and Alyosha Karamazov represent real historical trends in Christianity.

With Christianity on both sides of the apartheid struggle one is not surprised that, instead of offering hope for reconciliation, it adds to the bitterness and intransigence of the contention, as in Ireland.

Nineteen eighty-five was a year that brought these strains into dramatic focus.

At the beginning of the year the report of the Eloff Commission was made public. Eloff, as it is nicknamed, was a pointed inquiry of the government into the plans, activities, and private records of the South African Council of Churches with a view to legally squeezing the life out of the vigorous protests, particularly the sanctions-disinvestment campaign, spearheaded by its then general secretary, Bishop Desmond Tutu.

At the beginning of April, at its first annual conference, "From Protest to Challenge . . . Mobilization to Organization," SACC's secular sister, the United Democratic Front, had made the following demands of its own government:

- the immediate scrapping of the 1913 and 1936 Land Acts and the Group Areas Act of 1966 and an end to all forced removals.
- the dissolution of the homelands and the ending of the migrant labor system.
- the scrapping of the tricameral parliamentary system and all bodies created under the Black Local Authorities Act of 1982.
- the establishment of a unified and democratic education system.
- the repeal of the pass laws and all other restrictions on freedom of movement.
- recognition of the rights of workers to organize into unions, to strike, to bargain collectively, to security of employment, to housing, social welfare, pensions, and maternity benefits.
- the release of all political prisoners, the lifting of bans on individuals and organizations, the return of exiles, and the lifting of all restrictions on freedom of speech and assembly.
- the disbanding of the South African Defence Force, the South African Police and all other arms of repression.
- the scrapping of all security laws.

Shortly thereafter, riot police had surrounded and stormed into Khotso House, the SACC administrative offices, in a search for "subversive" material.

By August 1985 the United Democratic Front had issued a memorandum to foreign government, foreign business, and organized South African business urging much more strict steps toward isolating South Africa by:

- breaking diplomatic ties;
- expelling and excluding South Africa from all international forums;
- immediately terminating the policy of constructive engagement followed by the United States, the United Kingdom, and West Germany;
- immediately ceasing military, technological, and intelligence support to the government;
- extending economic sanctions and sports boycotts;
- cutting off all forms of assistance to South Africa's government and domestic business, including those of the homelands.

By June of the same year, Chief Buthelezi's powerful Inkatha, which, although theoretically open to all, is fundamentally the Zulu political party and often at odds with the UDF, had its own demands. These were couched in the form of a declaration of intent urged on President Botha as a precondition of any negotiations with blacks:

- to amend the South African constitution in such a way that no one group would have a favored position over any other group.
- to devise a form of universal adult suffrage acceptable to all the peoples of South Africa.
- to grant full citizenship to all South Africans equally.

Less extreme than the blanket transformation sought by the UDF, Inkatha obviously was hoping for some sort of federation of tribal states, including one for the whites and Natal, where most of KwaZulu is located, for themselves. This tribalism is at the root of the black distrust of Buthelezi, since the other tribes are dispersed much more and see tribalism as a divide-and-conquer strategy exploited by the whites for centuries. Nonetheless, the point here is that organized demands of a radical nature were coming at Pretoria from every angle in 1985, and SACC was prodding and pushing and proclaiming most of them through sophisticated and widespread employment of multimedia methods.

During the political tumult of 1985, even the SABC Editorial Commentary beat the drum of the failure of apartheid and the need to adapt to new pressures and opportunities, as if it were criticizing government racist policies instead of urging a less obviously offensive formulation for domination:

[The government] will be required to move purposely on the position of Blacks outside the national states, the most intractable and urgent political problem with which the country is faced. (January 25, 1985)

The traditional influx control system is ineffective. Despite being enforced by a large bureaucratic machinery and tens of thousands of prosecutions annually, it has made no discernible difference to the rate of urbanisation of the black people—a rate dictated on the one hand by the need to earn a livelihood and on the other by the need for labour in a growing economy.

[The system is characterized by] ruthless repression, economic depression, mass famine in the rural areas and unmanageable social unrest. (January 29, 1985)

It is simply not possible to justify, logically or humanely, a policy that would strip of his citizenship a person who has always lived in this country and always will live here, as will his children and their children. To do so at all is a mere legal fiction, one that is so much at odds with economic and social realities that it can never find expression in a workable constitutional system. (April 23, 1985)

By autumn, SACC had printed in its magazine Καιρος [New Testament Greek, "providential opportunity"] a theological statement on the political crisis in South Africa, signed by over 150 theologians, clergy, and church professionals, that came to be known as the *Kairos Document*. It represented a formal declaration of theological war, damning not only apartheid, but the establishment version of Christianity used to condone racism. The document went on to bless violent actions on behalf of justice when all other means failed. By the end of the year, at a meeting of international church figures from the World Council of Churches convened by SACC in Harare, the capital of nearby Zimbabwe, the entire assemblage called upon the Pretoria government to resign. The combined thrust of their own official Harare Declaration and their espousal of the expository *Kairos Document* is to put SACC in a very militant position hardly distinguishable from that of the banned ANC. It is a position that SACC feels it has been forced into by the increasing intransigence of the government despite all manner of pleading and diplomacy aimed at dismantling apartheid peaceably.

Both sides see their opponents not only as politically wrong, but as morally evil, betrayers of Christ, hypocrites, liars, close to devils. Ecclesiastical apartheid is the most virulent of a string of apartheids based on the fundamental racist version.

In this, as in so many other worldwide conflicts and movements, South Africa offers us an extreme and dramatic instance. For the differing views of apartheid represent broader differences about the nature of Christianity itself which is coming to a head in the advanced countries and the Third World as well.

The larger trend is unmistakable. From South America to South Asia, immense numbers of formerly colonized peoples see the churches as relics of European domination; at the same time, in America and Europe, new classes of educated secularists see the churches as nationalist museums, tightly interwoven in the fabric of state and establishment power. The world struggle for a new and more just order is also a struggle within the churches between those who see Christianity as a message to the world to change itself and those who see Christianity as a response of individuals to the challenge of living a pure and selfless life within an inevitably corrupt structure. These views are intellectually compatible, with some traditionally fancy theological footwork, but they are practically antagonistic and cannot justify the same policies or programs.

Like a fleet of dreadnoughts, the mainstream churches are now in the midst of a sweeping, awkward turn to meet new currents despite their immense historical inertia. Although a reaction to events, the turn is neither mindless nor ahistorical, but is negotiated through the medium of theology, the church effort to make its mysteries communicable and contemporary. This is why a change in policy requires a change in theology. Liberation needs liberation theology.

The Kairos Document provides a clear set of distinctions about the political relevance of different versions of Christianity. Liberation theology is the ideology of the "partisan church." Christianity, in this view, obliges its members to side with the underclass and fight repression wherever it exists using the most efficient means, violent or otherwise. The apartheid regime is utterly without any redeeming feature and must be erased. This theology stands in contrast to "church theology," according to the document, which stands as a "third force" between oppressors and their victims and serves as a mediator to bring the two sides into some sort of harmony or reconciliation. In doing this, the church accepts the rules of the game established by the oppressor and thus is a collaborator in injustice. The worst theology is called "state theology," whereby the church offers justifications for the status quo—the theology of careerist military chaplains, battleship-blessing cardinals, and, of course, of the Dutch Reformed Church theorists of separate peoples working out their unique, God-ordained separate developments, under the tutelage of superior European culture. Charity is the preeminent Christian virtue, for this group, because it leaves justice to the politicians.

This is the view of Ronald Reagan. The church is great at private works of charity and the state needs it to provide the "safety net" that the government has no business providing, since it is not in the charity business. So, when the Catholic bishops speak out against poverty in America or when clergy seek to give sanctuary to illegal aliens or when Anglican Bishop Paul Moore speaks out against nuclear armament, the church is naively exceeding its otherwordly mandate. This judgment coincides exactly with the view of the Botha government. Christianity is a personal thing that helps people survive and even thrive within the existing social order, which God has blessed because it exists and is maintained by dulv constituted authority.

Whether sincerely held or not, this view contemptuously dismisses the traditional prophetic role of religious leaders, from the Old Testament prophets like Jeremiah and Ezekiel through Christ himself to such diverse historical and contemporary figures as Martin Luther and Martin Luther King, Jr. Although failing to see its relevance to his native Poland, the present Pope seems to agree at least in part with the Reagan view, condemning Latin American priests, for instance, who become politically active against the system, but remaining silent about his Vatican financiers and their involvement in the Banco Ambrosiano scandal.

The Christian supporters of the Nationalist regime come principally from three South African versions of the Dutch Reformed Church: the Nederduitse Gereformeerde Kerk (NGK), the Nederduitse Hervormde Kerk (NHK), and the Gereformeerde Kerk in Suid-Afrika (GKSA).

The NGK is by far the largest, with a membership of 1.7 million; NHK has 246,000; GKSA, the only one with black members, has only 128,000, two-thirds of them white.[2] Although they differ among themselves, the three churches are often grouped together as the Dutch Reformed Church by the foreign media. In fact, NGK is affiliated with three dependent and racially separate churches—the "coloured" NG Sendingkerk [Mission Church], the Indian Reformed Church in Africa, and the black NGK in Afrika (NGKA), thus having a sort of apartheid of its own. The NG Sendingkerk, of which Dr. Allan Boesak, former president of the World Alliance of Reformed Churches and vice-president of SACC, is assessor, has repeatedly urged the NGK to drop its color bar and to have all the churches completely unified. In its locally well-known Belhar Confession, the Sendingkerk has condemned apartheid as a heresy. The NGK executive body rejected both moves, claiming that the racially separate churches were established under "the guidance of the Lord." This view of the NGK, which has been called "the National Party at Prayer," extends to the political apartheid of the state system. In rejecting

Church-State Apartheid

the move of the Reformed Ecumenical Synod (of which it is a member) to condemn apartheid at the Chicago meeting in 1984, the NGK, through its director of ecumenical affairs, Dr. Pierre Rossouw, made a distinction between racism, which it has condemned as a sin, and apartheid, which "the overseas churches" do not accept because they have an "incorrect understanding." For this stand, the World Alliance of Reformed Churches has suspended the NGK and the NHK from the membership since 1982.[3]

Although subsequently the NGK opened its own doors to blacks in theory, the NHK has as recently as May 14, 1986, refused to drop its theologically maintained color bar. It was only in October 1986 that the General Synod of the NGK pronounced that there was no "biblical justification" for apartheid and opened the doors of all its churches to all races. Significantly, the Synod stopped short of declaring apartheid a "sin," something that Allan Boesak had been calling for year after year. So although the change in official position, after so much temporizing, produced another crack in the facade of Afrikaner unity, in practice, social custom has kept the average congregation from any radical change in composition.

While the leadership has made some tentative steps in the direction of abandoning apartheid, the mainstream membership of the NGK still vigorously supports the regime, and a strong dissident movement on the right within the NGK seeks to preserve apartheid as a proper practice. The latter condemn the National Party and Botha for giving in to liberal pressure and abandoning a divinely sanctioned separation of races. A strident voice in this cause is *The South African Observer: A Journal for Realists,* which is fond of condemning the antiapartheid movement as a part of the larger heresy of the "social gospel," which itself is of course an invention of the communist devils.[4] Although there is no census of these extremists, they are not a minor fringe group, judging from the politically active Conservative Party, which has also condemned Botha for selling out, and the alarmingly large quasi-Nazi movement, the Afrikaanse Weerstand Beweging (AWB, Afrikaner Resistance Movement), which has staged rallies ominously (or, from a different viewpoint, pathetically) reminiscent of Hitler's Nuremburg rallies, complete with brown shirts and shoulder belts.[5] Both these groups are largely Afrikaner and tend to belong to one of the Reformed Churches.

By 1986 these extremists had actually come to blows with the nationalists in Pietersburg. At that time, Foreign Minister Pik Botha was scheduled to address a gathering of the National Party at a meeting hall during the visit of the Commonwealth Mission, which was urging the government to free Mandela and open up negotiations with the African National Congress. To the members of the far-right AWB, Botha was a dangerous liberal who just might sell them out. There were over one thousand of them outside the hall, followers of AWB leader Eugene Terre'Blanche, a huge man, former rugby player, policeman, and bodyguard to a previous prime minister, John Vorster. Many of the men were dressed in the AWB uniform. Others were in Stetsons and riding boots, carrying whips. Some waved placards bearing Old Testament quotations which seemed to endorse apartheid. When the Nats arrived, dressed for dinner, push became shove, then flying fists. Only the police were able to defeat the rightist demonstrators. They did not use rubber bullets.[6]

It would not be fair, and it would certainly be too simple, to drag in these extremists without mentioning the uncounted members of the Reformed Churches who stay on as members yet arduously oppose apartheid and place their lives and careers on the line to do so, something that many other opponents of apartheid do not have to face. Beyers Naude is a famous example of a radical conversion in this regard: his entire life was changed and he was ostracized by the leadership of the country and the churches that he was felt to have betrayed. He briefly regained prominence, having replace Tutu as transitional general secretary of SACC. But there are many lesser figures, such as the Reverend Nico Smith, who with his wife went to live in a township to serve his black NGKA parishioners as an equal, a living of the real social gospel of personal service.[7]

What the Kairos Document has aptly called the "state theology" of much of the South African Dutch Reformed Churches is fortunately not characteristic of the vast majority of church leaderships in the world when it comes to apartheid. Most Christian churches the world over see apartheid as a great sin, but they assume the second role mentoned by the Kairos Document, the "church theology" of mediation between oppressors and victims. For some, this is an anemic position that smacks of collaboration with Mammon. Accordingly, the World Council of Churches has gone a step further in the direction of liberation theology to advocate a "partisan church" in the antiapartheid struggle. Within South Africa, the South African Council of Churches, closely allied to the crusading United Democratic Front, is the embodiment, and the model, for the "partisan church."

Both WCC and SACC came to the hard place where they now stand because they walked, and were pushed, step by step through a series of decisive reactions to events.

The events are well known to the world: Sharpeville (1960), Soweto (1976), and the current continuing crisis set off by the campaign to boycott the constitutional referendum of late 1983 and the subsequent bitter reaction to its adoption. The corresponding ecclesiastical reactions are less familiar, but they are driving a great deal of the apartheid struggle and its media wars today.

One hundred and eighty-six blacks were wounded and sixty-seven were killed by police fire in Sharpeville, and the world press sent the news around the world in a shock wave. Both the event itself and the world reaction to it panicked the Nationalist regime into banning the ANC, arresting Nelson Mandela, Albert Lutuli, and Robert Sobukwe, and declaring a state of emergency.

Joost de Blank, Tutu's predecessor in more than one sense as archbishop of Cape Town and Anglican primate, reacted himself by writing to the executive of the World Council of Churches demanding that in the light of events the Cape and Transvaal synods of the Dutch Reformed Church be expelled, since they supported government apartheid and practiced it themselves. Hard as it is to believe now, the WCC thought at the time this was a hasty and hot demand and eventually, nine months after Sharpeville, convened what has come to be known as the Cottesloe Consultation, from December 7 to 14, 1960, to see if the Dutch Reformed Church and her ecclesiastical critics could come to terms and take a forthright yet mutually acceptable stand against injustice in South Africa.

A U.S. officer of the WCC, Franklin C. Fry, presided over the meeting and its General Secretary Visser't Hooft was in attendance. Ten delegates from each of the five member churches of South Africa were present along with eighteen black participants and eight lay delegates, including Alan Paton. It was rumored that the NHK delegation was in constant consultation with Prime Minister Hendrik Verwoerd of South Africa.[8]

The upshot was rather tame. The consultation issued a statement calling for open worship for all races in all churches, criticizing the pass laws and racial job reservation, and asking for a reenfranchisement of the "coloured." The reaction of the government in this churchly country, where the statement was a media event, was far from reserved. Since the Dutch Reformed Church was fully represented at the consultation, Prime Minister Verwoerd personally expressed his grave displeasure with the NGK delegation, and he was joined by Dr. Koot Vorster, brother of the future prime minister, and Dr. Andries Treurnicht, soon to become a deputy minister in the government and now the head of the ultraright Conservative Party.

The result was that the DRC voluntarily withdrew from the WCC, and "liberal" clergymen of these churches were left without institutional support. This in turn eventually led to Beyers Naude's leaving his high position in the NGK (acting moderator of the Transvaal Synod) and in the Broederbond in order to found the Christian Institute in 1963, a multiracial group that began the trend of media warfare against apartheid through the publishing of reports and papers and the establishment of publicized study programs that called attention to the injustices of the system and the fundamental immorality of apartheid itself.

The 1976 Soweto school boycott and riots, provoked by the introduction of Afrikaans as a subject for black study, was the next precipitating event. The Christian Institute published two factual reports about that time and its trouble, with the characteristic question mark of titles under censorship threats: *Is South Africa a Police State?* and *Torture in South Africa?* The government reaction was to ban Naude and many of his colleagues, disband the Christian Institute, and close down its journal, *Pro Veritate* [For Truth].

At the same time, the leading black daily, *The World,* was shut down, as we have seen. Just as *The World* returned under another name with the same cast of characters doing essentially the same job, so the work of the Christian Institute was taken up by the existing South African Council of Churches, which since the early seventies had begun to take a less irenic role in seeking justice. Indeed, one of the provocative reports of SACC's early days, *Apartheid and the Church,* had been a joint venture with the Christian Institute. The cast of characters could not be quite the same, however, since their bannings were more durable than those of the journalists.

The current crisis follows the same pattern, but it is more diffuse. Although the series of states of emergencies was sparked by police killings in the Langa township near Uitenhage in early 1985, the number of incidents has been almost countless since then. The national event that began the present cycle was the campaign to boycott the constitutional referendum in late 1983 and the resentful aftermath of the new constitution's being adopted, since it virtually foreclosed the hope of any franchise for blacks and only gave the other races a cruel charade of representation.

Through this painful historical path the South African Council of Churches has come to form with its ally, the United Democratic Front, the chief organized focus of opposition to apartheid. Because it is exiled and impoverished, the African National Congress is not in the same position (although recognition by the United States government might change this drastically). It is alleged, but unproven, that SACC has aided and comforted the ANC, which only makes the point that SACC-UDF, not the ANC, is the power to contend with.

As we have seen, SACC is a principal player in the apartheid media wars, financing films, newspapers, and magazines as well as staging various meetings and events that call attention to grievances against the system. SACC has commissioned various special reports on squatter camps, relocations, health services, etc., that have been distributed internationally. The Interchurch Media Programme, headed by Rev. Bernard Spong, has been a spearhead facilitator of local church media programs, from small newsletters to slide shows to video, which combine the advantages of high-tech with the indigenous African sense of family and community; the special attention the program has received from the Security Police and the unjustified harassment of Spong and his underpaid workers show that they are considered effective.[9]

Yet when Rev. Jerry Falwell visited South Africa, the conservative Baptist clergyman and strong supporter of President Reagan felt that SACC was acting hypocritically and that many of the "real" Christian leaders he had talked with, for instance, were opposed to the imposition of economic sanctions and the disinvestment in South Africa, one of the major demands of SACC and of the Christian lobbyists against apartheid in America.[10]

Falwell is, of course, a spectacular example of American "state theology" and would hardly be expected to endorse any of SACC's initiatives. But he does raise the question of to what degree SACC *represents* Christians, churches, and blacks (Christian or not).

It is clear that the media, following their own intrinsic needs for clarity and drama, and without any necessarily biased political animus, can assign greater or lesser status to individuals as "black leaders." Desmond Tutu was catapulted by his position as general secretary of SACC to the Nobel Prize and to the Anglican primacy of South Africa, but as he has insisted over the years, he has no power, he is not the head of any political party. What of his church?

According to the 1980 census, less than 5 percent of South African blacks belong to the Anglican Church, whose membership is largely "coloured" and white. There are twice as many black Catholics, a body which cooperates with, but does not belong to, SACC. Father Smangalisu Mkatchwa, a black priest who serves as the executive secretary of the Catholic Conference of Bishops, has been very active with the United Democratic Front and has been detained by both the South African and Ciskeian authorities, as well as tortured by the latter. Only 10 percent of whites belong to the Anglican Church, but they tend to be English, middle class, and influential.[11] The Anglican Church has been outstanding in its constant efforts to reform apartheid peacefully, and its election of Tutu, given their membership, is a powerful political statement. Yet, though the Anglican leadership may speak for what they consider the best moral interest of the blacks, they cannot claim to represent them in any demographic sense. The numerically largest black political party, the Zulu Inkatha, is headed by an Anglican, hereditary Chief Mangosothu Gatsha Buthelezi, but he is not favored by the mainstream coalition of white and black opponents of apartheid.[12] Indeed, most people are not aware of Buthelezi's religious affiliation and consider it irrelevant.

Chief Buthelezi is not only a hereditary Zulu chief, he was originally a member of the ANC Youth League. Many forget that it was on the advice of Albert Lutuli and other ANC leaders that he participated in the setting up of KwaZulu as the "homeland" of his people. But Buthelezi refused to go along with the government's attempts to make it "independent," again folowing ANC policy. Buthelezi also had a brief flirtation with Steve Biko's Black Consciousness Movement.

After he broke with Black Consciousness in the early seventies, Buthelezi resurrected Inkatha, a then-dormant Zulu ethnic society. Because of his control of the KwaZulu adminstration, Buthelezi was able to reward loyal Inkatha members with patronage positions, and by 1985 Inkatha had about a million members.

Buthelezi's current isolation from the rest of the black opponents of apartheid and the Nationalist regime stems from the 1976 Soweto uprising. The Pretoria crackdown on dissenters and the banning of the ANC left a power vacuum into which he moved. This was bitterly resented. The force of this resentment was manifest when Buthelezi attempted to attend the funeral of a black radical, Robert Sobukwe of the separatist Pan Africanist Congress. He was stoned and spat upon by jeering young radicals who accused him of being a sellout. Thomas Karis, one of the leading experts on black politics in South Africa, notes that Buthelezi left in a crying rage, that he is a very sensitive man, and that the lasting effect of this experience on his political attitudes "is difficult to overstate."[13]

Since then, Inkatha has grown in power and influence and cautiously opposes Pretoria in ways that always leave open the possibility of a deal that would place the Zulu faction in an advantageous position in any new form of government. Buthelezi is still a formidable opponent of apartheid and has visited with many European and other heads of state, including Ronald Reagan, to seek an end to the current disfranchisement of all blacks, Zulu, Inkatha, or other. His Zulu power base, identification with approved "black self-government" in KwaZulu, and lack of deference to ANC or UDF initiatives have made him a figure of distrust for the mainstream opposition. But by no means can he be considered a minor figure in the antiapartheid struggle. Whatever his acceptability to the informal SACC/UDF/ANC coalition, there can be no doubt that he is a real leader of the largest single organized faction of blacks in South Africa and that he is opposed to apartheid.

Over one quarter of the black population are not Christian. Of the three quarters who are, almost half belong to the independent African churches, an indigenous mixture of African and Western religious traditions.[14] These groups are many and varied. The largest of them, the Zion Christian Church under Bishop Barnabas Lekganyane, holds a massive Easter assembly at its center in Moria, where more than one million gather. In 1985 State President Botha was an invited and honored guest. And as Chief Buthelezi pointed out in 1984, not a single indigenous church or synod had called for sanctions or disinvestment, further raising doubts about the representativeness of SACC, not merely of blacks but of its own member churches, whatever their racial composition.[15]

In terms of membership, SACC clearly does not represent the majority of blacks. But what about in terms of policies and beliefs? SACC, together with the UDF and the ANC, has pushed very hard for sanctions and disinvestment as a desperate, but necessary and effective, means of fighting apartheid. Is this the majority black view?

What *do* black South Africans think about sanctions and disinvestment? Everyone concedes that for the sanctions and disinvestment to work the blacks must suffer consequent economic deprivations. Archbishop Tutu, and a great many European and American opponents of apartheid not in South Africa, say that the blacks are already suffering a great deal under apartheid and a temporary increase in hardship will be well worth the price, for them, of eventual liberation.

It can be agreed that blacks hate apartheid, that they would favor any stratagem that might effectively rid them of its grinding injustices; can it also be agreed that they would hope to accomplish this without any needless intensification of their own suffering? There have actually been some opinion surveys of blacks in South Africa on these very questions.[16]

The London Sunday Times commissioned two polls a year apart which asked the same question: "Do you think other countries are right or wrong to impose economic sanctions unless South Africa agrees to get rid of the apartheid system?" In August 1985, 77 percent of 400 blacks in Witwatersrand, Pretoria, and Durban replied that sanctions would be rightly imposed. In July 1986, only 29 percent of 615 mixed rural and metropolitan blacks felt they would be rightly imposed. The second survey asked exactly the same question, but the sample, a larger one, included rural as well as urban blacks, and a second question was added: "Do you know or care about sanctions?" Thirty-nine percent said they either did not know or care about sanctions. This became the largest answer; 32 percent still opposed sanctions and 29 percent favored sanctions. It is of interest that *The New York Times* reported this same survey as showing blacks "about evenly divided" on the question of sanctions.[17]

In June 1984, 74 percent of 551 black male industrial workers felt it was "a bad thing" for "groups of people in America and England [to] try to encourage banks and organisations *not* to put their money in factories which are in South Africa." In November of the same year, 84 percent of male and female blacks in all major metropolitan areas of South Africa except Cape Town also felt such actions were a bad thing. This survey was conducted by South African academics known for their opposition to apartheid. In the same year the South African Human Sciences Research Council asked a stratified probability sample (similar to the sampling technique used in America to predict election results) of 1,478 black adults of both sexes: "Should the outside world apply an economic boycott against South Africa or not?" Eighty-two percent said that such a boycott should not be applied. The same question was repeated to a similar sample in May 1985 and 76 percent still felt the same way. Earlier in 1985 the same question was asked of a different sort of sample, which overrepresented more educated blacks; 63 percent were against the boycott. In July 1986, a major South African corporation asked a sample of adult blacks made up half of mining workers and half of other black adults in the Pretoria-Witerwatersrand-Vereeniging area: "Do you think large companies should be involved in bringing about political or social change in South Africa or should they concentrate on industrial growth?" If a person favored a company being involved in political or social change, further questions were asked about how. Two-thirds of the sample favored the companies seeking change but only 6 percent of the adults and 3 percent of the miners agreed that one of the methods would be to "not invest more money in South Africa or withdraw from South Africa until certain changes have taken place."

A more complex survey, which gave respondents a chance to nuance their responses, was designed and carried out during September 1985 by the Orkin Community Agency for Social Inquiry working with the Institute for Black Research and Research Surveys. Twenty-four percent of a stratified probability sample of eight hundred black adults in all the major metro areas of South Africa agreed with disinvestment as identified with the positions of the ANC, UDF, and other antiapartheid movements. Forty-nine percent agreed with the position that firms should invest, but only if they pressure the government to end apartheid and recognize trade unions chosen by the workers. This position was identical with that of SACC, and it was so known to be at that time. By 1986 SACC had virtually embraced the UDF-ANC view.

These figures represent the central tendency of polls taken in South Africa during the sanctions-disinvestment campaign.[18]

Alan Paton, the distinguished novelist, human rights activist, and former leader of the disbanded multiracial South Africa Liberal Party, called Bishop Tutu's "political morality" into question because of his constant pushing for sanctions and disinvestment.[19] Before the U.S. Congress took action Helen Suzman, the perennial Prog of Parliament and one with an international reputation for her dedication to equal human rights for all South Africans, strongly argued against sanctions and disinvestment in the lead article of *The New York Times Magazine* for August 3, 1986.[20]

By early 1987, South Africa was experiencing a slight economic upturn due, probably, to the availability of resources and capital assets at bargain rates as disinvestment proceeded apace. For instance, when Barclays Bank of the United Kingdom "disinvested" its 40 percent share of Barclays Bank of South Africa, the shares were snapped up at bargain rates by a South African consortium of businesses, spearheaded by the South Africa–based multinational conglomerate, Anglo-American. It is the not unfounded belief in Pretoria that both sanctions and disinvestment will promote "inward industrialization" as they did in the earlier arms embargoes, which stimulated South Africa to become a net exporter of high-tech arms after developing its own industry by means of a parastatal corporation (ARMSCOR). As for the hardships of sanctions and disinvestment, Pretoria is happy to pass them on to the frontline states, who depend on South Africa's economy for millions of dollars of guest-worker wages repatriated home and on South Africa's infrastructure to get and send products.[21] (About half of Zimbabwe's foreign trade must go through Durban's port facilities via South African railway connections.)

It is for these reasons that some opponents of apartheid see the development of Mozambique's seaports and rail and road corridors (particularly the crucial Beira corridor, 650 kilometers of rail, road, and pipeline between Harare, Zimbabwe, and Mozambique's port of Beira) as far more useful than sanctions or disinvestment. Furthermore, the United States, which has trumpeted its passage of a sanctions-cum-disinvestment bill, still supplies Jonas Savimbi's guerrillas, who are fighting South Africa's battles against the multiracial government of Angola, another crucial frontline state. It has even been alleged that in parallel with the secret and illegal Iran and Contra arms deals, U.S. interests are sending high-tech weapons to South Africa for Savimbi's use.[22]

No one can know the future, of course, and whatever happens, it will be difficult to assign major causes in a situation so complex. The only point that I wish to make here is that SACC, one of the major and constant indigenous forces against apartheid, has pushed hard for measures that would not seem to be endorsed by its own Christian constituency and about whose efficacy and morality there is some reasonable doubt in responsible quarters.

In view of these criticisms and constituencies, why were these measures seen as so crucial and urged with such passion by the international antiapartheid movement? The question is raised because it sheds light on the relevance and role of Christianity as embodied by SACC and its international affiliates in the fundamentally moral struggle against legalized white supremacy.

Whatever the moral or political value of sanctions and disinvestment, they were urged because of the leadership of SACC (and the ANC and UDF), and were achieved, in the action of the U.S. Congress, at least, because the black American caucus and the antiapartheid lobbyists in America saw them as things that America could *do*. SACC is supported almost entirely by overseas funds from the mainstream churches of Europe and America. Sanctions and disinvestment were also measures that these sponsoring churches could directly support in their own countries, measures that foreign media were in a position to report on with relative ease, since government and lobbyists need and serve the media.

Like the Live Aid program of rock concert support for Ethiopia, both the media and the political economies which support them are geared to the dramatic event and geared further to the events of the center as opposed to the events of what I have been calling the periphery, those areas outside the major market commitments of multinationals and not coincidentally beyond the high-tech coverage mechanisms of the generally richly capitalized international major media. It is a cliché that the media cannot deal with trends, that the spotlight of attention is always moving on, even though the problems remain—such as injustice in Vietnam or El Salvador. Apartheid is not an event, but a pattern of daily life under a bizarre hybrid of paternalism and repression. States of emergency are events; votes in Congress or Parliament are events.

Whatever the substantive merits of disinvestment and economic sanctions as *direct* instruments for erasing apartheid, the sanctions-and-disinvestment *campaign* was a brilliant strategy that captured and held world media attention for far longer than coverage of one more unjust system would ever merit. It thus mobilized world opinion against apartheid and set in motion countless initiatives that give great promise, in concert, of overthrowing the racist regime.

I wish to stress that the sanctions and disinvestment campaign of SACC-UDF-ANC has proven most effective against apartheid not because of the substantive effects of these financial actions (which are questionable), but because of their potential for mobilizing vast constituencies to try any number of means to thwart Pretoria and because of their psychologically isolating effects on the Nationalist Party and its supporters. It was essentially a media strategy, but by no means does this imply that it was therefore all image and no reality. Indeed, my growing conviction over the years is that image *is* reality in a wholly new way that we do not yet understand. (My additional thoughts on aspects of this situation are presented in "Excursus: Managing Appearances." pp. 200–202.)

In saying that events in the First World (the various national campaigns) would more likely be covered because of media logistics, which is indeed true, I have no intention of denigrating the minority, but not inconsiderable, media efforts to cover apartheid on the ground. We must recognize the heroism of journalists (cameramen and reporters have died on the job) and the willingness of major media organizations to spend money on a hot topic, however difficult and arduous field coverage may prove. The point is that the coverage must have some link with the central constituencies of the media, and the link must be readily perceived and facilely presentable. This, sanctions and disinvestment provided. By contrast, coverage of Chinese students demonstrating against the government in Shanghai and Beijing proved a brief blip. But if there had been a large Chinese-American congressional contingent, coupled with a motivated and muscled coalition of Chinatowns, both the nature of the coverage and its media shelf life would have been dramatically enhanced.

SACC showed considerable savvy in recognizing that a new phenomenon could be turned to the advantage of the repressed blacks of South Africa, who might not have been aware of the opportunity that SACC exploited in their behalf. Its strategists realized that international conflicts, ethnic interests, humanitarian causes, the continued viability of embattled regimes on the right and left—all these political issues—are increasingly not so much argued or urged, but rather presented manipulatively through cocktail parties, slide shows, rock concerts, music videos, and other tools of political public relations. Haircuts and haberdashery are drawing the attention of the Gorbachevs and Ortegas of this world since they have seen how far it has carried such diverse figures as Rajiv Gandhi and Ronald Reagan. Pope John Paul and Archbishop Desmond Tutu, in their varied and just causes, have little to learn from Madison Avenue.

The final push for the campaign was due to the very nature of SACC. SACC is strongly internationalist in both constituencies and funding; it must live on foreign largesse and must not only act in a good cause but also appear to act in a good cause in a way that is tangible to a very broad supportive constituency.

It may well be true that the prophetic role of church leaders permits, even requires them, to do what is in their view good for their flocks, even though the flocks might not quite see the good with the same moral clarity. SACC's lobbying for measures that do not seem terribly popular with its domestic membership may be accounted for in this way. But quite aside from these theological considerations, the positive choice of the measures of disinvestment and sanctions is directly connected with the pragmatics of SACC's position on the political grid of world media priorities.

The authors of the Eloff Commission report, issued in 1984, were not surprised by SACC's campaign, since they concentrated on SACC as a propaganda force acting to destabilize the apartheid establishment.

Although Bishop Tutu was predictably outraged by the report of the Eloff Commission, saying that it was "blasphemous" for any secular authority to pass judgment on the churches,[23] the recommendations of the report were unpredictably mild. Many had feared that SACC would be declared an "affected organization," meaning that it could not receive funds from overseas, a virtual death sentence for an organization whose support was almost totally foreign. The Eloff Commission avoided doing this on the realpolitik grounds that it would be impractical, since member churches could still receive funds, and counterproductive, since it would only create more sympathy for SACC internationally. With uncharacteristic generosity, the report conceded that SACC was an organization that provided many necessary charitable services to needy South Africans, but deplored the alleged political litmus test it applied to recipients—most being opponents of the regime, political prisoners and their families, etc.[24]

Subsequent to the release of the report, the August 21 edition of *The Star* indicated that SACC drought relief was being held back from Zululand because Chief Buthelezi's Inkatha movement was "on the SACC blacklist." In November, Buthelezi charged that SACC's joint screening committee was the "primary tool" for blocking "Christian aid for the programme of self-help development which KwaZulu and Inkatha were trying to foster."[25] The Eloff Report maintained that SACC denigrated Inkatha overseas so that it would not siphon off financial assistance that might go to SACC; this astounded Buthelezi, who had refused to testify against SACC before the commission, even though, he said, SACC had done its "damnedest to vilify" him abroad.[26]

What the Eloff Commission did recommend was either a new law or an amendment to the Internal Security Act which would make advocacy of disinvestment or economic sanctions a crime under some such title as "economic sabotage." In late 1986 this came about under one of the numerous emergency regulations that have made so many types of utterance "subversive," and thus punishable under existing law.

If the law had been in effect during the entire stewardship of Desmond Tutu over SACC, he would have been a spectacular repeat offender. During the 1986 and 1987 state of emergency, he has continued to urge both measures of retaliation against his own country in no uncertain terms. To date, his eminent international and ecclesiastical position has kept him out of jail.

Eloff devoted a great deal of space to Desmond Tutu and considered him the primary propagandist of the antiapartheid movement, mightily assisted at that time by his base in SACC. There is a certain truth to this charge. Tutu has a natural talent for using the media; he is a moving preacher, a witty and telling debater, a great manipulator of would-be piercing interviews, and a natural coiner of the one-liners that media people love to quote. Above all, he is a brave man, willing to say what he feels he must, no matter what the consequences to his own safety or comfort. His new position as archbishop of Cape Town does not seem any less powerful and protected.

The report also devotes some space to Dr. Wolfram Kistner, a name with no recognition value outside of WCC circles and his own church. He is director of SACC's Justice and Reconciliation Division and, in Afrikaner eyes, the mastermind behind the massive antiapartheid propaganda effort associated with WCC and Tutu. (This recalls the view that Joe Slovo, a white, must be the brains behind the ANC.)

Kistner, unlike Tutu, is a campaign strategist. It was he who was instrumental in calling SACC's attention to the importance of the international media and in getting expert media advisers from all over the world, principally from Germany, to formulate a strategy that the Eloff Report quotes with grudging admiration as the "communications project document":

According to Bishop Desmond Tutu, General Secretary of SACC, South Africa is . . . in the midst of a massive psychological warfare. . . . Since mass media establishment is the main theater of operations of the psychological warfare in South Africa, it is particularly important for SACC to be able to handle the media in an appropriate manner. . . . This indicates four different targets for SACC communication strategy:

- the general public in South Africa, represented there through the mass media establishment in particular;
- and through the alternative media at the grass roots sections;
- but also through the international media with their correspondents;
- and finally the SACC itself, member churches and their co-workers as well as the widespread net of SACC staff.[27]

Kistner has always put great emphasis on actions that call into question the legitimacy of the government, as when he suggested to a conference of ministers that they might not wish to register as marriage officers any longer since it was a form of recognition of an evil government. He has been very much influenced by Paolo Freire's notion of consciousness-raising and by the general Latin American approach to grassroots media.[28] One recalls the affinity of *Grassroots* with *La Chica Prensa.*

During his testimony before the Commission of Inquiry, Kistner was forthright about his advocacy of civil disobedience, as were many others who testified in behalf of SACC, including the now well-known envoy of the archbishop of Canterbury, Terry Waite. Although this evident thrust of SACC, especially its encouragement of conscientious objection in a country desperately short of trustworthy armed men to carry its growing military burden, was a matter of outrage to the government, the commission singled out the use of funds as the point of state correction and recommended that SACC be subject to the restrictions of the Fund Raising Act, which might well prevent SACC from using its funds for its obvious political purposes. To this end, in a classic South African legalism, the commission suggested that the relevant statute might be changed to require "spiritual" purpose be proven by the regulated organization, since "religion" might well be interpreted in the dread "social gospel" sense.

After the report was released, it sparked a lively debate in Parliament,* where the Pinelands member, Dr. Alex Boraine, had a spirited exchange with the then minister of law and order, Louis le Grange. Boraine was comparing SACC to Israel under the pharaohs when the minister accused him of advocating disobedience in a Christian state. When Boraine replied that there was not one Christian state in the world, Le Grange seemed genuinely bowled over by the assertion. It was Boraine's turn to be stunned when Le Grange announced he had a copy of Boraine's private notes, acquired by "his staff," that is, Security Police.[29] So much for the legitimate government's respect for legitimacy; Boraine may have been too outraged to see that the minister's actions had totally undercut the minister's position.

It is ironic that the government should try to undermine SACC by questioning its legitimacy. Does the National party, so obsessed with protocol and procedures and constitutionality, rule by means of law, or by means of brute power with a security apparat that mimics and undercuts, anonymously, illegitimately, the visible government?

In the media rhetoric of democracy, the terms "white minority rule" and "the black majority" obscure the issues of justice and truth. If the Nationalist Party represented a white majority, it would hardly legitimate its racist policies; just so, a black majority government would hardly be justified in instituting an apartheid of

*Reaction outside parliament to the Eloff Commission report offered an encapsulation of the apartheid media wars up to that point. For an overview of editorial opinion showing the range from oppositionist to loyalist, see Appendix 2.

its own. Any honest assessment of the situation indicates that there is no clear organized *majority* of any color, only contending and confused factions of every color. In the end, it is not who has the most guns, or the most bodies, or the right color that achieves legitimacy. It is those who speak for justice and seek it by honest and just means.

NOTES

1. South African Institute of Race Relations, Survey of Race Relations in *South Africa, 1984*, p. 911.

2. Main Committee Investigation into Intergroup Relations, *The South African Society: Realities and Future Possibitilies* (Pretoria: Human Sciences Research Council, 1985), p. 36.

3. South African Institute of Race Relations, op. cit., pp. 905, 907.

4. *South African Observer.* 21, no. 1 (June 1986): 2.

5. Richard Usher, "White Rightists Challenge NP," *Africa News,* 26, no. 12 (June 16, 1986): 11–12.

6. Allister Sparks, "South Africa: Apartheid, Apartheid Uber Alles," *Washington Post National Weekly Edition,* June 9, 1986, pp. 16–17.

7. South African Institute of Race Relations, op. cit., p. 906.

8. John W. de Gruchy, *The Church Struggle in South Africa* (Grand Rapids, Mich.: William B. Eerdmans, 1979), p. 66.

9. Bernard Spong, *Interchurch Media Programme Annual Reports,* 1983, 1984, 1985 (Johannesburg: Khotso House, 1984, 1985, 1986). Mr. Spong shared many of his experiences with me in personal interviews during 1983 in South Africa and during 1986 in New York.

10. Beth Spring, "Falwell Raises a Stir by Opposing Sanctions Against South Africa," *Christianity Today,* October 4, 1985, p. 52.

11. Main Committee Investigation into Intergroup Relations, loc. cit.

12. Geoffrey Wheatcroft, "Toward Racial Reform in South Africa," *New York Times,* December 21, 1986, p. 13. See also South African Institute of Race Relations, op. cit., p. 917.

13. Thomas G. Karis, "Black Politics: The Road to Revolution," *Apartheid in Crisis,* ed. Mark A. Uhlig (New York: Random House, 1986), p. 123.

14. Bernard Lategan, "The Republic's Religions: Preaching Beyond the Pulpit," *Indicator South Africa,* 3, no. 3 (Sunner 1986): 14.

15. South African Institute of Race Relations, loc. cit.

16. Lawrence Schlemmer. "The Sanction Surveys: In Search of Ordinary Black Opinion," *Indicator South Africa* 4, no. 2 (Spring 1986): 9–12.

17. Adam Clymer, "Poll in South Africa Shows a Rise in Whites' Distaste for Apartheid," *New York Times,* August 3, 1986, p. A1.

18. Schlemmer, op. cit., p. 12.

19. *South African Digest,* November 16, 1984.

20. "What America Should Do about South Africa," pp. 14 ff.

21. John D. Battersby, "Sanctions: A War of Attrition," *Africa Report,* January–February 1987, pp. 4–9.

22. First reported in the British daily *The Independent,* December 9, 1986.

23. South African Institute of Race Relations, op. cit., p. 912.

24. The document's official title is *Report of the commission of Inquiry into South African Council of Churches.* The commission was chaired by C. F. Eloff and is thus referred to as the Eloff Report. The document is 450 pages of repetitive testimony, spuriously precise, with an excessive number of sections and subdivisions. I obtained a copy of the document and managed to read through it. Both proponents and opponents of the government's view made a great deal out of uncovered illegal financial maneuvers involving the revered John Rees, the white layman who transformed SACC by bringing in so many blacks and making sure that they were treated equally in wages and in access to the highest positions, including his own. All admit that for years the financial management and accounting of SACC was at best amateurish, and there is no doubt that, in the instance Eloff hammers at, serious impropriety existed. Nonetheless, I think it would be foolish to be distracted by what is a minor point in the debate and the conflict from a larger perspective. The government report itself is not accessible to those outside South Africa without considerable difficulty, but there is a special summary available from the government printing office in Pretoria ("Report of the Commission . . . Churches: Short Summary Concerning Financial Matters"). The Annual Survey of the South African Institute for Race Relations, an indispensable and objective reference source for anyone writing about South Africa, offers a brief and accurate summary of the main points in its 1984 number (pp. 911–14). One of the last issues of the now banned SACC newsletter, *Ecunews* (March 1984), was devoted entirely to a summary of the report, which of course cannot be from a disinterested point of view, and of reactions to it.

25. South African Institute for Race Relations, op. cit., p. 916.

26. Ibid., pp. 913–14. In 1986, what Conor Cruise O'Brien has called the "Buthelezi Option" had received serious attention in South African and some American media *(CBS Sixty Minutes, Atlantic Monthly)* although the Botha government has recently rejected the possibility (cf. Wheatcroft, *supra).* Briefly, it is that the entire province of Natal, a rich and large area of South Africa that includes the third major city, Durban, and that has a principally English and Indian population among non-blacks (Indians so consider themselves, for the most part, although the antiapartheid movement considers all nonwhites black), become an independent "homeland" for all races in it, and that it be ruled by Buthelezi under some form of constitutional monarchy (Buthelezi is a hereditary chief and the non-Zulu population would insist on democracy). Cf. Karis, "Black Politics."

27. *Eloff Report,* pp. 244–45.

28. Marjorie Hope and James Young, *The South African Churches in a Revolutionary Situation* (Maryknoll, N.Y.: Orbis Books, 1981), pp. 94–95.

29. John Scott, parliamentary observer for the South African Associated Newspapers, reported this debate in his column for February 28, 1984.

CHAPTER SEVEN

Communicating Legitimacy

The Afrikaner oppositionist novelist, J. M. Coetzee, remarked wistfully to Conor Cruise O'Brien that he used to wonder why South Africa could not have become another Brazil.[1] Chester Crocker, the architect of the now discredited "constructive engagement" policy of the Reagan administration, remarked on the *McNeil-Lehrer News Hour* that South Africa was not the fifty-first state. Former U.S. Representative James Symington, whose law firm lobbies for the South African government, has compared Americans' perception of South Africa to a "time machine" through which they painfully reenact their experience of the American civil rights struggle of the sixties.[2] When I first saw Pieter Dirk Uys, the cabaret satirist, do his hilariously bitter drag number of an Afrikaner matron, I could not help but think of *Cabaret*, the American musical made from Christopher Isherwood's cycle of short stories about Berlin in the early days of the Nazi party. There is desperate humor in the snug bunker while outside Jews were being kicked to death as the great dark political night of the twentieth century was gathering.

Because South Africa is so distant from the Atlantic community, yet so historically and economically tied to it, one searches for the reassurance of familiar stereotypes, and one can easily find them. But do they reveal or conceal this land?

I had come to South Africa by way of Brazil, taking off from Rio under a glorious southern winter moon and gliding by Table Mountain on a dazzling sunny morning. Rio and Cape Town also present obvious parallels. Spectacular mountains marching to the sea, miles of beach, luxury hotels, bustling cosmopolitanism. Perhaps this is the setting for what Coetzee may have had in mind. I had my own eye peeled for telling comparative images and was immediately struck by what I thought would be a poetic and powerful metaphor for political reality.

In Rio, walking down the packed streets, my eyes frequently lifted up to the many great volcanic columns that punch up dramatically through the city to hundreds or even thousands of feet. Corcovado, on top of which is the famous statue of Christ, is one. Sugar Loaf, not so high, is another. I was puzzled by the frequent plumes of smoke, some with flame, that rifled the air high up on these towers. It turned out they were caused by small hot-air balloons, raised by on-board paraffin flames, that had crashed into the sides and started brush fires, too high to be put out or to threaten life. The balloons were jubilant gestures with no great purpose beyond amusement and of course were against the fire code. They were not noticed much by the inhabitants, who were likely to be killed by one of the many careering autos if they took their eyes off the street.

In Cape Town I also noticed some smoke plumes on the distant slopes of Table Mountain, as it rises behind and above the city. Were paraffin balloons a mark of the southern hemisphere? I was told that there were homeless people living in caves on the mountainside, and their presence was tolerated in this land of regulated residences because they helped to put out fires which were beyond easy reach of the fire department. It was believed they set the occasional fire to solidify their rather filmsy legal grounds for squatting.

Perfect! The social systems of each country in a nutshell! The colorful comparisons could come pouring out of the word processor! But they would be so terribly misleading. Brazil and South Africa certainly have taken divergent paths in both the cultural and political handling of multiracialism, but the former is far from a happy land of freedom and the latter is regrettably not unique in repressing its inhabitants.[3]

As Edward Jay Epstein and others have noted, the news business, particularly the television news business, must struggle to present the new not only in terms of the familiar, but in terms of readily digestible themes.[4] Looking over recent years of South African news videotape from ABC, CBS, BBC, UPITN and other mainstream organizations, I was struck by the resourcefulness of the coverage, its attempt to get footage of the unusual, the efforts to balance crisis with color. Inevitably, of course, one is overwhelmed with images of angry blacks, jogging in place with upraised fists, of coldly infuriated Afrikaners, desperately trying to explain the obvious in terms of the doublethink that apartheid breeds; of police charging with whips and dogs, of celebrated victims of apartheid, like Winnie Mandela, whose understandable desire for vengeance and settling the score comes through whatever rhetoric of reconciliation is being offered. When the state of emergency of 1985 and 1986 extended the control over reporters, the control itself became a familiar theme, leaving the substantive issues of the struggle behind, a result not entirely displeasing to the censors.

Modern media are too sophisticated and too consciously dedicated to balanced reporting to deal in blatantly misleading stereotypes. The bias comes out in the themes, the implicit comparisons of present events with previous stories. This is frequently an unconscious process, similar to the way generals tend to fight the last war and reporters are prone to cover the last election. The overwhelming theme of the apartheid struggle is the framework of the American civil rights struggle, since it is both familiar and reasonably appropriate, complete with an activist and brave clergy.

South Africa is being judged by European and American standards, not by Third World standards. Since most press coverage of foreign affairs takes a First World viewpoint, this is hardly surprising. There is the further reason that South Africa is both a First and Third World country, the whites and some few of the other races living in an advanced industrial economy, the blacks and some few of the other races living in the poverty of the homelands and the majority of the townships. The National Party has sought to choose its themes and its comparisons according to its own propaganda needs. When they wish to be seen as bulwarks of civilization in a savage continent, then they are indubitably of the First World. When they wish to be seen as a transitional country, trying to rise up to difficult standards for which they are not yet ready, then they are a Third World country. Ironically, it should be noted that this double standard is characteristic of the Third World, which for the most part consists of countries with a small elite class of fabulous wealth (as in Brazil, the Phillipines, India, for example) which lives on estates with townhouses in the capital city and a huge underfed and underhoused class of urban proletariat and peasants. Whatever the form, aid for the poor rarely comes from the indigenous wealthy but rather from international agencies or First World countries through the not unprofitable brokerage of the indigenous wealthy.[5]

The propaganda of the apartheid media wars, as in all modern media warfare, is the struggle for the appropriation of the most useful theme, which in turn requires the exploitation of selective contexts. In the old wars of debate and rhetoric, the person who set the state of the question, defined the terms, had a winning advantage. In the media wars of public relations and imagery, the person who sets the themes and contexts for the scenarios acquires the tacit consent, if not the approval, of the world media audience. Tacit consent is often all one can hope for and all one really needs, for it prevents mobilization of countervailing forces. So long as the American public saw the Vietnam War as some sort of repeat of the Second World War, opposition was sporadic and ineffectual.

An outstanding example of context shaping and theme choosing appears in Paul Johnson's masterful polemical essay, "The Race for South Africa." Originally appearing in the conservative *Commentary*, it was understandably reprinted in the South African government's *South Africa International*.[6]

Johnson is a former editor of the *New Statesman*, and a prolific writer of books of great sweep, among them an immense history of Christianity and a chronicle of the twentieth century, both packed with confident judgments about complex issues. I have briefly chatted with Johnson and can report that his reputation for not being tentative seems fully earned.

The article in question appeared during the debate in the U.S. Congress about sanctions. (It should be noted that sanctions are trade restrictions imposed by governments, political acts having economic consequences; disinvestment decisions, apart from those of government pension funds or other state holdings, are economic moves by private corporations having political consequences and motives, too, no doubt.) Like Helen Suzman's *New York Times* article referred to in the last chapter,[7] it was apparently intended to influence the debate, which, of course, it failed to do. Given the manner of its presentation, the article may have influenced the vote *for* sanctions in a minor way, for it assails the American blacks' defensiveness about Africa and abrades the political sensitivity American whites have about seeming to patronize blacks.

Given this, it seems to me that Johnson's point was not intended so much to influence the congressional debate but to put forward, without squeamishness, the scenario and the context within which he, and many conservatives, feel the international apartheid debate should proceed.

For Johnson, South Africa is not so much to be classified as First or Third World, but as African. South Africa is typically African in six ways:

- It is suffering a population explosion.
- It is *tribally* divided.
- Its cities and towns are under great immigration pressure from the countryside.
- It addresses these problems with a brutal form of social engineering that is both repressive and fundamentally anti-capitalist.
- The repression is applied on a tribal-racial basis.
- The repression and the form it takes is justified by a quasi-mystical official state philosophy–religion.

Johnson sets great store in tribalism as a uniquely African feature, noting that no other continent is so fragmented and that colonialism set up artificial larger units that violated tribal borders and cultural differences. The modern black states created from former colonies have inherited this unworkable, ungovernable mixture of traditions, religions, and political loyalties. He ticks off the no doubt real diverse ethnic groups in such places as Nigeria, Rwanda, Uganda, Sudan, and Chad, and notes the attendant civil strife and bloodshed and lack of stable government.

Without missing a beat, Johnson glides from this to the statement that whites are the second largest group in South Africa, after the Zulus, being careful to point out that the Zulus and the whites are further divided into diverse ethnic groups. I do have trouble with this step. How are the Germans and English and Dutch and French and Jews and Greeks formed into one race or tribe, whereas the blacks are not permitted this level of social organization? I suppose it is one way to maintain that "whites" are a larger "group" than the Xhosa, the third largest, by this mathematics.

One of the effects of the rural pressure on urban centers is the terrific crime rate, which no one disputes. But how does one present the crime rate and in what context? Johnson indicates that Lagos, Nigeria, and a half-dozen other black cities have a much higher murder rate than any place in South Africa, but that the rate in Soweto, with 1,454 homicides in 1985, is alarmingly high and taxes the thinly stretched police force. He notes that all governments feel they must act ruthlessly in "shantytowns" lest the entire city become "ungovernable."

Careful readers of the world press are well aware of the civil warfare and repressive dictatorships of Africa, granted that less is reported about them than about South Africa, because anti-establishment reporters are less tolerated in places like Zaire or Uganda. Political scientists and serious students of Africana may also be aware of the state creeds of various repressive states, such as Senegal's Negritude, Tanzania's Ujaama, or Zaire's ridiculous Mobutuism. Johnson takes these acknowledged realities, so diverse and difficult to classify, and shamelessly converts them all into identical apples in that large African basket which before was so multifarious and varied ("No other continent is so fragmented"). Apartheid, we are breezily informed, is just South Africa's version of this universally African political ethos.

A lesser talent would be trapped here. If it is in the nature of Africa to spawn brutal and repressive regimes, to harbor ungovernable cities with mind-boggling murder rates, then surely civilized intervention is called for. One remembers the French paratroopers arresting the mad "Emperor" Bokassa and the multilateral African effort that toppled the insane demogogue Amin. Forward the ANC, with American and European aid!

But Johnson is ready for this. South Africa is the same—but different. It shares six characteristics with the rest of Africa (its faults). It is different from the rest of Africa in four ways (virtues, perhaps?):

- It is rich because of its mineral wealth.
- It has a modern industrial economy.
- It has a large black middle class.
- It has a rule of law and is a democracy.

Johnson admits that the last point is subject to serious qualifications, but (and now we are back in the Third World context again) South Africa is the only country in Africa where there is a separation of powers, where despite draconian emergency decrees black litigants can and have successfully sued the state. At this point, Johnson's tactical command of comparative statistics ("[T]here are more black-owned cars in South Africa than there are private cars in the whole of the Soviet Union [?!]. . . . more black women professionals in the Republic than in the whole of the rest of Africa put together") fails him utterly. There is no mention of the numbers of detainees held without trial relative to the number of successful black litigants, but one could say that there are more detained blacks in jail now than there have been successful or even unsuccessful black litigants in the history of the Republic.

One must always bear in mind, when reading tendentious essays of this type, that the manipulating of assumed background is a tactic far more effective than presenting the arguments of the foreground. It is dictated by the importance of getting people to see the facts in the context of the author's choosing. I believe the following to be the most audacious appropriation of a useful context I have seen in any polemical writing: "South Africa has a parliamentary constitution with a limited franchise, rather as Britain had in the early 19th century. Like Britain then, and unlike the rest of Africa now, it has been moving toward democracy rather than away from it." Johnson goes on to salute the new constitution's granting of a limited franchise to Indians and "coloured" and offers: "No one doubts that the blacks, who already have the vote in local government elections, will get it in some form in central government elections." Since South Africans as diverse as

Percy Quoboza and Zach de Beers have both expressed such doubts on international television, we can doubt the literal truth of the last statement.

The Commonwealth Mission, or "Eminent Persons Group," which visited South Africa some months after these doubts were expressed (June 1986) would seem regrettably to bear them out. After trying to get the Nationalist regime to negotiate with the ANC, the mission was informed that groups rights, "homelands," the new tricameral legislature, and population registration—all foundation stones in the wall of apartheid—were to be considered irremovable. One man, one vote in a unitary state would be out of the question. The Commonwealth Mission formally stated:

> From these and other recent developments, we draw the conclusion that while the Government claims to be ready to negotiate, it is in truth not yet prepared to negotiate fundamental change, not to countenance the creation of genuine democratic structures, nor to face the prospect of the end of white domination and white power in the foreseeable future. Its program of reform does not end apartheid, but seeks to give it a less inhuman face. Its quest is power sharing, but without surrendering overall white control.[8]

Outside of government spokespeople, the general observation on the new constitutional arrangement is that the legislature—white, Indian, or "coloured"—has been eviscerated by the executive. When two out of three houses declined to support the new security legislation of 1986, the "impasse" was constitutionally resolved by the "President's Council," a group of appointed delegates whose name tells all. As mentioned earlier, the National Security Council, with a large military contingent, is the effective ruler of South Africa today (insofar as anyone is effective). When Conor Cruise O'Brien asked an Afrikaner specialist in military intelligence what future circumstances might possibly lead the South African Defence Force to throw off civilian control, he was met by a deadpan: "You are supposing that there is civilian control at the moment."[9]

Despite what I believe are fundamentally wrong assessments of both the political and moral significance of apartheid, Johnson does make some valid points about the likely substantive effects of disinvestment and sanctions. Others have said that such measures will hurt the innocent. Johnson has pointed out that it won't hurt the guilty, whom he considers to be the hard core of isolated Afrikaner landowners and farmers; they believe in apartheid as a divine truth, and seek isolation and self-sufficiency anyway. Johnson also makes the telling point that advanced capitalism and apartheid are at fundamental odds. Both O'Brien, hardly a capitalist tool, and Johnson agree that apartheid is bad for business, since it constricts the range of free markets.

All the same, it seems a shame that a man of Johnson's stature should so distort the realities of South Africa if his only purpose was to try to thwart the sanctions-disinvestment tactic.

The argument one most often hears for these actions, of course, is that economic sanctions and disinvestment, as effective economic steps, would damage the South African economy to such a degree as to render the country unmanageable and thus bring about the downfall of the current regime. Many doubt this; there are just too many trading partners available outside the sphere of the antiapartheid movement. Halton Cheadle, the civil rights lawyer and labor organizer, told me in a private conversation, right after the U.S. Congress decided to impose sanctions and during the steamrolling movement among private companies to disinvest, that, in the short run at least, the effect would be to spur the indigenous economy of South Africa by providing productive assets to local investors at bargain rates.

The General Secretary of the Congress of South African Trade Unions (COSATU), Jay Naidoo, made it quite clear at the congress's 1987 convention that much so-called disinvestment was actually "corporate camouflage" for management's evasion of its obligations to indigenous labor. He called for complete disclosure of information to the unions and negotiated withdrawal of foreign investment so that workers would "get what's coming to them." With this understanding, COSATU endorsed both mandatory sanctions and total disinvestment."[10]

Although the more important psychological and public opinion effects of sanctions are hard to predict,[11] the known amount of American investment provides a yardstick for measuring the strict economic effects of disinvestment. On these grounds, both the proponents and opponents of American investment in South Africa would seem to have exaggerated its scale.

When Coca-Cola, for instance, pulled out of South Africa, only 460 of the over 4,000 South Africans involved in manufacturing, selling, and distributing Coke could have been affected, for that is the number that works for the *American* company; the rest work for the South African owner of the Coca-Cola franchise. Overall, about one black out of every 120 in the workforce is employed by Americans. So, if all the American companies were to pull out immediately and if, an unlikely event, all their employees were instantly put out of work, less than one percent of the labor market would be affected. When it comes to paying full wages for those detained by the Security Police, a few South African firms do so; but no American firms do (some pay a portion).

Many American firms pursue policies that defy apartheid, but in a climate of increasing misunderstanding and mistrust by the black militants of the townships. Seven million dollars was spent by a consortium of American firms for Planned Advancement of Community Education Commercial College in Soweto. Initially a great success in preparing blacks for advanced positions, it had by 1985 become a target of the general school boycott; two months after the students burned an American flag, the college suspended operations.[12]

The sanctions-disinvestment issue is raised here again because it provides a finite lens for our examining the dynamics of the debate without our being daunted by the diffuse nature of the apartheid media wars.

The Christian Century cited with approval the testimony of U.S. Episcopal Bishop John Walker at the U.S. Senate hearings of August 1986 on the proposal of sanctions. A close friend of Archbishop Tutu and a sworn foe of apartheid, the Bishop stated:

> Our agony over the plight of black people often has trapped us into taking actions that may be more pronounced in their symbolism than in their capacity to bring about substantive change.[13]

None of these considerations count for much among the leading forces of the antiapartheid movement outside of South Africa nor among the main opponents of the regime within South Africa: the SACC, the Council of South African Trade Unions (COSATU), the United Democratic Front (UDF), and all the complex interlocking coalitions they represent, who have pushed very hard for sanctions and disinvestment.

Lenoard Thompson, Charles J. Stillé Professor of History Emeritus at Yale and the director of the Yale-Wesleyan Southern African Research Program, who has a reputation for moderate and informed judgement based on immense scholarly experience, is a foursquare proponent of sanctions and disinvestment. He is one of those who believe sanctions made a serious contribution toward the downfall of the Smith regime in Rhodesia. He believes any additional suffering the blacks may endure as a result of this policy would be marginal and bearable. He further believes that it is in the best interests of the United States to impose sanctions and encourage its businesses to leave South Africa, because not doing so is badly hurting U.S. credibility with the Third World. He feels sanctions and disinvestment would give an "immense boost to the black people of South Africa."[14]

The case against the imposition of sanctions-disinvestment because the economic effects would alter politics in a way inimical to the anti-apartheid struggle is made by Helen Suzman, a doughty opponent of apartheid and of the National Party in the old and new forms of Parliament. She presents a succinct position that both opposes apartheid and economic punishment of the entire country and of the many countries that depend on the economic health of South Africa:

> Unpalatable as it may seem to the sanctions lobby, the most practicable way to get rid of apartheid and to achieve a nonracial democratic society in South Africa is through an expanding, flourishing economy. The process of integrating blacks as skilled workers into such an economy would be expedited. Their economic muscle would then, through increased trade-union action, be a potent force not only in the workplace, but also in the sociopolitical sphere. Strike action and consumer boycotts—both of which can be used as temporary expedients, unlike disinvestment and mandatory sanctions—are the most powerful weapons for blacks to use to resolve important issues like political power-sharing.
>
> Indeed, consumer boycotts have already been used to great effect in some parts of the country, such as the eastern Cape Province, where many white-owned shops were brought to the brink of bankruptcy. Conversely, if blacks are unemployed and have nothing to spend, such boycotts would be meaningless. It is astonishing to me that those advocating punitive actions do not realize that, if successful, they will have undermined the most significant power base that blacks could acquire. . . .
>
> It may well be that such arguments fall on deaf ears, and that they are advanced in a lost cause. Nevertheless, they deserve to be made in the interest of millions of moderate South Africans of all races who abhor apartheid, who have long fought the abominable practices of race discrimination and who are striving for a peaceful transition to a peaceful democracy. For them, at least, it is surely not too much to ask that they be spared the violence and misery of a scorched earth policy.[15]

On January 8, 1987, the seventy-fifth anniversary of the founding of the long-suffering African National Congress, it seemed the earth might be scorched a bit sooner than Helen Suzman envisaged. Whether sparked by the U.S. Congress's vote on sanctions or not, both the ANC and the Pretoria government were further than ever from conciliation. In his anniversary address on Radio Freedom, the ANC station in Lusaka, Zambia, Oliver Tambo, president of the ANC, called on blacks to carry out armed attacks against strategic targets in white-controlled areas to help create a "mass revolutionary basis" in black areas, by which he clearly meant active combat forces. He also called on white civilians to join with ANC blacks in these attacks, calling them "white compatriots" for "democracy" against "racist tyranny."[16] He did this when U.S. Secretary of State George Shultz was in Africa, the George Shultz who days before his leaving to visit various black African governments voiced the "serious concern" of the Reagan Administration about ANC ties to Moscow. In fact, the U.S. State Department released a special report on the anniversary of the ANC, almost as Tambo was speaking, in which it noted with alarm that about half of the ANC Governing Council are active members of the South African Communist Party.[17] Together, the statement and the report constitute a rather shabby courting of the paranoia of the extreme right, whose support helped put Reagan in the White House.

Many American scholars of black South African politics, particularly Thomas G. Karis, one of the leading experts, find the evidence of strong Moscow ties to the ANC, of the type alleged in the State Department report, to be flimsy and the reasoning to be tendentious.[18]

Since media influence on popular perceptions is a vital factor here, Karis's dissection of the alleged Moscow link is worth recounting.

On July 26, 1986, *The* (London) *Economist* maintained that, of the thirty members of the ANC Executive Committee, at least ten and possibly fifteen were members of the South African Communist Party (SACP). This and similar statements are good examples of the mainstreamed mistake so typical of the increasingly incestuous international media, who pick up an "interesting" or "dramatic" allegation from perhaps an at first acknowledged source, and then pump it though repeatedly without attribution until it becomes what Norman Mailer has called a "factoid." This particular assertion seems to have begun with Senator Jeremiah Denton's (Republican, Alabama) Subcommittee (Judiciary) on Security and Terrorism, which uncritically relied on information supplied by the South African government and its intelligence agencies in 1982. In June 1986, after the South African government had distributed a booklet listing twenty-three members of the ANC Executive Committee as either communists or their "active supporters," Congressman Dan Burton (Republican, Indiana) promoted nineteen to actual membership and opined that perhaps as many as thirty (the full committee) were communists. Two months later, the CIA declassified its biographies of ANC Executive Committee "communists," at the request of Senator Jesse Helms (Republican, North Carolina).

Karis grants that three members of the ANC Executive Committee are publicly acknowledged members of the South African Communist Party: Joe Slovo, the number three military man in the ANC, is SACP chairman and white. Steve Dhamini and Dan Tloome, the other two, are elderly former trade unionists and long-time ANC supporters. He further grants that there may be some others, but hardly as many as ten, and that there is no evidence for considering any more to be members of the party.

It must be remembered that the ANC, like the UDF, and the SACC, is a *coalition* of a number of different groups, parties, and organizations—a characteristic of the apartheid society and its politics. The ANC, as editor Joe Latakgomo said of Desmond Tutu, would ally with the devil himself to fight apartheid. The SACP, for its part, acknowledges a two-step plan: First, alliance with the antiapartheid forces to remove the National Party racist government; then, after a transition of indefinite length, a move toward socialism. Karis, like virtually all other specialists in the field, sees the ANC leadership, the black trade union movement, and other antiapartheid groups as having resorted to a wary use of communist support, after being rebuffed by the West in the seventies and eighties, on the principle that "the enemy of my enemy is my friend."

The ANC is a widely supported and dispersed organization, perhaps more so because it cannot legally exist within South Africa. It has twenty-eight offices from Melbourne to Moscow. Scandinavians supply 20 million dollars annually. Several million dollars more in refugee aid is provided by various United Nations agencies. Other aid in lesser amounts comes from the governments of Italy, Austria, several Third World nations, Oxfam, The World Council of Churches, and several Catholic aid agencies. Nonetheless, Soviet-bloc military support accounts for over half of ANC overall support.[19]

One of the CIA's top candidates for communist agent among the ANC leadership is Alfred Nzo, whom they describe as a "self-avowed communist." Professor Karis heard Nzo personally deny this and declare himself an African nationalist. The CIA biography cites as proof of its characterization Nzo's public remarks in praise of the international policies of the Soviet Union and his long-standing opposition to United States actions in Vietnam, Grenada, Nicaragua, Mozambique, Angola, and elsewhere. Nzo also favors the Palestine Liberation Organization and the Non-Aligned Movement.

These positions, though hardly right wing, do not require subversive intent or membership in the Communist Party. In fact, it is rumored that even some loyal American citizens have not been enthusiastic supporters of American military activities overseas.

More troubling than ANC's real or alleged links with the South African Communist Party is its apparent loss of control of the "comrades" and "children" of the townships, whose fury is without strategy or sanction and has led to indiscriminate "necklacing" in South Africa. The inflammatory rhetoric from ANC's Radio Freedom in Lusaka, is a sorry attempt to stay ahead of its increasingly chaotic constituencies. William Murray's recent well received survey of the South African struggle states:

What is taking shape across the country, without any help from Moscow and very little from Lusaka, is a loosely organized, radical mass movement of youngsters who operate outside any law and without identifiable leaders. They see themselves as socialists and their enemy as white capitalism. . . . In some ways, the unrest has taken the ANC by surprise, and they are certainly not in control of it or in any position to be able to control it. . . .

In Mamelodi (a black township near Pretoria), young black gangsters indulged in the fanciful charade that they were comrades 'engaged in the struggle' but instead they terrorize residents in the name of the UDF. . . . [Other such gangsters in the eastern Cape region formed] clandestine people's courts to 'punish' those alleged to have hindered 'the struggle,' meting out primitive sentences on wrongdoers. For those condemned to death, a tire doused in petrol was draped as a 'necklace' around the head and shoulders of the accused and then set alight.[20]

The 1987 anniversary of the ANC was also the day the National Party regime chose to shut down *The New York Times*'s Johannesburg bureau by denying a work permit to Alan Cowell, the incumbent bureau chief, and a visa to Serge Schmemann, his scheduled replacement. The reason given was the disadvantage to Pretoria of the alleged continuing negative coverage of its policies and subsequent adverse effect on American public opinion, which contributed to the sanctions vote in Congress.[21] It can be no coincidence that Tambo arrived in Washington twenty days after his call for violent uprising to confer with members of Congress and Shultz. Whatever the signal Congress intended to send, the sort of signal Tambo received is clear. To add that bizarre South African touch to these all-in-one-day happenings, Pretoria issued the latest example of its concern for law and order even as it restricted the press still further. The day before Tambo spoke, all the major English-language papers ran full-page advertisements calling on the government to recognize the ANC. Rather than simply arrest the perpetrators of the ad or close down the papers or (for it must have known) just prevent distribution of the papers in advance, the government enacted a new regulation making it "subversive" from then on to issue a report or carry an advertisement that would "improve the image" or "defend the policies" of any banned organization.[22]

By the end of January 1987, when Botha officially opened Parliament, two days after Tambo met with George Shultz, the rule of law and the censorship of the press in South America had come full circle. On January 29 the Supreme Court had declared the January 9 banning of any advertisement that might enhance the image of an outlawed organization an unconstitutional expansion of police power. Pretoria struck back the very next day with an emergency proclamation that gave the police commissioner unlimited powers of censorship over anything he chose. The game of legal piece-by-piece removal of freedom of the press was over, and the pretense of respect for free expression was stripped away with finality.

Ironically, on the day of the press banning, the SABC on both radio and television quoted the banned Oliver Tambo, and the government gave all the media permission to use quotes from Tambo that they had selected. This unprecedented coverage of an official "unperson" was occasioned by Tambo's aforementioned meeting with U.S. Secretary of State George Shultz on January 28, a meeting that right-wing pressure on the Reagan administration had kept in low profile. Tambo's remarks, which had been made in Washington, D.C. (at Georgetown University), but separate from the meeting, were called "shocking." Among other things, he said that the "killing of some whites" would be "beneficial" because it would get whites used "to the idea of bleeding."[23] Neither the context nor the many balancing statements Mr. Tambo has made about solidarity with whites against tyranny were permitted to be quoted.

In his official address at the opening of Parliament on that same busy and fateful media day, State President Botha declared that there would be elections on May 6 for the White Assembly. He said this in the face of numerous defections from the Nationalist Party from the left and the right. The papers for that day carried the news that his ambassador to Great Britain would resign his position in order to campaign against the Nationalists for dragging their feet on announced reforms, such as that of the Group Areas Act, the basis of residential segregation that looked more entrenched than ever.[24]

When events are both so fast-moving and so long in being precipitated, it would be imprudent to pontificate on their precise meaning, and it would be fatuous to offer a prediction. I offer a narrow reading of the current situation from the viewpoint of a student of media wars, of modern mass propaganda, and of the reactive role of leaderships to it.

Pretoria lost the media war on two fronts: the domestic and the international.

It must be said that this victory of the free press, this refusal to be effectively muzzled, required two domestic factors within South Africa: first, journalists who were and are willing to go to jail, to lose their jobs, to lead unglamorous, impoverished lives, in order to tell what they see as the political truth; second, a government that keeps a scintilla of respect for the idea of a free press and always holds back from the ultimate solution—unmitigated totalitarianism. As Gandhi said, he was fortunate in his opponents. A John Dugard or a Percy Qoboza could simply not exist in Albania or Uganda or Iran and, *per impossibile,* if such a one ever did, his or her career would be short and silent. To imagine the Pol Pot government expelling *The New York Times* bureau chief requires patently absurd presuppositions about the prior establishment of a bureau.

The Pretoria government has lost the war of images on the international stage of public opinion, principally among American opinion leaders, the arena they are most concerned with, because the odds against them were overwhelming and because they have neither the skill nor the stomach for the slick public relations stratagems that might have given them a limited chance to kill the sanctions movement in Congress.

The odds: They were up against a wide and deep coalition of First World blacks and their passionately dedicated white Christian allies. They were up against the international solidarity of trade unions. They were up against the Second World of socialist states and communist superstates, who see, and wish the world to see, apartheid as capitalism unmasked: a vivid black-and-white demonstration of the exploitation of labor. At the same time, and woe betide anyone benighted enough to provoke both these antagonists, they were up against the mainstream of multinational capitalist corporations, who realize that apartheid, in a world of unregulated international capital markets and globally mobile labor "platforms," is an outdated and impractical nationalistic method of exploiting labor.

Finally, and most appositely, they pitted themselves most foolishly against both ends of the international media world: mainstream high-tech information conglomerates, like the BBC, *The New York Times,* the major wire services, American television networks, and European state-operated electronic news-gatherers, on the one hand, and small-bore "liberationist" journalists from churches and new-left organizations, on the other hand. At one and the same time they faced the mouse, the poorly paid amateurs putting together technically incompetent anti-apartheid handouts, and the mountain, Richard Attenborough, commanding prodigious artistic and technical forces, who filmed the new *Gandhi*, the life of Steve Biko, *Cry Freedom*, in Zimbabwe.

Unable to smother the voices and forces of opposition, what of Pretoria's ability to tell its side of the story, if not to the world, at least to the movers and shakers of the world, where money and realpolitik talk? On this score, I don't believe the government ever had a chance, because of long-term Afrikaner traditions and recent political history.

The first week I was in Jo'burg, Charles Barry of *The Star*, with characteristic generosity, arranged for a luncheon meeting with a number of journalists and broadcasters at the Country Club, a central symbol of white privilege, where golf and cricket are played on clipped greenswards and delicate fish are forked over snowy linens while deals are made. Robin Knoxe-Grant, then head of English programming for SABC, was there, and I believe it was he who raised the question of Muldergate, largely, I thought, to forestall my raising it.

Muldergate, to refresh our memories, also known as Infogate, was the revelation, chiefly through investigative reporting, of gross misappropriation of public funds for the purpose of funding a variety of clandestine propaganda plots from 1972 to 1978. The most notorious of these involved the establishment and continual subsidy of a progovernment English-language newspaper, *The Citizen*, going so far as to hide its need for subsidy by falsifying circulation figures. Some of the other schemes involved the attempted purchase of American newspapers in California and Washington, D.C. As mentioned earlier, the revelations ruined the careers of Connie Mulder (who may join Captain Boycott, more ironically, as an enricher of the English language), the responsible minister of information, and brought down a prime minister (Vorster). No one went to jail, however; *The Citizen* is still in print and *The Rand Daily Mail*, which played the role of the *Washington Post* in this parallel to Watergate, was to die later under mysterious circumstances.

Visiting Americans in journalism were at the time of my visit (1983) still eagerly inquiring about the finer points of the debacle. English-speaking journalists were then relishing the discomfiture of the formerly self-righteous Afrikaners, who, with the powerful state apparat behind them and the SABC virtually one long paid commercial for the regime, still found it necessary to play dirty.

Knoxe-Grant, of relentlessly British mien, was an employee of the state broadcasting apparat, whose bosses were and are deep-dyed Broederbond. His combination of apologetics and eagerness to get the subject behind us, it seemed to me at the time, was more than just the weariness of a local with a tourist topic. Muldergate, beyond its political significance, raised again the bitterness of the past, when the Afrikaners were looked upon by English speakers as loutish simpletons, unfamiliar with the niceties of afternoon tea, tacit rules of office behavior, and how to get on in the great world.

Reading the excellent accounts of the scandal and observing the characters involved, especially the very visible "deep throat," Eschel Rhoodie, Mulder's agent and tempter, one is struck by its klutz-content, not foreign to the archetypal Watergate botched burglary and later red-wigged disguises.[25]

I bring this up in the current context of the lost propaganda war, because I think it accounts in part for Pretoria's failure as a lobbyist in Washington. High-style government PR is a preeminently British game. Poor Ambassador Herbert Beukes, clutching his teacup, would be no match for the Prince of Wales. Muldergate made the Nationalists hypersensitive about swanky PR ploys.

Before the infamous "gate" suffix found its way to Connie Mulder, it was briefly attached to Korea, referring to the mid-seventies scandal of big bucks being lavished on chosen Congressmen and high-powered Washington law firms by the Asian dictatorship—money well spent, since it produced millions of dollars of support in one form or another for this authoritarian bulwark against communism. Other staunch opponents of creeping socialism such as former President Marcos of the Philippines and the former terrors of Haiti, Papa Doc and Baby Doc Duvalier, were equally generous to public relations firms throughout the United States.

In the market mentality of the hired gun, all money is green. Burson-Marsteller, a public relations firm in Washington, D.C., served the Argentine junta, as J. Walter Thompson briefly, through a subsidiary, served the Chilean junta.[26] Saudi Arabia and Japan between them spend over twenty million dollars a year on commercial and political lobbying. The South African government spent a bit over one million dollars in 1985. Separate business lobbies for South Africa (who may themselves be opposed to apartheid) like Intergold and the South Africa Foundation together spend less than that on strictly political lobbying. The

South Africa Tourism Board spends about two and a half million, and Intergold has a huge budget, for its commercial ventures, of twenty-four million dollars.[27] Intergold spent its political money, in vain, it turned out, to keep the Krugerrand from being banned in America.

Pretoria's money went principally to three lobbyists: Baskin & Sears (later just Sears alone) received $500,000; Smathers and Symington, $350,000; Black PAC, $390,000.[28] Philip Baskin was a Mondale fund-raiser during the 1984 campaign, and John P. Sears was Ronald Reagan's first campaign director in 1980. James Symington was a Congressman from Missouri, and George Smathers was a U.S. Senator from Florida. Black PAC, a Republican political action committee, is headed by a black American, William A. Keyes, formerly a Reagan White House aide.

There is no doubt that these lobbyists, and others, slowed the U.S. Congress in voting sanctions against Pretoria and pumped blood into the Reagan administration's dying "constructive engagement" to the last possible minute. No doubt they can keep alive U.S. support for the enemies of the enemies of apartheid, using the communist bogey, in Angola, Namibia, Mozambique, and possibly even Zambia. But the money and the slick argument could not have overcome the powerful coalition of interests so fundamentally opposed to apartheid. Pretoria's weakness is that it could not project its own sense of moral uprightness beyond the tiny *laager*.

The tactics of all the lobbyists were faultless; they contacted key players in all the constituencies, and they did so persuasively and with style. The problem lay with the compelled strategy: they could not be in favor of apartheid. They had to be able to demonstrate that the most reliable team for the demolition of the apartheid structure were its architects and those who had benefited most from it. They had to share moral revulsion and then point out the prudence of delay in ridding the world of its chief perceived racist scandal. Back home, Pretoria was, by its own lights, going at breakneck speed in demolishing a variety of legal props of apartheid that had barred races from intermarrying, devised racist residential districts, and restricted jobs and ownership on racial grounds; the regime even stretched to the point of dismantling the underpinning of the homeland policy: separate racial citizenships.

To Pretoria's surprise, these real legal measures were perceived as cosmetic because they were so patently ineffectual. The world could not believe that their enactors were not fully aware of their ineffectuality.

The law. The Nationalists were paying the price of pretending that the law was the key to the creation and the destruction of apartheid. The hundreds of laws, against the press and against the blacks, were bizarre constructs mostly hammered together after the fact to prevent a cultural or social or political move that would have weakened the politicosocial structure that had been fashioned long before 1948 by the father of modern racism, colonialism, in South Africa as in India. The Afrikaners thought they could make the arrangement permanent—legitimate—by rigging a Kafkaesque web of silly rules from 1948 onward at the same time that the rest of the world was discarding the legal underpinnings of racism and replacing them with more up-to-date instruments of exploitation and subjugation derived from other criteria of willed superiority, such as class, ownership, nationality, party membership, revolutionary loyalty, sheer brute possession, or, most effective of late, religion. Since 1948 these varied ideologies had managed to spark a number of quite sizable massacres, remarkably like racist pogroms in effect, in places as diverse as Nigeria, West Irian, Cambodia, China, and elsewhere.

The United Nations played a key role in this media war because it provided an image for all the players of the world audience. Derided by its isolationist detractors as a debating society with hypocritical double standards, politicized beyond the point of parody, seen as a tool of the Soviets by conservatives in the United States, condemned as a front for the Atlantic Alliance by the Third World, the United Nations was crucial precisely because of these perceived shortcomings in the apartheid media wars. More than in most contexts, here image is decidedly reality. Racism was one topic on which all three worlds not only could agree but were eager to appear to agree. South Africa's location and population placed it outside any indisputable sphere of influence, like NATO or the Warsaw Pact or the non-aligned nations. With all of the severe political problems, to say nothing of hot wars, going on in the world among member states of the United Nations, it has three separate entities focused on the apartheid struggle, a Special Committee of the General Assembly, an Ad Hoc Committee trying to come up with some sort of international convention against apartheid in international sports, and a special Centre Against Apartheid, which not only provides information about the problem but also has a branch specifically dedicated to promotion of antiapartheid activities. Only the transnational corporations and the Palestinians merit so much special bureaucratic attention at UN Plaza.

Once one has cynically examined all the realpolitik reasons for the failure of Pretoria in the media wars, one is still left with the force of moral argument on the world stage. A truly cynical view would hold that world media could by no means have an effect on a powerful government in place and in charge, as Pretoria still is. But they did.

The neo-Marxist view of the global media is that they are the lackeys of First World transnational corporations, with an outmoded understanding of news as the exceptional event. At the same time that these media make headlines of disasters, they place these headlines in a context of conventional expectations about the values of the world as seen through Western bourgeois spectacles. The overwhelming effect is to legitimate further the status quo. The state-security view, often associated with the North American and Latin American right, is that the media are irresponsible sensationalists, with no sense of loyalty to local forms of order, with a schoolboyish penchant for ridiculing the grown-ups who have to make sure the trains run on time. This view not infrequently is exaggerated by a form of rightist paranoia to the point where journalists are seen as actual agents of subversion, in league with rebels and traitors against the state.[29]

That these radically opposed extremes each have touched a truth about the media is beyond cavil. But the media, like the world, are incorrigibly plural. Swimming against both of these strong currents is an international camaraderie of perpetually indignant truth-seekers, burning to know and itching to tell the rest of us what they find out, in the often disappointed hope that when the public learns of abuse or injustice, it will move to correct it.

The apartheid media wars seem to have brought out the best in world media and to have confounded the cynics of left and right. Newspapers owned and operated by major corporations who were and are involved in businesses which revolutionary change would damage never let up on the Nationalist regime, devising stratagem after stratagem to evade the purpose of hundreds of restrictive press laws. The very real price that Argus and SAAN have paid for their opposition may not appease Marxist critics or dissuade even moderates like John Dugard from asking for more, but it does show that journalists have fought apartheid, and have fought it bravely.[30]

That Pretoria has lost this phase of the apartheid media war, of course, does not automatically mean that anyone else, like the ANC, has won it. What it does mean, no matter what the future holds, is that regional and local struggles, if they can be brought to center stage, will be subject to a moral judgment, not necessarily a correct or perfectly informed moral judgment, but a moral judgment nonetheless. Look around. All those conflicts, from the superpower Cold War to the regional fights from Ireland to Israel to Iran to Pakistan to Nicaragua, are not only played out on the ground with fists and bullets; they are played out on the screens and pages of the world. It is depressing that most of what we hear is the result of laboriously contrived deception, but it is encouraging that both the good and the evil feel they must make their case before some kind of vague world opinion, an opinion that cannot be measured, but that must be taken into account, into final account. When the devil feels he must conceal his horns and wear top hat and tailcoat, the moral world, however feebly, has extended sway over raw nature, red in tooth and claw. If one believes that hypocrisy is the tribute that vice must pay to virtue, then the growth of world PR, like the growth of world media, is something to salute—while no doubt covering one's wallet.

Using the slow and limited press of the nineteenth century, the Abolitionists managed to outlaw slavery internationally. Satellites and color television are undermining legal racism internationally. Amnesty International's campaign against torture, like the other media wars, operates on two premises: the effectiveness of public relations techniques and a fundamental human decency that universally rejects cruelty and injustice.

The apartheid media wars provoke a reflection about this wider context.

NOTES

1. Conor Cruise O'Brien, "What Can Become of South Africa?" *Atlantic Monthly,* March 1986, p. 50.

2. Sanford J. Ungar, "South Africa's Lobbyists," *New York Times Magazine,* October 13, 1985, p. 115.

3. Amnesty International provides a depressingly universal survey of human rights abuses annually which can serve as some sort of standard of comparison. On Brazil in particular, cf. Joan Dassin (ed.) *Torture in Brazil: A Report by the Archdiocese of Sao Paulo.* Translated by Jaime Wright (New York: Vintage Books/Random House, 1986). Jane Kramer baldly states that the Brazilian *ditadura* from 1964 through 1985 was noted for its sadism, social terror, and corruption, and since then is best remembered for its stupidity ("Letter from the Elysian Fields," *New Yorker,* March 2, 1987, p. 40).

4. Edward Jay Epstein, *News from Nowhere: Television and the News* (New York: Random House, 1973).

5. Cf. Peter Worsley, *The Three Worlds: Culture and World Development* (Chicago: University of Chicago Press, 1984), esp. pp. 315–322. Richard Critchfield, *Villages* (Garden City, N.Y.: Anchor Press, Doubleday, 1981), esp. pp. 225–235. Peter Berger, *Pyramids of Sacrifice: Politi-*

cal Ethics and Social Change (Garden City, N.Y.: Anchor Press, Doubleday, 1976).

6. *Commentary,* September 1985, pp. 27–32; *South Africa International,* January 1986, pp. 119–28.

7. Helen Suzman, "What America Should Do about South Africa," *New York Times Magazine,* August 3, 1986, pp. 14 ff.

8. "Excerpts from Report on South Africa Issued by Commonwealth Mission," *New York Times,* June 13, 1986, p. A13.

9. Conor Cruise O'Brien, op. cit., p. 63.

10. "COSATU's Call for Sanctions," *SACTU News Flashes,* no. 33, August, 4, 1987, p. 4.

11. The Comprehensive Anti-Apartheid Act, passed by Congress on October 2, 1986, required the State Department to submit a report to the President by April 1, 1987, listing those countries that supply arms to the government of South Africa. The President was then obliged to review the report with a view to stopping military aid to any country on the list. Israel was a standout on the list, because it is both a very large supplier of arms to South Africa and the major recipient of United States military assistance.

As a result, there has been a continuing struggle within the Israeli government. The vast majority wish to maintain their low-visibility high support of Pretoria for reasons of solidarity with the important (about 120,000) Jewish population and for reasons of realpolitik, since South Africa and Israel have supported one another in the past and are both, for different reasons, outcast nations. A small minority, led by Yossi Beilin, the political director general of the Israeli Foreign Ministry, and Amnon Rubinstein, the minister of communications, feel that the U.S. concern for not seeming to support a racist regime and the inevitable obliteration of apartheid under some form of black rule together make both a practical and moral case for cutting off trade, or at least arms trade, with South Africa. The majority, which includes the ruling party and the major opposition party, would at most allow some token reductions and a tightening of the already considerable cloak of secrecy around the relationship between the two countries. The publicly known commercial trade in 1986 involved about one hundred million dollars worth of exports from Israel and about forty-four million dollars worth of imports from South Africa. But the secret arms trade is said to amount to hundreds of millions by itself and to be an important part of Israel's extensive, and aggressively marketed, arms industry.

On March 18, 1987, the Israeli government announced it would not sign any future military contracts with South Africa, but existing contracts and clandestine deals would keep the trade going far into the future. This measure went far enough to maintain the flow of U.S. aid. In the unlikely event that the minority truly and completely wins its case, this would definitely be a serious blow to Pretoria. Cf. Thomas L. Friedman, "Israelis Reassess Supplying Arms to South Africa," *New York Times,* January 29, 1987, pp. A1, A6.

12. Cf. Michael Massing, "The Business of Fighting Apartheid," *Atlantic Monthly,* February, 1987, pp. 26–32.

13. *The Christian Century,* November 19, 1986, p. 1021.

14. Leonard Thompson, "What Is To Be Done?" *New York Review of Books,* October 23, 1986, p. 7.

15. Helen Suzman, op. cit., p. 17.

16. Sheila Rule, "South African Rebel Leader Calls for Widening of 'Armed Attacks,'" *New York Times,* January 9, 1987, p. A2.

17. Neil A. Lewis, "U.S. Says South Africa Rebels are Obligated to Communists," *New York Times,* January 9, 1987, p. A2.

18. Thomas G. Karis, "South African Liberation: The Communist Factor," *Foreign Affairs,* Winter 1986–87, pp. 280–287. Cf. also Tom Lodge, "The African National Congress in South Africa, 1976–1983: Guerilla War and Armed Propaganda," *Journal of Contemporary African Studies,* 3, 1–2 (1983–84).

19. Mark A. Uhlig, "Inside the African National Congress," *New York Times Magazine,* October 12, 1986, pp. 20ff.

20. Martin Murray, *South Africa: Time of Agony, Time of Destiny* (London: Verso, 1987). Cited with endorsement by Leonard Thompson, "Before the Revolution," *New York Review of Books,* June 11, 1987, p. 26.

21. "South Africa Bars Times Correspondents," *New York Times,* January 9, 1987, p. A3.

22. "South Africa Tightens Curbs on Newspapers," Reuters Wire, January 9, 1987; also, Nigel Wrench reporting from Johannesburg by satellite on National Public Radio *Morning Edition,* January 9, 1987.

23. Nigel Wrench, live by satellite from Cape Town for National Public Radio *Morning Edition,* January 30, 1987.

24. John Madison, live by satellite from Cape Town for National Public Radio *Morning Edition,* January 30, 1987.

25. Cf. William A. Hachten and C. Anthony Giffard, *The Press and Apartheid: Repression and Propaganda in South Africa* (Madison, Wisc.: University of Wisconsin Press, 1984), chap. 10. Richard Pollack, *Up Against Apartheid: The Role and the Plight of the Press in South Africa* (Carbondale, Ill.: Southern Illinois University Press, 1981), passim.

26. Greg Goldin, "The Toughest Accounts: How Madison Avenue Sells Foreign Dictators," *Mother Jones,* January 1985, pp. 27–29.

27. Cf. Sanford J. Ungar, op. cit., p. 112.

28. Ronald Grover, "Nice Work If You Can Stand It: Lobbying for Pretoria," *Business Week,* September 30, 1985, p. 47.

29. The long-lived debate over a "New World Communication Order," sparked by UNESCO and kept alive by the Third World elites and Second World owners of state media, is the current context for this perennial conflict. I refer the reader to: Cees J. Hamelink, *Transnational Data Flows in the Information Age* (Amsterdam: Chartwell-Bratt Ltd., 1984); John A. Lent, editor, *Third World Mass Media: Issues, Theory and Research,* Studies in Third World Societies no. 9 (Williamsburg, Va.: Department of Anthropology, College of William and Mary, 1979); Armand Mattelart, Xavier Delcourt, and Michele Mattelart, *International Image Markets: In Search of an Alternate Perspective,* trans. David

Buxton, Comedia Series no. 21 (London: Comedia Publishing Group, 1984); John C. Merrill, *Global Journalism: A Survey of the World's Mass Media* (New York: Longman, 1983); Jim Richstad and Michael H. Anderson, eds., *Crisis in International News: Policies and Prospects* (New York: Columbia University Press, 1981); Robert L. Stevenson and Donald Lewis Shaw, eds., *Foreign News and the New World Information Order* (Ames, Iowa: Iowa State University Press, 1984).

On some representative areas and countries, see Robert McDonald, *Pillar and Tinderbox: The Greek Press and the Dictatorship* (London: Marion Boyars, 1983); R. C. S. Sarkar, *The Press in India* (New Delhi: S. Chand & Co., 1984); Frank Okwu Ugboajah, ed., *Mass Communication, Culture and Society in West Africa* (New York: Hans Zell/K. G. Saur, 1985).

30. Dugard was harshly critical of editorial opinion in much of the English press during the campaign for the referendum on the new constitution. "[T]hey do not give a damn. Profit, not politics, is their prime concern." Cf. South Africa's *Sunday Express*, Oct. 7, 1984.

CHAPTER EIGHT

World Media and Global Conscience

The embarrassing parallels to South Africa's apartheid system in other countries, including our own, and the moral demands focused on South Africa by the rest of the world through media pressure place an old question in a very new context: Is there a natural law of universal human morality that underlies and overrules any national law?

Modern international recognition of such a fundamental morality has been expressed in a series of conventions and accords from Geneva to Helsinki under the more recognizable modern rubric of "human rights," accelerated by the United Nations enshrinement of the language in the Universal Declaration of Human Rights shortly after the foundation of the organization (1948). Since then, scores of national constitutions and dozens of particular global and regional conventions have adopted the principles of the UN declaration, to the point where it has the force of customary law within nations, according to many legal scholars.[1] Most appositely in the context of this book, it was the ruling of the International Court of Justice against South Africa's rapacious and cruel rule over Namibia, made in 1971, that explicitly applied the UN declaration to the heretofore sacrosanct "internal affairs" of UN member states.

The idea of universal and fundamental moral law is behind the campaign against torture of Amnesty International today and was the driving engine of the Abolitionist Movement against slavery in the last century. Neither initiative sought to *prove* that slavery and torture were morally wrong—that was and is assumed as obvious. Just so, the American Founding Fathers assumed it a self-evident truth that all men are created equal. To deny these kinds of truths is to deny one's own humanity.

This universality has been mightily accelerated by the new global media environment. Dramatic examples abound.

In the eighties, the plight of starving Ethiopians was broadcast to the world. That knowledge produced shame, and that in turn led to an international rock concert which itself was sent by satellite simultaneously from Hong Kong to Hollywood. Sales of the record and other proceeds from the event and the song, "We Are The World," went into an international private effort to bring food to the victims who inspired the drive and the deed.

In the spring of 1985, the American Broadcasting Company's *Nightline* broadcast from South Africa by satellite to the world interviews and conversations among leaders and dissenters, a number of whom could not have met under other circumstances without breaking South African law. In trying to explain themselves to Ted Koppel, they were all, from Botha to Qoboza, implicitly accepting the moral judgment of the great world beyond South Africa. This understanding has even managed to infect the SABC, which has had discussion shows with the minister of information and fractious editors like Tertius Mybergh, who burst into derisive song when the minister suggested that foreign television news really entertained rather than informed. The specific program was not particularly enlightening, but it sprang from an assumption that opposing sides can and do share legitimacy, an assumption not nearly as evident beyond the studio walls.

The international campaign against apartheid is thus part of a larger and longer movement that has been enormously accelerated by the growth and sophistication of global communications and international news media.

From one perspective the global media environment we all share can be seen as the culmination of a broad historical trend, despite serious setbacks, toward a global consciousness, a more universalist outlook, which can only strengthen the conviction that we are one, that we *are* the children of this planet, and thus aid the growing concern for human rights and the sanctity of the individual.

The media foster this healing perception in two ways.

First, the global media system subjects local barbarisms to the censure of international elite opinion. The same kind of pressure that South Africa felt was also placed on the junta in Argentina. Granted that an Iran ignores or defies such opinion, even a traditionally xenophobic giant like Russia, blinking in the new light of *glasnost,* is increasingly concerned about how its policies are playing on the great stage of the world. The inside, as it were, is exposed to the fresh air of the outside.

Second, the outside is delivered to the inside. Undreamed-of material standards are shown in living color to the drab Third World, igniting unrest and revolution as well as shifts to high productivity economies and high expectancy polities. It took centuries for Greco-Roman civilization to spread to the Indus and the Thames; the process of diffusion was so long in developing that the changer and the changed produced third realities, modern Europe to the west, cultures as diverse as Russia's and India's to the east. European colonialism by contrast was a blitz campaign of less than five hundred years. The marriage of the microchip and the satellite in the service of global media have made current cultural diffusion a matter of decades and years. The impact is not only swift, it is also direct and uniform, so syncretistic adaptation is replaced by rough-and-ready substitution. Korean students demonstrate as if they were French.

Despite the resultant dislocations, should we not applaud a development that can serve as the basis for a universalist morality that may do away with torture as official state policy, just as the universal spread of uniform medical procedures has done away with yellow fever?

Regrettably, the role of the media in the world is manifold and certainly cannot be seen in utopian or mystic terms. Some cautionary, but by no means dismissive, notes must be sounded. For one thing, to draw hope from the technical potential of global mobilization for worthy causes is not to ignore the maudlin and manipulative dimensions they inevitably contract, as in the bafflingly vacuous "Hands Across America" event. More seriously, to note these signs of apparent integration among cultures, across oceans, and most difficult of all, across desks, is not to gloss over the divisive uses of modern communications technology, especially the propaganda radio employed by all nation-states.

The global media are certainly not automatic forces for good in the world, but I do believe that they have an intrinsic bias toward global unity and equality. This can promote a positive moral effect despite the intentions of the users. Paradoxically, the very effort to "win hearts and minds" for narrow causes provokes unanticipated notions of global solidarity because of its operational assumptions about common motivations for loyalties.

Their danger, to my mind, springs from exactly this same intrinsic bias.

The mass media require *masses*. They not only *can* reach immense audiences, they also *must* reach immense audiences in order to recoup their enormous capital costs. With this bias toward larger and larger audiences, the technology encourages users and producers to overcome the principal nontechnical obstacle to worldwide communication: language.

But language is the traditional vehicle for morality. *Habeas corpus* is not just a Latin tag for a technical rule, it is the time-traveling capsule that preserves an idea of justice, fairness, logic, and proof. Yet some uses of global media require the obliteration of cultural connotation, and thus ultimately of moral evaluation. In casting down barriers to turn things inside out, global media run the risk of tearing the heart out of civilization. Without safeguards and countervailing interests, the end result could be a world of neither inside nor outside, neither right nor wrong, just policies and problems. We have a current example of this amoral antiseptic attitude in Patrick Buchanan's description of the Iranian arms deal as merely "controversial," since it did not work and provoked opposition.

This style of global media environment is not so much like a global village as it is like the concourse of a vast international airport, whose only common language consists of aseptic ideograms for luggage and toilets.

The unanswered question is whether the new internationalism will be acultural, in the sense of amoral, or transcultural, in that it will obliterate tribal taboos. Will the new global media environment make of Mother Earth a dread global anthill, as envisioned by George Orwell and E. M. Forster, or will it usher in a period of respect for the law of nations, the common morality so yearned for by philosophers and jurists from classical antiquity to today?

It depends on which class of interests determines the kind of language, and thus the type of moral outlook, that will dominate world media content.

If the language powers of the world were exclusively government or corporate apparatchiks, Orwell's prophetic warning would long ago have come to pass in full. At this very moment, the U.S. government has produced a pamphlet for the edification of those who might be subject to a nuclear attack or some sort of Chernobyl disaster. The pamphlet is classic Orwell. It states that radiation will occur; that radiation produces fever; that water and aspirin help reduce fever. True, but hardly the truth, since in effect it is advising Americans to take aspirin for nuclear disaster.

Fortunately, language is not solely in the hands of such people. The South African community media, la chica prensa in South America, novelists, poets, and playwrights around the world, newly aware of each other's work through international journals and conferences, and groups like PEN, the international writer's organization, Amnesty International, and the various civil and human rights groups springing up in virtually every nation, even the most unlikely, may well prove to be the collective David who wrests control of modern communications technology from both the ideologues of hate and the bland amoral exploiters of the world as mere market.

In the meantime, we cannot enjoy the luxury of simplistic moral judgments about what is the dominant trend in world media influence.

Although the children of light and the children of darkness are conveniently differentiated when one compares, say, Amnesty International's use of public relations techniques with that of Lieutenant Colonel Oliver North and his shadow irregulars, in many instances the distinction is not so clear-cut. The political and moral ambiguity of the bitterly controversial *Graceland* produced by rockfolk composer and performer, Paul Simon, spotlights the Janus face of world media.

Simon's *Graceland* tour, starring a number of versatile South African black musicians who specialize in *mbaquanga,* "township jive," has appeared in stadiums and theaters all over the world. It has played in England, Western Europe, the United States, and even in South Africa's neighbor to the north and possible model for the future, Zimbabwe—the black-ruled independent country with a sizable white minority that rose from the ashes of Ian Smith's white supremacist Rhodesia.

In addition to South Africans from the townships, the *Graceland* company features long exiled black South Africans Miriam Makeba, who sings "Soweto Blues," and trumpeter Hugh Masekela, who plays "Bring Him Back Home," referring to Nelson Mandela. The tour has played to packed and pounding fans. In Rotterdam, the Netherlands, which has been very active in anti-apartheid causes and in fundraising for the struggle, the tour opened to standing ovations and the rhythmic Dutch chant of "oh-wey" from the white European crowd. In Harare, the capital of Zimbabwe, in a stadium guarded by the army against possible terrorist bombs or other forms of violence, the black crowd went wild with enthusiasm, despite the scorching heat, abetted by the bright lights of a videotaping destined for worldwide cable distribution. Each show ends with both performers and audience rising to sing what has become the anthem of the antiapartheid struggle, *N'Kosi Sikeleli Afrika* (God Bless Africa).[2]

Ray Phiri, *Graceland* guitarist and leader of the Soweto band Stimela, says that the Zimbabwe appearance of *Graceland* was the biggest hit of his life; "Our music gives the people hope." Phiri is happy to acknowledge that he has been given tremendous exposure to the world outside of South Africa "because of Paul Simon." He adds that a song like " 'Homeless,' is talking about our very present [South African] situation . . . You don't get up and say things are bad without offering a solution. I respect people who come up with solutions, not people who come up with big wind that means nothing."[3]

Hugh Masekela finds the *Graceland* tour a form of liberation. He says "one of the things that made the world realize what was happening to African-Americans in the United States was music. At the time they were being lynched, long before civil rights. Yet Duke Ellington, Count Basie and Miles Davis could make this incredible music in spite of all that. It was through them that you knew about the plight of the people."

Simon feels that "a strong artistic community within South Africa is important to ensure freedom of expression. If there is a change in the form of government, there still has to be freedom of expression. The strongest way of ensuring that is to have a thriving community of really powerful internationally known artists."[4]

Simon is the producer of the *Graceland* tour, not the star. *Graceland* is a variety show featuring South African musicians, with South African bands and the now famous a capella Zulu song-and-dance troupe, Ladysmith Black Mambazo, whose hit international album, *Shaka Zulu*, Simon produced.

Simon paid the South African musicians triple New York union scale.

One third of the proceeds from the final part (eight appearances) of the *Graceland* tour will be sent to Allan Boesak's "Children of Apartheid," a fund set up to aid detained children. The rest is marked for the United Negro College Fund and charities in each city where the tour has appeared.

Simon has written to the United Nations Special Committee Against Apartheid pledging his continued support of the boycott as he understands it, since he has turned down million-dollar contracts to perform in Sun City, and considers himself an artist who has refused to perform in South Africa. "To go over and play Sun City would be like going over to do a concert in Nazi Germany at the height of the Holocaust, but what I did was to go over essentially and play to the Jews."

To the astonishment of not a few supporters of the struggle and to the baffled outrage of Simon himself, he has been severely criticized by the ANC, the UN, and other key forces in the antiapartheid struggle. Why is that? I believe it is because the critics do not have the tour in mind, but the record album, *Graceland,* which has sold over six million copies worldwide and has hit the top of the charts in South Africa (where it is significantly uncensored). Although inextricably linked, the tour and the album are separate realities, the latter much more the creature of the global media money machine. Since it is a much greater slice of their personal performing experience, the tour is what the performers feel *Graceland* is all about.

Neither Masekela nor Makeba appear on the album. Simon is featured on most of the album cuts. The songs are neither political nor topical; many are not even about South Africa in any sense. Some of the musicians on the album are not South African and two of the groups, Los Lobos and Good Rockin' Dopsie and the Twisters, are from Los Angeles and Louisiana, respectively. Although the original tapes for much of the music were made in Johannesburg, the album credits only studios in New York, London, and Los Angeles.

In fact, it is a middle-class "white" album which may partake of the latest form of "radical chic,"—a painless shot of pseudo-struggle awareness. One recalls Barney Simon's *Born in the R.S.A.*, a politically conscious play that has toured Europe and North America. One of the characters, a white university student with kinky sexual tastes who turns police informer, speaks for many when he says that South Africans have become the world's celebrities, whom everyone else observes from a safe and moralistic remove, as if apartheid were "a sado-masochistic scene played out in a leather bar."

Most of the crowds in the United States have been predominantly white.

Jeanette Mothobi, of the ANC Mission to the UN, says that ". . . in South Africa you cannot in any way separate culture from politics, from economics. . . . We maintain that in the present moment in South Africa you cannot talk about artistic endeavour when people are dying."

James Victor Gbeho, Ambassador to the United Nations from Ghana and chairperson of the Subcommittee on the Implementation of the UN Resolutions and Collaboration with South Africa, points out that exiled black South African music stars like Hugh Masekela and Miriam Makeba have been singing protest songs for twenty-five years but he doubts that they have had any political effect whatsoever within South Africa. And therefore Gbeho believes that Simon cannot justify his actions by claiming that they are part of the struggle against apartheid: "When he goes to South Africa, Paul Simon bows to apartheid. He spends money the way whites have made it possible to spend money there. The money he spends goes to look after white society, not the townships."[5]

The *Graceland* tour was picketed in England, and prominent English musicians signed an open letter to Simon requesting that he apologize for breaking the boycott. They included Paul Weller of the Style Council, General Public's Dave Wakeling, Billy Bragg, and Jerry Dammers of the Specials (who co-wrote the Brit hit, "Free Nelson Mandela").

Allan Boesak defends Simon and sees both the tour and the album as positive factors in the antiapartheid struggle. On July 6,

1987, he told National Public Radio's *Morning Edition* that the cultural boycott forces should be less rigid, and he applauded Oliver Tambo's personal statement that some cultural exchanges with South Africa aid in the struggle.

Graceland guitarist Ray Phiri feels that many long-term exiles who support the struggle with calls for sanctions and boycotts "have become so outdated that they don't know what to do, what we want." One can sympathize with Phiri and the other musicians, who are bewildered by the criticism: "If they [the ANC, UN, and others] say they are helping South African musicians by keeping them away from the world, how is that help?" He adds that opinions like those of Ambassador Gbeho are "stupid and naive."[6]

The position of the ANC and UN, and their followers in the cultural boycott, is neither stupid nor naive. But it does appear to be politically inflexible and moralistically narrow. There is a sort of puritanical demand for purity of motive and tangible polemical value in every musical note, a stern requirement that every play be an effective protest. Ambassador Gbeho would have Miriam Makeba and Hugh Masekela give mechanistically obvious evidence that their art has tangibly injured Pretoria. The cultural boycott supporters did not object to *Woza Africa,* as they did to *Graceland,* because the tour of black protest plays were overtly and at times crudely polemical, even though they, too, played largely to a white middle-class audience.

But there is a further difference between protest plays and *Graceland*. The former, like the alternative press, are community-based and divorced from the polished multinational media machine. Does a connection with big money destroy the moral worth of protest? It will be interesting to see the fate of Richard Attenborough's planned blockbuster film, *Biko,* filmed in Zimbabwe and undoubtedly a project that contributed to the local economy there.

The reality will remain murky, at least to the honest. There is no doubt that mass media impose a format and an agenda on moral crusades that can be corrupting, as observers of televangelism have realized. It is my hope that the experiences and outlook of the community media, especially those in South Africa, will have a humanizing effect on the high-tech bureaucrats of opinion and entertainment.

In this context, the lessons of the apartheid media wars are as portentous for the moral growth of the globe as for the anti-apartheid struggle itself.

NOTES

1. C.f., Denis J. Driscoll, "The Development of Human Rights in International Law," *The Human Rights Reader,* edited by Walter Laqueur and Barry Rubin (New York: New American Library, 1979), pp. 41–56.
2. David Fricke, "Paul Simon's Amazing *Graceland* Tour," *Rolling Stone 503,* July 2, 1987, pp. 43ff.
3. *Art. cit.,* p. 48.
4. *Art. cit.,* p. 59.
5. *Art. cit.,* p. 48.
6. *Ibid.*

Excursus

Managing Appearances

The concern of public relations professionals, advertisers, and politicians with image and appearance as instruments for persuading people about important matters in the real world of events and decisions is matched by the growing scholarly and intellectual interest in signs and symbols as makers, not merely conveyers, of the world we live in.

Appearances now carry a burden perhaps too great.

For instance, before the diversity and division of the modern world, with its intimate mixture of silent strangers, the language of clothing, "the dress code," consisted mostly of nods of agreement or reminders of the familiar. But now individuals sail the high seas, as it were, of a fluid intercultural world and, like ships, must bristle with flags of intention and explanation. Like marriage and money, fashion is being stretched to cover a field of duties and difficulties hitherto borne comfortably by broader institutions in more confident cultures.

Balzac saw fashion as a language, but it now takes a Roland Barthes or an Umberto Eco to decipher the intricate uniforms fashion designers have provided for the lost middle classes of the advanced nations: cowboy, tycoon, traditionalist with liberal views, teenage tough, honest laborer, jovial professor, aesthete, and on and on. Those charming nursery books of yesteryear that showed children the stereotypical garb of firemen, nurses, ballet dancers, and policemen no longer can comfort children or adults with the clear categories of an imaginable future. For one thing, job uniforms have been replaced by designer adaptations, often to accommodate the degenderizing of crafts and professions: the fireman is now the sexually ambiguous firefighter, the nurse may well be a man, and so forth. For another thing, the bewildering cosmopolitan menu of affiliations and occupations would exhaust any schoolbook effort toward the reassuringly straightforward.

Over a generation ago, John Kenneth Galbraith, under the pseudonym of Mark Epernay, poked fun at the solemn triviality of social scientists with his mythical Sociometric Institute. The institute assuaged the agonies of hostesses and diplomats by assigning to various individuals a numerically determined *prestige horizon* that permitted secure ranking at the most diverse gatherings. At last, ferryboat captains would know how to address morticians, and ancestral dukes could be seated on the proper side of film stars. I recall trotting out this elaborate academic joke in the early seventies only to have it received gratefully as a needed service. What was the phone number of the institute?

This not really ridiculous earnestness carried for me a further signal. Not only are we at sea in trying to establish the pecking order for others; we are equally, perhaps especially, confused about our own position. In a secular society in which there is no vertical relationship to some ultimately clarifying, and thus comforting, transcendant standard, one's "position" on the horizontal plane of the social order is also one's meaning, one's very self.

Originally, "Style is the man" was a corrective cliché for "Clothes make the man." Unlike the instant attractiveness a good wardrobe might provide, true "style" was the outer result of an inward force, an expression of character. Now character is a not very compelling inference one might or might not draw from observable characteristics. The glass of fashion is truly become the mold of inner form.

The world may always have been a stage, but now set designers and special effects technicians get top billing.

Fashion has thus assumed throughout the world the central significance it once had at Versailles: the art of managing appearances with a view to controlling actions. It amounts in fact to a sociophilosophical revolution that has literally turned our view of reality inside out.

Aristotle, the scholastics, and Kant converted Plato's *idea* to inner substance and then into the secret noumenon, the inner heart which can only offer clues of its nature to the groping senses of inquirers who are by definition permanent outsiders. This professional thought confirmed common sense. Language discounts the surfaces of things as "superficial" and "skin-deep."

But now our wafer-thin technologies, with their remarkable power to simulate life's every sight and sound, are eroding this once entrenched human attitude.

Freud's serious concern with the trivial accounts of everyday life, the superficial, as keys to character is an early sign of this shift. He saw slips of the tongue, stumbles of the foot, harsh words blurted out in rage, as no mere chinks in social armor but as enactments of the real self. The face, surely, tells us more than the heart ever could, had we chests of glass.

It may thus be that Castro's battle fatigues, Reagan's Second

World War bomber jacket and cowboy boots, and the operatic uniforms favored by Latin American dictators tell us more about each man's political views than any number of speeches. It may be that the visual media in so relentlessly focusing on "personality" are giving us truer pictures of candidates for office than they would if they focused on "issues." Coverage of "personality" is reporting on what politicians wear and do, whom they socialize with, what their hobbies and little pet hates are—the superficial. Those very things, in short, that Freud (and every parent) sees as the key to character. When real issues are extremely complex and all political decisions are of necessity compromises to be executed by a technological elite that forms the permanent government, then surely character is of greater importance than position papers written by hired "information specialists."

Ronald Reagan's little joke about bombing Russia, slipped out through an inadvertently open mike, surely tells us more than White House press releases about the significance of "Star Wars."

In the disturbing investigations and speculations of Julian Jaynes, language preceded self-conscious thought in human evolution. Acknowledged intentions, plots, plans, the entire human project—all are based on the technology of language.[1] The inside came from the outside. Life imitates art, as we increasingly see in our crafted media world of images and symbolic gestures.

Seen from the perspective of these reflections, the sanctions-disinvestment campaign can be viewed as not only a wise, but as an inevitable strategy to overthrow Pretoria. To my mind, it is the threat of sanctions and disinvestment, not the actions themselves, that are effective.

NOTES

1. Julian Jaynes. *The Origin of Consciousness in the Breakdown of the Bicameral Mind* (Boston: Houghton Mifflin, 1976).

Appendix 1

Editorial Opinion on the National Council Bill and Crossroads Violence

Die Burger:
The National Council Bill, which is published today for general information and comment, is a particularly important reform initiative, which can decisively lead South Africa out of the present situation of unrest to a more peaceful future in which the country's full potential can be realised.

The Minister of Constitutional Development regards the proposed council as a starting point for power sharing, which can result in a government of greater national unity.

About thirty members will serve on the Council: cabinet members, representatives of the self-governing states and 20 nominees. Ten of the 20 will be nominated by any organization, institution, or interest group representative of Black people who live permanently in South Africa, and the other ten will be nominated by the State President who will be the council's chairman.

The council will receive wide powers, among which will be the right to consider all matters, inclusive of existing and proposed laws, as well as all steps which the executive authority takes or proposes as long as the council deems it to be in the national interest.

Apparently the council, if it achieves consensus, will be able to make recommendations to the government concerning matters of national importance. Such consensus decisions will have to be implemented, and through this the council's prestige and status will increase. From the start it can therefore be a powerful instrument to ensure the equal inclusion of Black South Africans in a new constitutional dispensation.

May 23, 1986

The same proposal viewed by the moderate English *Sunday Tribune:*

As he tinkers with constitutional models in an effort to bring about a government of national unity in a Nationalist-controlled way, President Botha has devised the National Statutory Council. It is to be charged with the task of planning the constitutional dispensation to provide participation in government for all South Africans.

The Council will be chaired by the President. Among its members will be ten people appointed by the President from a list of nominations to represent Blacks and a further ten people who could make a "contribution."

Here lies the rub.

Such a council could be the salvation of a country in which politics are polarising at an alarming rate, but there must be trust; trust that when Mr. Botha talks about power-sharing, he means full and effective sharing and is not playing with words in an apartheid context; trust that the council will have the power to divert the government from unacceptable stances; trust that any new constitution proposed by the council will not be hampered by the prejudices of the past.

One way of gaining this trust is for the President to resist the temptation to appoint members of the council. If he is sincere about the council, he will realize it is not up to him to select leaders, but up to the Blacks themselves.

If the council is to have any chance of success, the key lies in the credibility of the Black membership. If the Blacks demand Nelson Mandela, then for the sake of the country, the President should release Mandela to take his place on the council.

Mr. Botha has anticipated such a demand. Among the qualifications for membership of his National Council is that no one should have a jail sentence of longer than a year or be a member of a banned organisation. If Mr. Botha can make such qualifications, he can also throw them out. By doing so he would start along the road towards the trust he so desperately needs if he is to go down in history as the man who saved his country from certain destruction.

May 25, 1986

Die Volksblad:

Therefore the sigh in many hearts and the necessary prayers that the National Council should not be sunk by suspicion even before it has been composed and can start functioning. May the council be given a chance to prove that reasonable South Africans, people who meet each other as equals and in good faith, can discuss their points of view, conditions and misgivings together and reach acceptable agreements. May the council not also be seen as another "Tower of Babel" incapacitated by misunderstandings.

Built on the belief that an Almighty God decides the fate and future of this country—not on the sand of hatred, discrimination, and unfairness—the National Council can become a monument for peaceful coexistence.

May 23, 1986

And now the Afrikaner view of the Crossroads violence:

Beeld:

. . . The police's present role in Crossroads is to keep the quarrellers apart, but it should also be a lesson for people who maintain that peace and order will return automatically to the Black residential areas as soon as the police and army withdraw.

Accelerated urbanisation will most probably make the development of further "informal settlements" unavoidable. The question is whether it should not rather take place from the outset under the protection of recognized authority. . . .

May 23, 1986

Die Volksblad:

A haphazard settlement of poverty-stricken people such as this is, of course, an obvious starting point for radicals who wish to kindle revolution. The inhabitants have little to lose, many are unemployed and desperate. Law enforcement in such an area is very difficult. The law of the jungle applies in the Crossroads, where a social organization has taken root around a number of leaders who each controls his own faction to some degree.

Radicals, mostly youths, have through terrorism, intimidation, necklace murders and firearms, established a culture of violence. They dictate boycotts, stay-away actions and keep the area in turmoil.

Now reaction has set in. Black people who want to be left in peace to earn their daily bread are using clubs, hatchets and arson to revolt against the "Comrades" or "Makabanas" as the young radicals are known. They refuse to continue living in fear that their families and property will be burnt out when they return from work, and they want to rid the area of radicals. They also do not welcome the presence of police in the area. . . .

May 22, 1986

A black paper, *Evening Po⌐ᵗ·*

Security Forces already have ⌐irtually unfettered powers of arrest and detention, yet the Government finds it expedient to add yet another repressive measure to the statute book. . . . innocent people could be locked up for three months before reasons for their detention have to be given to a review board.

This Bill is unnecessary and should be scrapped.

May 23, 1986

Appendix 2

South African Editorial Reaction to the Report of the Eloff Commission

A neat summary of the ecclesial split was offered by Dr. Abraham Luckhoff, religious editor of the moderate Afrikaner paper having the largest circulation, *Rapport*. Luckoff is a minister of the NGK and one of 123 NGK theologians who have signed a maverick antiapartheid statement. His column for February 19, 1986, stated in part:

> In short it amounts to this: The average member of the Afrikaans churches sees the SACC as a revolutionary organization which makes political statements for the promotion of the black man at the expense of the Whites.
>
> The pro-SACC minded people again see the Afrikaans churches and especially the NGK as the spiritual partner of the National Party which provides theological and biblical sanction for its policy—a policy which according to them favours the white and which declares the black man to be a third-rate citizen in his own country.
>
> The great point of conflict is thus politics. This was the reason why the NGK had resigned in the early forties from the then Christian Council (the predecessor of the SACC) and why Afrikaans churches have until now not seen their way open to join SACC.

Die Kerkbode, the official journal of the NGK, for February 22:

> . . . There is something wrong about SACC, and that its theological point of departure (premise) is doubtful, is clear. In the past there have been various appeals to Afrikaans churches to join the organization.
>
> The findings of the Eloff Commission offer few reasons for the NGK to seriously consider joining under these circumstances.

During my stay in South Africa, Afrikaner journalists recommended that I take a look at *Beeld,* because of its journalistic excellence; I did visit the editorial offices and was treated most courteously by senior members of the staff, some of whom pointed out that the government was then (1983) in dire straits because it was forced to spend so much money on black townships and homelands (among other costs). Their editorial reaction to Eloff on February 16:

> This is a devastating, but deserved judgement which the Eloff Commission expresses on the SACC. . . . And the SACC and its General Secretary, Bishop Tutu, cannot complain that they received that which they did not seek. . . .
> There are few countries in the world which will allow an organisation with money from other countries to undermine the authority of the State, especially when such an organisation reveals little viability in those countries.
> Yet, one can only imagine what fuss it will cause if the South African Government acts against that crowd, as they should and as every other country in the world would probably have acted if they were in our shoes.
> It is probably precisely what our enemies have hoped for, because it will give them a beautiful propaganda weapon.
> Perhaps one should, when action is discussed, seek consolation in the fact that the influence of the SACC does not reach very far, if it receives so little financial support here.
> On the other hand, even Bishop Tutu surely does not expect that he can continue totally unhindered with his activities. After all, we are not so stupidly indulgent.

Die Vaderland, from Jo'burg on February 16:

> Against the background of its Christian and ecclesiastical confession, the Commission presents the actions of the SACC.
> An overseas propaganda campaign for political, economic and cultural pressures on South Africa; attempts to discredit the State, the Defence Force and the Police; a campaign for civil disobedience; support for attempts to withdraw investments from South Africa; support for prospective draft dodgers; support for black power and similar organizations; and close contacts with the ANC. . . .
> From the evidence it collected, it seems only too clear that if the practical aspirations and actions of the SACC—in contrast to its confession—should succeed, it would cause great damage to South Africa and also its people.
> It would have consequences which are totally in conflict with the Christian principles which the organisation professes.

Rapport, the largest circulation Afrikaans paper, is a joint venture of both Perskor and Nasionale Pers and appears only on Sunday; its editorial control is in the same hands as that of *Beeld.* It had this to say on February 19:

> That the SACC is moving dangerously close to ANC accents of a revolutionary emphasis, as appears from their campaigns, their use of

words, their proteges and their identification with powers which want to overthrow South Africa is true. . . .

The State has the right and duty to investigate SACC because it is the duty of the State to counteract revolution in its territory.

The Eloff report can be read in such a manner (and it is read in such a manner by some, whether it was intended or not) that the SACC should confine itself to the spreading of the Gospel.

This means by definition the churches should keep their hands from political, social, and economic matters, that the SACC must be not involved with the "liberation struggle" which is intended to thwart the Government in its declared efforts to achieve change through an evolutionary process.

Such a viewpoint is unacceptable to us. The church has everything to do with the horizontal life of its people: their housing, material welfare, and political rights.

The church has the right to protest against systems, also the right of resistance and it is expected that the church should provide leadership also to help assure political life for its people.

The Sowetan, the largest black newspaper in the country, edited by Joe Latakgomo, the heir of the banned *World* and *Post,* for February 29:

There are many decent people, who are completely apolitical, who believe the SACC has done a splendid, Christian job and that this must be kept up. Such people, if they were called to hold their inquiry, would deliver a completely different verdict—of that we are certain. . . .

It is alleged that Bishop Tutu supports the ANC even if he has said he does not like violence. It is thus inferred that he also supports the Communist Party.

Our reading of the situation is that Bishop Tutu will support even the Devil himself if he (the Devil) attacked apartheid and tried to change some of the more deplorable oppressive laws. Bishop Tutu has even supported the Government in ways that have made him something of a sell-out amongst some radical blacks. That, we believe, is the role the SACC through Bishop Tutu, should play.

On February 16, *The Star,* the flagship of the Argus Publishing Company, which also publishes *The Sowetan,* was the only major paper to tie the Eloff recommendations to the problem of censorship:

Where the Commission did neither the SACC nor the country a service was to recommend yet more censorship under the Internal Security Act. The Commission wants to forbid all citizens from advocating disinvestment in this country. To do so would destroy the argument in favor of investment. Such a law would render instantly invalid the strong case put up by the proinvestment lobby. Worse: such a law would bring George Orwell's "1984" thought control fears right into South African homes in 1984—and justify Bishop Tutu's allegations and the people's deepest fears.

Bibliography

Addison, Graeme. "The Drum That Roused the Black Consciousness." *The Star* (Johannesburg), May 16, 1981, p. 14.
———. "'Total Strategy' and the News of the Angolan War." Journalism Department, Rhodes University, May 1979.
———. "The Union of Black Journalists: A Brief Survey." Journalism Department, Rhodes University, September 1977.
Ainslie, Rosalynde. *The Press in Africa: Communication Past and Present.* New York: Walker, 1966.
Ascherson, Neal. "Selling Apartheid: The Facelift in South Africa." *Ramparts,* July 1975, pp. 11–13.
Barnett, Ursula. "Censorship in South Africa Today—From Bad to Worse." *Publishers Weekly,* September 22, 1975, pp. 78–80.
Barton, Frank. *The Press of Africa: Persecution and Perseverance.* London: Macmillan, 1979.
Battersby, John D. "Botha Landslide Worries Foes." *The New York Times Review of The Week,* May 10, 1987, pp. 2.
Beckett, Denis. "The MWASA Strike: Beneath the Surface Lie Bottomless Depths." *Frontline* 1, no. 7, pp. 4–7.
Blackwell, Leslie, and Brian Bamford. *Newspaper Law of South Africa.* Cape Town: Juta, 1963.
Braestrup, Peter. "Duty, Honor, Country." *The Quill,* September 1985, pp. 15–21.
Brink, Andre. "Censorship and Literature," In *Censorship,* edited by Theo Coggin, p. 44. Johannesburg: South African Institute of Race Relations, 1983.
———. "Censorship and the Author." *Critical Arts,* June 1980, pp. 16–26.
Broughton, Morris. *Press and Politics of South Africa.* Cape Town: Purnell and Sons, 1961.
Brown, Trevor. "Did Anybody Know His Name? U.S. Press Coverage of Biko." *Journalism Quarterly,* Spring 1980, pp. 31–38.
———. "Free Press Fair Game of South Africa's Government." *Journalism Quarterly,* Spring 1971, pp. 120–127.
———. "The South African Press: No News for 170 Years?" Paper presented to Association for Education in Journalism, University of California at Berkeley, August 1969.
Chafee, Zechariah, Jr. *Free Speech in the United States.* Cambridge, Mass.: Harvard University Press, 1967.
Charles, Jeff; Larry Shore, and Rusty Todd. "The New York Times Coverage of Equatorial and Lower Africa." *Journal of Communication,* Spring 1979, pp. 148–55.

Cheh, Mary M. "Systems and Slogans: The American Clear and Present Danger Doctrine and South African Publications Control." *South African Journal on Human Rights* 2, part 1 (March 1986): 29–48.

Chimutengwende, Chenhamo. *South Africa: The Press and the Politics of Liberation*. London: Barbican Books, 1979.

Clymer, Adam. "Poll in South Africa Shows a Rise in Whites' Distaste for Apartheid." *New York Times*, August 3, 1986, p. A1.

Coplan, David. B. *In Township Tonight: South Africa's Black City Music and Theatre*. White Plains, N.Y.: Longman, 1986.

Corrigan, Edward C. "South Africa Enters into Electronic Age." *Africa Today*, Spring 1974, pp. 15–28.

"COSATU Marks First Anniversary." *Africa News Special Report*, December 8, 1986, pp. 6ff.

Cowell, Alan. "The Struggle: Power and Politics in South Africa's Black Trade Unions." *The New York Times Magazine*, July 15, 1986, pp. 14ff.

Couzens, Tim J. "History of the Black Press in South Africa, 1836–1960." Paper, Yale-Wesleyan Southern African Research Program (SARP), n.d.

———. "A Short History of the *World* and Other Black South African Newspapers." Johannesburg: University of the Witwatersrand, 1977.

Curry, Jane Leftwich, and Joan R. Dassin. *Press Control Around the World*. New York: Praeger, 1982.

De Gruchy, John W. *The Church Struggle in South Africa*. Grand Rapids, Mich.: William B. Eerdmans, 1979.

Devenish, G. E. "A Critical Review of Inroads into Press Freedom in South Africa." *Business SA* 15, (May 1980): 30–35.

Driver, Dorothy. "Control of the Black Mind Is the Main Aim of Censorship." *South African Outlook*, June 1980, pp. 10–13.

Dugard, John. *Human Rights and the South African Legal Order*. Princeton, N.J.: Princeton University Press, 1978.

———. "A National Strategy for 1980." Presidential Address to the S.A. Institute for Race Relations, Johannesburg, 1980. 12 pp.

Edgar, Patricia, and Syed A. Rahim, eds. *Communication Policy in Developed Countries*. Boston: Kegan Paul International (in association with the East-West Center of Honolulu), 1983.

Edlin, John. "The Perils of the Profession." *Africa Report* 32/2 (March–April 1987): pp. 27–29.

Frederickson, George M. *White Supremacy*. New York: Oxford University Press, 1981.

French, Howard. "On the Newstands." *Africa Report* 32/2 *(March–April 1987): p. 49.*

Fricke, David. *"Paul Simon's Amazing Graceland* Tour." *Rolling Stone* 503 (July 2, 1987): pp. 43, ff.

Fussell, Paul. "The Smut Hounds of Pretoria." *New Republic*, February 23, 1980, pp. 20–23.

"Gandar Trial: Ex-Prisoner Describes Torture by Warder." *IPI Report*, May/June 1969, pp. 14–15.

Gerhart, Gail M. *Black Power in South Africa*. Berkeley, Cal.: University of California Press, 1978.

Giffard, C. A. "Circulation Trends in South Africa." *Journalism Quarterly*, Spring 1980, pp. 86–91, 106.

———. "The Impact of Television on South African Daily Newspapers." *Journalism Quarterly*, Summer 1980, pp. 216–23.

――――. "South African Attitudes toward News Media." *Journalism Quarterly*, Winter 1976, pp. 653–60.

Ginwala, Frene. "The Press in South Africa." *Index on Censorship*, no. 3, 1973, pp. 27–33.

Gordimer, Nadine. "New Forms of Strategy—No Change of Heart." *Critical Arts: A Journal for Media Studies* 1, no. 2 (June 1980): 27–33.

――――. "A Writer in South Africa." *The London Magazine*, May 2, 1965, pp. 22–23.

――――, John Dugard, et al. *What Happened to Burger's Daughter, or How South African Censorship Works*. Johannesburg: Taurus, 1980.

Hachten, William A. *Muffled Drums: The News Media in Africa*. Ames, Iowa: Iowa State University Press, 1979.

――――. "Policies and Performance of South African Television." *Journal of Communication*, Summer 1979, pp. 62–72.

――――, and Anthony C. Giffard. *The Press and Apartheid: Repression and Propaganda in South Africa*. Madison, Wisc.: University of Wisconsin Press, 1984.

Haysom, Nicholas, and Gilbert Marcus. "Undesirability' and Criminal Liability under the Publications Act 42 of 1974." *South African Journal on Human Rights* 1, part 1 (May 1985): 37.

Henry, W. A. *American Institutions and the Media*. New York: Gannett Center for Media Studies, November 1985.

Hepple, Alex. *Press under Apartheid*. London: International Defence and Aid Fund, 1974.

Johnson, Shaun. "Barometers of the Liberation Movement: A History of South Africa's Alternative Press." *Media Development* 32, no. 3 (Summer 1985): 18–21.

Karis, Thomas G. "South African Liberation: The Communist Factor." *Foreign Affairs*, Winter 1986/87, pp. 280–287.

Kitchen, Helen. "Some Observations on U.S. Media Coverage of South Africa in the 1980's." *International Affairs Bulletin* 4, no. 3 (1980): 10–17.

Kramer, Jane. "In the Garrison." *New York Review of Books*, December 2, 1982, pp. 8–12.

Lacob, Miriam. "South Africa's 'Free' Press." *Columbia Journalism Review*, November/December 1982, pp. 49–56.

Lamb, David. *The Africans*. New York: Random House, 1982.

Laquer, Walter, and Barry Rubin, eds. *The Human Rights Reader*. New York: New American Library, 1979.

Laurence, John. "Censorship by Skin Colour." *Index on Censorship*, March–April 1977, pp. 40–43.

Lodge, Tom. "The African National Congress in South Africa, 1976–1983: Guerilla War and Armed Propaganda." *Journal of Contemporary African Studies* 3, 1–2 (1983–84).

――――. *Black Politics in South Africa Since 1945*. White Plains, N.Y.: Longman, 1983.

Magubane, Peter. *Magubane's South Africa*. New York: Knopf, 1978.

Marcus, Gilbert. "An Examination of the Restrictions Imposed on the Press and Other Publications Which Appear in Practice to Affect Members of the Black Group More Severely Than Other Groups." Human Sciences Research Council, Johannesburg: University of the Witwatersrand, n.d.

————. "*S* v *Simoko* 1985 (2) SA 263 (E): A Black and White View of South Africa." Centre for Applied Legal Studies, Johannesburg: University of the Witwatersrand, 1986.

Mathews, Anthony. *The Darker Reaches of Government.* Johannesburg: Juta, 1978.

Merrill, John C., ed. *Global Journalism: A Survey of the World's Mass Media.* New York: Longman, 1983.

Mervis, Joel. "The Nightmarish World of South Africa's Journalists." *IPI Report,* November 1979, pp. 12–14.

Milton, John. "Areopagitica." In *Complete Poetry and Selected Prose of John Milton,* pp. 677–724. New York: Random House, The Modern Library, 1950.

Momoh, Prince Tony. "The Press and Nation Building." *Africa Report* 32/2 (March–April 1987): p. 57.

Murray, Martin. *South Africa: Time of Agony, Time of Destiny.* Verso, 1987.

Neier, Aryeh. "Selling Apartheid." *The Nation,* August 11, 1979, pp. 104–6.

Nordenstreng, Kaarle. *The Mass Media Declaration of UNESCO.* Norwood, N.J.: Ablex, 1984.

North, J. "Death of a Daily." *New Republic,* Sept. 9, 1985, p. 12.

O'Brien, Conor Cruise. "How Long Can They Last?" *New York Review of Books,* November 5, 1982, pp. 17–31.

Page, Phillip, and Arthur Goldstuck. "Forbidden Music: Songs Against Apartheid." *Ear: Magazine of New Music,* April–May 1986, pp. 4ff.

Peterzell, Jay. "Can the CIA Spook the Press?" *Columbia Journalism Review,* September–October, 1986, pp. 29–34.

Phelan, John M. *Disenchantment: Meaning and Morality in the Media.* New York: Hastings House, 1980.

————. *Mediaworld: Programming the Public.* New York: Continuum Books, 1977.

"Planning for Life After Apartheid." *Christian Century,* November 19, 1986, p. 1021.

Pogrund, Benjamin. "The South African Press." *Index of Censorship,* August 1976, pp. 11–16.

Pollak, Richard. *Up against Apartheid: The Role and the Plight of the Press in South Africa.* Carbondale: Southern Illinois University Press, 1981.

Potter, Elaine. *The Press as Opposition: The Political Role of South African Newspapers.* Totowa, N.J.: Rowman and Littlefield, 1975.

Randall, Peter. *Survey of Race Relations in South Africa 1982, 1983, 1984.* Johannesburg: South African Institute of Race Relations, 1983, 1984, 1985.

Report of the Commission of Inquiry into Mass Media, PR 89, 3 vols.; and *Supplementary Report of Commission of Inquiry into the Mass Media,* PR 13. Pretoria: Government Printer, 1981, 1982.

Report of the Commission of Inquiry into the Reporting of Security News from South African Defense Force and Police. PR 52. Pretoria: Government Printer, 1980.

Roach, Colleen. "Annotated Bibliography on a New World Information and Communication Order." *Media Development* 32, no. 1 (1985): 36–43.

Rothmyer, Karen. "The McGoff Grab." *Columbia Journalism Review,* November/December 1979, pp. 33–39.

———. "The South African Lobby." *Nation,* April 19, 1980, pp. 455–58.

Rubin Barry. "Press under Apartheid." *IPI Report,* February 1981, pp. 8 ff.

———. "The Uncertain Future of South Africa's Press." *Washington Journalism Review,* November 1980, pp. 41–45.

Saul, John S., ed. *A Difficult Road: The Transition to Socialism in Mozambique.* New York: Monthly Review Press, 1985.

Seligman, Daniel. "Keeping Up." *Fortune,* April 14, 1986, p. 114.

Serfontein, J. H. P. "Press War in South Africa." *Africa,* February 1981, p. 64.

Shaw, G. *Some Beginnings: The Cape Times, 1876–1910.* Cape Town: Oxford University Press, 1975.

Shlemmer, Lawrence. "The Sanction Surveys: In Search of Ordinary Black Opinion." *Indicator SA* 4, no. 2 (Spring 1986): 9–12.

Shumach, Murray. *The Face on the Cutting Room Floor: The Story of Movie and Television Censorship.* New York: William Morrow & Co., 1964.

Sidle, Winant. *Report of the Joint Chiefs of Staff Commission of Press Coverage of Military Operations,* 1985.

Silk, Andrew. "Black Journalists in Johannesburg." *Nation,* November 5, 1977, pp. 454–56.

Silver, Louise. "Criticism of the Police: Standards Enunciated by the Publications Appeal Board." *South African Law Journal* 95 (1978): 580–83.

———. "The Statistics of Censorship." *South African Law Journal* 96 (1979): 1120–126.

———. "The Statistics of Censorship." *South African Law Journal* 97 (1980): 125–37.

———. "A Guide to Political Censorship in South Africa." Occasional Papers 6, Centre for Applied Legal Studies. Johannesburg: University of the Witwatersrand, April 1984.

Smith, Anthony. *The Geopolitics of Information.* New York: Oxford University Press, 1980.

Smith, H. Lindsay. *Behind the Press in South Africa.* Cape Town: Stewart, 1945.

"South Africa and Zimbabwe: The Freest Press in Africa?" *A Report by the Committee to Protect Journalists.* March 1983.

Steif, W. "Stop the Press" *Progressive* 48 (December 1984): 32–34.

———, and T. Mechling. "A Precarious Freedom." *Commonweal* 112 (August 9, 1985): 429–31.

Sterling, Christopher H. *Electronic Media: A Guide to Trends in Broadcasting and Newer Technologies, 1920–1983.* New York: Praeger, 1984.

Stevenson, Robert L., and Donald Lewis Shaw, eds. *Foreign News and the New World Information Order.* Ames, Iowa: The Iowa State University Press, 1984.

Stuart, K. W. *The Newspaperman's Guide to the Law.* 3d ed. Durban: Butterworth, 1982.

———, and W. Klopper. *The Newspaperman's Guide to the Law.* Johannesburg: Mainpress, 1968.

Switzer, L. S., and Donna Switzer. *The Black Press in South Africa and Lesotho.* Boston: G. K. Hall, 1979.

du Toit, Andre. "The Rationale of Controlling Political Publications." In *Censorship*, edited by Theo Coggin, pp. 80–129; esp. p. 92. Johannesburg: South African Institute for Race Relations, 1983.

Thomas, Donald. *A Long Time Burning: The History of Literary Censorship in England*. London: Routledge & Kegan Paul, 1969.

Thompson, Leonard. "Before the Revolution." *The New York Review of Books*, June 11, 1987, p. 26.

———. *The Political Mythology of Apartheid*. New Haven: Yale University Press, 1985.

———. "What is To Be Done?" *New York Review of Books*, October 23, 1986, p. 7.

———, and Andrew Prior. *South African Politics*. New Haven: Yale University Press, 1982.

Tomaselli, Keyan. "From Laser to the Candle." *South African Labour Bulletin* 6, no. 8 (1981): 64–70.

———. "Oppositional Filmmaking in South Africa." *Fuse*, November–December 1982, pp. 190–194.

———. "Progressive Film and Video in South Africa." *Media Development* 32, no. 3 (Summer 1985): 16.

———. "The Semiotics of Alternative Theatre in South Africa." *Critical Arts* 2, no. 1 (1981): 24–28.

———. *The South African Film Industry*. 2d ed. Johannesburg: African Studies Institute, 1980.

———, and Ruth Tomaselli. "Change and Continuity at the SABC." *South Africa Indicator: Political Monitor* 3, no. 3 (Summer 1986): 19–20.

Uhlig, Mark A. "Inside the African National Congress." *The New York Times Magazine*, October 12, 1986, pp. 20 ff.

Ungar, Sanford J. *Africa: The People and Politics of an Emerging Continent*. New York: Simon and Shuster, 1985.

de Villiers, Les. *Secret Information*. Cape Town: Tafelberg, 1980.

Washburn, Patrick S. *A Question of Sedition: The Federal Government's Investigation of the Black Press During World War II*. New York: Oxford University Press, 1986.

Wauthier, Claude. "PANA: The Voice of Africa." *Africa Report* 32/2 (March/April 1987): pp. 66–67.

White, Landeg, and Tim Couzens, eds. *Literature and Society in South Africa*. White Plains, N.Y.: Longman, 1984.

Wilcox, Dennis L. "Black African States." In *Press Control Around the World*, edited by Jane Leftwich Curry and Joan R. Dassin, pp. 209–32. New York: Praeger Special Studies, 1982.

———. *Mass Media in Black Africa: Philosophy and Control*. New York: Praeger, 1975.

Wilkins, Ivor, and Hans Strydom. *The Super Afrikaners*. Johannesburg: Jonathan Ball, 1978.

Willenson, Kim. "Frolic in Honduras: The Pentagon Press Pool SNAFU." *Washington Journalism Review*, July 1985, pp. 17–19.

Woods, Donald. *Asking for Trouble—An Autobiography of a Banned Journalist*. New York: Atheneum, 1981.

———. *Biko*. New York and London: Paddington Press, 1978.

———. "South Africa: Black Editors Out." *Index on Censorship*, June 1981, pp. 32–34.

Zille, Helen. "South Africa Gags 2 Student Journalists, Bans Their Anti-

Apartheid Paper." *Chronicle of Higher Education,* April 28, 1982, p. 12.

————. "Student Press Is the Chief Victim of South Africa's Censorship Law." *Chronicle of Higher Education,* November 1979, p. 19.

van Zyl, J. A. F., and K. G. Tomaselli. *Media and Change.* Johannesburg: McGraw-Hill, 1977.

INDEX

advertising, influence of, on media
"advertorials," 27
influence on film, 117–18
influence on television, 59
neutrality to attract blacks, 81
to reach black consumers, 59, 68–
70, 75
African National Congress (ANC)
ally of early union coalition, 22
black activism moves to, 73
calls all nonwhites black, 20
calls to end banning of, 33–35
encourages Buthelezi's power, 155
criticizes *Graceland*, 196–98
Eloff Commission on, 207–8
exiled and impoverished, 154
1950 parade fired on, 31
Pan Africanist Congress breaks
from, 69
Post accused as vehicle for, 75
question of communists in, 63, 176–
79
SACC agrees with aim, 158–59
Sharpeville causes banning, 152
subject of protest play, 10
Tutu urges nonviolence of, 124
Afrikaners, 12–17, 23, 44–52, 58, 153.
See also National Party, Dutch
Reformed Church
apartheid
Afrikaners attempt to suppress, 16
books on, 87
church as leader against, 19, 147,
149–50
exploitation of tribalism, 16–17
groups in, 20–21
petty apartheid relaxed, 4, 14–15
result of capitalism, 86, 91–92
Argus publications, 37, 41, 46, 48, 60,
64, 70, 73–75, 186

banning, 5, 7, 24, 45, 80, 84, 107, 109–
14
Beeld, 48, 57
Biko, Steve, 31, 66–72, 134–36, 198
Black Consciousness Movement. See
Biko, Steve

black press
black journalists, training of, 77–78;
unions of, 66–67, 72, 74, 77, 82
call for end to black supplements, 75
history of, 68–69, 93
kept alive by Argus, 73–74
marketing influence on, 68, 75, 81
power of, 67–68
worse harassment of, 35, 66, 72,
109, 116
See also community newsletters,
labor unions, MWASA, *The
Sowetan*
Boesak, Dr. Allan, 21, 25, 88, 149–50,
197–98.
See also SACC, UDF, Dutch
Reformed Church
books, 18, 86–88, 106, 109, 111–12
Botha, P.W., 5, 18, 23–24, 29, 32, 43,
44, 66, 149, 203
Botha, Pik, 29, 39, 55, 150–51
boycott, 50, 176
Brink, Andre, 58, 107–8, 137
Broederbond, 44, 50, 58, 62, 153, 183.
See also Afrikans
Buerk, Michael, 25
Business Day, 38–39, 73
Buthelezi, Chief Mangosothu Gatsha,
20, 72, 146, 155–56, 162, 166.
See also Inkatha, Zulus

Cape Times, 7, 37–38, 41, 48
Cape Town, 4, 6–7, 10, 12, 15
Cape Town, University of 25, 58, 69,
79, 89–90, 94, 122
censorship
banning laws, 5–9, 24–25
by fines on books, 18–191
by laws, 95, 99, 102–6
by police, 39–41
compared to U.S., 30–32
in rest of Africa, 8–9, 26–27
numbers of, 115
of films, 117–21, 130
politics the criterion of value, 110
use of registration, bonds, 41–42, 45,
77

CIA (Central Intelligence Agency), 30, 177–78
church
    leader against apartheid, 19–21, 26
    on both sides, 144, 147–51, 154, 161
    scope of influence, 9
    support of black publications, 83–85, 88
    support of oppositional films, 121–22
    See also SACC, Dutch Reformed Church
The Citizen, 38, 48
City Press, 34, 48, 75
"coloured", 12, 14, 15, 20, 41, 44, 48.
    See Afrikaners
communism, 68–69, 177. See also entry under African National Congress
community newsletters, 34, 69, 82–85, 163
"consensus" political pressure, 49–61.
    See also censorship
Conservative Party, 20, 24–25, 150, 152
COSATU (Congress of South African Trade Unions, 22, 25, 174
Cowell, Alan, 22, 35, 179
Christian Institute, 19, 85, 88, 151, 153
Crossroads, 10–11, 88–89, 204–5

Defiance Campaign of 1952, 31, 69
demonstrations, 124.
    See also labor unions, Sharpeville, Soweto
detention. See jails
Die Burger, 46–48, 115
disinvestment, 23, 156–60, 170, 173–76, 188, 202
Dugard, John, 7, 24, 94–95
Dutch Reformed Church, 14, 19, 21, 46, 144, 148–53
economic sanctions. See disinvestment
Eloff Commission, 19, 145–64, 166
English, 13–16, 33–34, 38–39, 45–48

film, 10, 85, 91, 107, 117, 119, 122–27, 131–32.
    See also videotape
The Financial Mail, 18
Frontline, 18, 19, 53–55
Fugard, Athol, 122, 138
funeral orations, 121

Giwa, Dele, 26
Gordimer, Nadine, 10, 87, 107, 127–31
government press relations, 33, 36, 38, 45, 50, 69, 183–84

government, structure of, 14, 24, 25, 31–32, 49.
    See also law
Graceland, 195–199

Harris, Kevin, 85, 88, 90
Heard, Tony, 7, 38–41

Inkatha, 20–21, 69, 72, 146, 155–56, 162, 166
Internal Security Act, 7, 31, 85

jails, 2, 3, 5, 16, 31, 40, 65, 85, 96, 172
Jeune Afrique, 27
Jews, treatment of, 61, 188
journalists, 25, 32–35, 40–41, 49, 65–67, 72, 74, 77, 82.
    See also black press, censorship, press, Publications Act, Publications Directorate
Klerk, Willem de, 23
Kruger, James, 71, 72
Koppel, Ted, 29, 192

labor unions, 21–25, 80, 87, 114, 122, 139, 181.
    See also COSATU, journalists' unions
Latagkomo, Joe, 41, 64, 75.
    See also *The Sowetan*
Lategan, Ester, 23
law, South African, 2–10, 24, 31, 39, 40, 94–95, 104–6, 113, 185
    See also apartheid, censorship, Internal Security Act, Publications Act
literacy, 17–18, 70, 87, 97
Lutuli, Albert, 10, 133, 152, 155, 198

McGoff, John, 76
Machel, Samora, 58
Mandela, Nelson, 24, 33, 40, 124, 152, 204
Manoim, Irwin, 39–40
Marxism, 9, 78
Masakela, Hugh, 195–198
Makeba, Miriam, 195, 197, 198
media, 8, 17, 49, 177, 160–61, 163, 169, 180–81, 186, 191–99.
    See also film, funeral orations, music, press, radio, theater, videotapes
Media Council, 42–43, 45
Mkatchwa, Father Smangalisu, 21, 126, 155
Mugabwe, Robert, 27
Mulder, Cornelius, "Muldergate", 38, 57–58, 76–77, 182–83